IDAHO GHOST TOWNS AND MINING CAMPS

Robert E. Ballard

Caxton Press

Idaho Ghost Towns and Mining Camps
ISBN# 978-087004-6476
© 2023 by Robert E. Ballard

First Edition

Library of Congress Control Number: 2023942860

Cover and book design by Jocelyn Robertson

Printed in the United States of America
CAXTON PRESS
Caldwell, Idaho

To my wife, Robin. Who accompanied me throughout my continuing quest to locate these isolated places while driving over some of the roughest terrain in Idaho. Her support, understanding and technical knowledge pushed me on. Through love and devotion, she provided me with the peace of mind needed to put my words into this book. Without her patience it would have not been possible.

TABLE of CONTENTS

ACKNOWLEDGMENTS

Steve Anderson, this book would have never gotten off the ground without him. It was Steve who first suggested and encouraged me to write a book on ghost towns of Idaho.

Larry Meadors, to my patient and resourceful friend who accompanied me on occasion and was continuously helpful in identifying Idaho plants.

Jon and Arlynn Anderson, taking full advantage of their vast knowledge of Idaho wildflowers, they were always there to answer my endless questions.

To my friend **Chis Bengtsson** for being my friend, always. From the beginning he was interested in the book's development. He is truly one of my biggest supporters.

Jane Hoff, for her welcomed suggestions and shrewd reasoning.

PREFACE

As you peruse this book, stop and let your imagination wander. Close your eyes and listen to the sounds of the streets that once bustled with activity. Listen to the sound of the mule teams as they pull the wagons loaded with heavy cargo heading for a mining camp outside of town. Listen to the sounds of the leather harnesses as the teams move slowly up the dusty roads.

If you listen carefully, you will hear the laughter of men who momentarily stopped inside one of the saloons that line the busy street to share their triumphs, or to learn where the latest strike is. You can hear the hard-soled boots on the boardwalk as the men hurry from one place to the next. Listen to the sounds of hammers and saws as skilled carpenters cut fresh lumber to build the many buildings in the fledgling community. The buildings are not all saloons; there is a mercantile, an assay office, hotel, freighting line, livery stable, feed and grain, post office and even a schoolhouse. There are no screeching tires, automobile engines or blaring horns from an impatient motorist.

All mining towns and communities didn't start out as busy as this. Nevertheless, they all started the same way when some persistent prospector discovered color in a creek or stream. Others then followed and soon a camp was born with canvas tents, dugouts, or a rock cabin. If the placer gold was rich and abundant, more people followed and with them came tradesmen, merchants, saloon keepers, more functional structures and civilization. Placer claims gave way to load mining, then hydraulic mining, then dredging. If the gold, or silver, or copper, continued to pour forth from the earth, the community grew. If the ore ran out, or the value dropped, the economy failed, and the town died. The result is a ghost town and that is what this book is about.

Anyone who walks into a ghost town experiences the same thing: loneliness and emptiness, decaying buildings slowly giving up their battle to the harsh winters and summer sun. The glass from the windows that once kept out the wind is gone while sagebrush protrudes though a splintering boardwalk. In some cases, stoves and utensils silently sit in the dust-covered rooms waiting for the owner to return. Things that were too heavy to carry or things of no apparent value were left behind by people who rushed to the next strike. You can sense that people were once there, that families once lived inside the now-deteriorating homes. You can still see the last vestiges of a picket fence that bordered a once well-groomed yard. People went to church on Sunday and celebrated afterwards with a picnic. There were dances and gatherings but now everything is still. Where did they go? Who were they? What happened to the children? What happened?

This is where I want to salute the stalwart groups and individuals who have sacrificed and given of their time to preserve these extraordinary places and have kept vandals and thieves from destroying and looting them. Many of the towns mentioned in this book are part of the National Register of Historic Places. I wish to give my personal thanks to the people who are associated with this organization as well as the people who visit these places and leave them as clean as they were when they arrived. One adage I am always faithful to is, "take only pictures and leave only footprints."

The pursuit of locating some of these out-of-the-way places has disadvantages and rewards. Getting to some may be difficult but, in most cases, the more difficult the pursuit the greater the rewards.

While searching the back roads in search of these forgotten places consider the fact that there is no cell service and for the most part you will be in isolated regions with no other traffic. It is good practice to carry emergency gear whenever you set out. Carrying a saw and length of chain or tow straps is essential in the event you encounter a fallen tree over the road. It's wise to have a shovel, axe, blankets, additional water and food. I carry a bug-out bag wherever I go that is loaded with emergency items such as candles, matches, duct tape, knife and extra clothing.

Idaho has a rich history in mining that has shaped the state. Mining is so important to the state's history that the image of a miner is depicted on the Great Seal of the State of Idaho. Tragically, the number one toxic polluter in the United States today is mining. However, an age-old law called the Mining Law of 1872 enables mining to continue, as it is still considered to be the highest and best use of the land. According to Bureau of Land Management, Idaho is not alone with this law: 18 other states operate under the same law. Today many environmentalist groups argue this century-old ruling and its ecological impact. Unless proper guidelines are followed, toxic wastes and heavy metals can be introduced into the waterways, having life-threatening impacts on fish, waterfowl and wildlife.

Resources are needed to keep up with the demand for automobiles, building, transportation and technology. Our society desperately needs these raw materials to continue growing. The largest molybdenum mine operating in Idaho was Thompson Creek Mine in Custer County. Currently it is inactive. Molybdenum is a critical component to steel production. Cobalt is essential with the production of batteries. As the demand for electric car batteries continues to rise so too must the demand for mining the materials to produce them. The largest deposit of molybdenum in the world has been discovered north of Idaho City. The CuMo Project anticipates pushing forward with an open-pit operation. Lessons learned from those early years of mining have taught environmentalists and mine owners to work together to ensure environmental damage that was seen in the past is not repeated.

Before you make a rash decision, let's consider halting mining operations in this country in favor of environmentalism. Would it be better to import natural gas, coal, cobalt, petroleum and steel from other countries? Don't you see what the outcome could be? If the United States relies on other countries for our basic raw materials, we become dependent on those countries. Importation from other nations is fine but not at the expense of our national defense. Responsible mining is essential and mining operations today go to great lengths to follow critical guidelines that are set up to protect our environment. Consider the significance other countries put on environmentalism and pollution control. Let me just say that other countries may not be nearly as attentive as the United States is when it comes to following environmental guidelines. On a global level, mining companies in the United States far surpass the concerns of other nations. Perhaps our forefathers were right when they initiated this law.

Read now how it all started, how the camps and towns grew and in many cases were abandoned. It is a fascinating story about the men and women who were here before us. Hopefully, some of you will follow where I left off. All the places in this book are still there. Don't allow their origins and memories to be forgotten.

Boise Basin Museum

Boise County Courthouse

BOISE BASIN

IDAHO CITY *Queen Of The Boise Basin*

You have all heard of the California Gold Rush, but how many of you have heard of the Boise Basin Gold Rush? It all started in 1862. As the Civil War waged in the east and brother fought brother, George Grimes and Moses Splawn discovered gold in Grimes Creek. The volumes of historical events that took place can hardly be told here, but I will try to give some insights.

The Boise Basin encompassed an area three hundred square miles wide, with Idaho City (originally called Bannock City) at the hub. Placerville, Centerville and Pioneerville soon came into being, but Idaho City saw the largest growth. It was officially founded October 7, 1862, by J. Marion More. By 1864, Idaho City was the largest city between St. Louis and San Francisco. With a population of seven thousand, it was the largest settled area in the Pacific Northwest. Miners, craftsmen, merchants and adventurers traveled to stake claims in and around the new community. The saloon was often the first public building constructed. It was a retreat from the day's work. Whether it be a plank of wood supported by two whiskey barrels surrounded by a canvas tent, or a single-room log cabin, the saloon was a meeting place. It was a place where a man could socialize over a drink or game of cards. In many cases it served as a night's lodging and even as a courtroom. Most of Idaho City's first residents were prospectors and miners from California who had left their claims after hearing of the fabulous new strike.

Crime reigned in the first years. Wells Fargo was robbed so often that they were forced to shut down their stage line for a year. One source stated that fifty murders occurred in a few months without a single conviction. In 1863 one citizen stated, "There is no jail in Bannock City but plenty of rope and trees."

Due to the plentiful water supply from nearby Elk Creek and Mores Creek, Idaho City quickly outgrew surrounding camps, earning it the title, Queen of the Boise Basin. Readily available timber made it possible to build permanent structures, turning the fledgling tent camp into a flourishing city. By 1863, there were 250 businesses in town with four sawmills, seven blacksmith shops, seven churches, a hospital, five community theaters, twenty-three law offices, forty-one saloons, four breweries, thirty-six grocery stores, two bowling allies, an undertaker, a watchmaker and *The Idaho World* newspaper, which is Idaho's longest-operating newspaper, established in 1863. Idaho City had the first Masonic Hall, first Catholic Church (St. Joseph's Chapel) and first jail in Idaho, which also served as the territorial prison for eight years. By 1864, strict law and order prevailed. Women established a presence, bringing with them social practices. Horseshoe Bend became a staging area for miners waiting for the early signs of spring to melt the heavy snows from Harris Creek Toll Road leading to the higher elevations.

A fire in 1865 destroyed four-fifths of the city. Another equally disastrous fire burned the city again in 1867, destroying the Boise Basin Mercantile. Every consideration was made with rebuilding the mercantile, which included a brick facade with iron windows and doors. Fire has never again threatened this structure, making it the oldest mercantile in Idaho.

Lode mining continued for decades after placer claims were exhausted, which prevented the Boise Basin camps from dying out. By 1868 Chinese immigrants made up half of Idaho City's population. A Chinese section flourished in Idaho City as in most mining camps across the western United States. An estimated 1,700 Chinese lived mostly along the lower end of town along Montgomery Street. By 1900, their number was down to seventy-five. The Chinese worked claims sold to them by white miners. They also worked in the laundries and grew and sold vegetables to white miners. The later 1800s saw a dramatic decrease in Idaho City's overall population as mines shut down.

Twentieth-century industrialization brought dredge mining, which ushered in a rejuvenation of gold production in the Boise Basin. These gigantic mechanical machines furrowed deep in the stream beds and unearthed gold that nineteenth-century technology could not reach. Evidence of the dredging years in the form of dredge tailings can be seen in numerous places outside Idaho City.

At an altitude of 3,907 feet, Idaho City is far from a ghost. Its current population is 485, and Idaho City has the distinction of being the county seat of Boise County.

A forty-five-minute drive from Boise, Idaho City can be accessed in one of two ways. One way is by traveling east up Harris Creek Road on the south end of Horseshoe Bend. The first 4.2 miles of Harris Creek Road is paved. At 15.7 miles, Harris Creek Road again turns to pavement. You will see the Star Ranch on your left and the homestead of the Ranft family. There is an historical marker here that

St. Joseph's Chapel, Idaho City

is worth the stop. Harris Creek Road will turn into Centerville Road at the Placerville Junction. Turn right here and drive for twenty-eight minutes to Idaho City. A half mile before entering the city limits, you will see the turnoff to the Pioneer Cemetery (Idaho City's cemetery). Take this detour and visit this cemetery. There are pamphlets available at the entrance for a self-guided tour to pay your respects to some of the intrepid souls that ventured west in those early years. The other route is to take exit 57 off I-84 onto Highway 21 and head north for thirty-four miles; an effortless journey compared to 1882.

Unlike other districts that went bust, Boise Basin lasted for several decades, and Idaho City endured where other boomtowns became ghosts. Reports state that three million ounces of gold were taken from gravel creek bottoms and hillsides of the Boise Basin. Some say only a fraction of the gold was recovered, with vast amounts of gold still unaccounted for. If this gold had been recovered, it could have rivaled the California Rush of 1849. Prior to 1933, gold was fetching $20 per ounce. In 1933 it escalated to $35 per ounce. California had fourteen years of production prior to the Boise Basin being discovered. Although California is credited with recovering more gold, you must first consider the vast topography of the California rush as opposed to the area known as the Boise Basin.

There are a few places to enjoy an excellent meal and an equal number of spots for overnight lodging. Cool your heels over a cold beer and hamburger at The Gold Mine Restaurant or enjoy a piece of the world-famous pie at Trudy's Kitchen across Highway 21. Sarsaparilla Ice Cream Parlor provides something for everyone. Idaho City abounds with places of interest and is steeped in history. I suggest first stopping by either the Idaho City Visitor Center, or Boise Basin Museum, to pick up a self-guided tour booklet, Bricks to Boardwalk. The Idaho City Visitor Center (Boise Basin Interpretive Association BBIA) is a must. Joyce Obland oversaw the visitor center for fifteen years. It was Miss Obland who kindly supplied a great deal of my information. Don't miss the opportunity to have an experienced docent at the center share important things to see as soon as you arrive in Idaho City. Private historical walking tours can also be scheduled with Rhonda Jameson, simplyfun@live.com.

Places like Idaho City Trading Post are available for that special gift, and Town Dump Antiques is the best antique shop I've ever been in. The owner of Town Dump Antiques is arguably Idaho's City most charming and celebrated citizen. Her name is Trudy, and it is a shame there aren't more like her! If you enjoy hiking, I suggest the Buena Vista Trail which encircles the Idaho City Airstrip. It is lined with Douglas fir and you will pass mounds of discarded river rock "dredge tailings," which are the scars left over from the gold-dredging years.

The annual "Idaho City Days" commences the first weekend in October. Sponsored by the Idaho City Chamber of Commerce, the open-air festival is in its seventh year and provides visitors of all ages the opportunity to meet craftsmen, antique dealers and artists, and offers an array of thrills, wonderful food and performers. The 2022 festival saw more than one hundred concession booths, with an estimated attendance of 10,000 visitors.

The Idaho City Chili Cook-Off is the first Saturday in March. Also, the Fourth of July has a full day of activities, including a wheelbarrow race, parade and a reading of the Declaration of Independence at the Idaho City Hall at noon. Hot dogs and beer are served at the Historical Center. Information for any upcoming events can be obtained at the Idaho City Hall on Main Street.

The *Idaho World* newspaper was founded in Idaho City in 1863 by Joseph and Thomas Butler, and is the longest operating newspaper in Idaho. The original building that was home to the Idaho World is located on Main Street and is on the National Register of Historic Places. A historical plaque appears on the front of the red-brick building. The weekly paper circulates inside of Boise County today, although arrangements can be made to receive it by mail anywhere. You can subscribe or pick up a copy at any grocery store in Boise County for seventy-five cents. The IOOF was built in 1875, and is the oldest Odd Fellows Lodge in Idaho.

Most of the back streets of Idaho City are strewn with relics from another era. Take photos and look through some of the shops and restaurants throughout town that beckon you from a time long since passed. You can easily spend an entire day.

Today, Grimes Creek, Mores Creek and Grimes Pass remain as reminders of another time. Our western United States is full of forgotten towns that were built by courageous men and women who had the adventurous spirit to travel to unmapped regions where no highway or settlement had been before them. These are the people who made it possible for us to be here. It is important to take the time to venture off the main highway sometimes, and step back in time and give thanks to these intrepid individuals who helped to make life as we know it possible.

PLACERVILLE

Gold was discovered in Grimes Creek in 1862. That same year the location of Placerville was settled and named for the rich placer deposits in the area. The three-hundred-square-mile area surrounding the discovery became known as the Boise Basin. Four primary cities were established within that boundary, with Idaho City being the largest, although Placerville was close behind with three hundred buildings and a population of 5,000 by 1863. Hard rock mining, placer and hydraulic mining were used here. There is extensive evidence of dredging on Mores Creek west of town on Centerville Road. Look for the familiar heaps of river rock (dredge tailings) which are the scars left by the twentieth-century dredgers that moved up and down the creek bottoms, gathering the precious metal from the sand and gravel.

It was soon realized that Placerville was not going to be another Florence, where placer claims were worked out in the first season. The placer gold went deep here. Eighty miles of ditches were dug to bring vital water to the sluices. Optimistic merchants, professional people and artisans set out for the diggings to establish businesses. By the 1890s, Placerville had five blacksmiths, a mercantile, seven restaurants, five meat markets (dispensing 4,000 pounds of beef daily), a bakery, post office, thirteen saloons, a watchmaker and eighty-seven framed and log homes. Placerville was destroyed by fire in 1899. The town was immediately rebuilt incorporating the latest building trends. In June of 1900 the town was almost wiped out again by fire, and again rebuilt.

Placerville is not a ghost, but is certainly worth a visit. As of this writing, Placerville has twenty-eight full time residents. It hosts a lovely general store named Donna's Place which also serves as the town hall. Skip and Donna Meyer own the mercantile, but Brian Davies runs it; Brian is also the town mayor. As a matter of fact, Mr. Davies has held the mayoral position for three consecutive terms but insists he will be standing down when the term finishes on January 24, 2023. Stop into Donna's Place for an ice cream or a refreshing beverage. Brian has most anything a traveler might need, including cold beer and conversation. There are two museums, the Henrietta Penrod Museum and, directly across the street, the Mercantile Museum. They are open Memorial Day to Labor Day on weekends only, from 12:00 PM to 4:00 PM. Both have their unique charm as do the volunteers who oversee them! The small team of volunteers look over the museums all year long. If you are planning a trip to Placerville during off-season, you may telephone Donna's Place and give them a time you will be there. One of the museum volunteers will return your call and meet with you at a predetermined time. During the summer months you may be fortunate enough to see a bearded resident or two seated on the museum's wooden front porch. Be sure to exchange some conversation with them. They are extremely friendly and are a wealth of historic information.

The building that the museum is located in was originally the Magnolia Saloon, one of three saloons in town. A fire destroyed a portion of the saloon in 1899. It was rebuilt the following year and continued as a saloon well into the 1930s. Henrietta R. Penrod purchased the abandoned structure sometime later and along with others, renovated the notable landmark. After renovation was complete, Ms. Penrod sold the saloon to the city of Placerville for one dollar on the promise it would be established as a museum. Born in Placerville in 1896, Ms. Penrod worked as the postmistress. She was laid to rest in the Placerville Cemetery in 1971 at seventy-four years of age. A historical plaque in front of the museum commemorates her memory.

There are two ways to get to Placerville from Boise. One is by taking Highway 21 off I-84. The other is by traveling east up Harris Creek Road on the south end of Horseshoe Bend—17 miles. The first 2.5 miles of Harris Creek Road is paved. At 7.2 miles you will see a concrete piling on the left side of the road. This is in commemoration of the Harris Creek Toll Road Gate that operated here between 1863 and 1907. The proprietors of the station were Thomas Reeves, Tom Pettingill, Felix Harris, Hank Hawkins and Phillip Fry. At 15.7 miles Harris Creek Road again turns to pavement. You will see the Star Ranch on your left and the homestead of the Ranft family. There is a historical marker here that is worth the stop. Harris Creek Road will turn into Centerville Road at the Placerville Junction. Continue straight for one mile to reach Placerville. Interesting note; as you enter Placerville you will notice Ranft Road on your left which is named after the family of the Star Ranch.

When women joined their husbands, they brought with them a domestic touch. Men's primary focus prior to this had been on two things, mine gold and eat! Tents made way for cabins and framed houses. During the early years of summer and lacking the luxury of glass, burlap was stretched across the windows to allow a breeze in but prevent flies and mosquitoes from entering. This later transitioned to windowpanes and curtains. Women also brought culture and a focus on schools, church and social gatherings. Relationships with neighbors were formed that endured for generations.

The Placerville townsite was laid out around a plaza in 1864 with a flagpole in the center. That plaza remains today. Don Thornton

Placerville Cemetery

Henrietta Penrod Museum

Pavilion/Placerville Veterans Memorial Plaza is in the center of town. The Episcopal church which still holds regular services is located on Granite Street west of town. Placerville has an active fire station next to the mercantile. There is no gasoline available in town. A must-see is the Placerville Cemetery. Take Granite Street west from Main Street one-quarter mile to Cemetery Road, turn left. Cemeteries tell a great deal about the town and the individuals who lived there. I was impressed at the size and opulence of the cemetery. The moment you see it you will marvel at its grandeur. It is clear that the residents who remained in Placerville through its decline looked over this cemetery, preventing scavengers from desecrating the hallowed ground. Nothing in this cemetery has been vandalized or disturbed and it is a testimony to the affluence that once reigned here.

If you continue on Alder Creek (dirt) Road (615) past the two museums east of town, it will take you to Garden Valley.

Three miles west of Placerville on Granite Street/Quartzburg Road is the site of Quartzburg. However, don't bother: there is a heavy steel gate one mile before you reach Quartzburg that bars the way. The current owner of the property doesn't want anyone past the gate and the formidable "No Trespassing" signs posted demonstrate his extreme sincerity. In cases like this you must respect the wishes of the property owner. I am told that some buildings still exist (see section on Quartzburg).

CENTERVILLE

The settlement of Centerville was near the site of the original gold discovery by the Splawn-Grimes party and was settled along Grimes Creek. It is located in Boise County at an altitude of 4,209 feet and was one of four towns inside the Boise Basin. As a matter of fact, the town received the name because of it being *centrally* located inside the Boise Basin.

There is Old Centerville and New Centerville. Both are off Grimes Pass Road. The beginning of New Centerville starts at the junction of Centerville Road and Grimes Pass Road, 4.2 miles south of Placerville Junction. Several homes and cabins exist in New Centerville where full-time residents live. To get to Old Centerville, drive 2.5 miles on Grimes Pass Road from Centerville Road. You will see a small dirt road to your left just prior to FS Road 349. Take this small, unmarked road for a hundred yards to the "site" of Centerville.

Very little exists except for a pile of rusted tin cans and a collapsed dwelling of some kind. A decaying and collapsed barbed-wire fence

Centerville

indicates a boundary for livestock at one point in time. It is a great place to park and enjoy a lunch under a canopy of Douglas fir trees. I have read that the scant remains of the Twin Sisters Mill may lay across Grimes Creek to the east of Centerville. If you're up for it, give it a try. As for me, the brush was too heavy and water too deep to cross.

To make your visit to Centerville worthwhile, visit Koppes Cemetery. Drive back to Grimes Pass Road. In a few hundred feet turn left onto FS Road 349. In half a mile you will see a small, unmaintained dirt road to your right. There should be a sign reading Koppes Cemetery. At the end you will see two chain-link fences surrounding two grave sites. This was once the Centerville Cemetery. In 1931 the Quartzburg Fire destroyed forty original wooden grave markers in this cemetery, leaving only a few marble markers. Several family members by the name of Koppes are interned here, one dating back to 1907. For that reason, the cemetery has taken on the name Koppes. The forty gravesites whose markers were destroyed in the 1931 Quartzburg Fire have been lost for all time.

At the beginning of the twentieth century, the demand for timber had surpassed mining in economic importance. However, getting the lumber to Boise sawmills was an issue. In 1914, the Intermountain Railway was built from Boise to New Centerville. The railroad tracks bordered the Boise River, Grimes and Mores Creeks. The

Intermountain Railway was discontinued in the 1930s and replaced by Highway 21.

If you continue north on Grimes Pass Road, you will come to Pioneerville (see section on Pioneerville).

GOLDEN AGE CAMP

Four miles north of Pioneerville and one mile east of Grimes Pass stands the incredible settlement of Golden Age Camp. Named for the Gold Age Mine, it sits on 640 acres off White Cap Road. Although on private property, the caretaker was kind enough to show me around.

Vandalism has never threatened these structures. Thanks to the altruistic efforts of the owners of this property and its caretakers, Golden Age Camp has been saved in time where others have vanished! As with all mining camps and towns, newer structures transitioned throughout different periods of mining history.

The Golden Age Mine was a hard-rock mine, principally gold and silver. It was first settled in 1915. The adit and numerous shafts south of the property that once provided air to the tunnels have long since been bulldozed. The camp lies between Grimes Creek and White Cap Road.

Seventy-five miners and mill workers supported the camp. The largest of the structures today is the two-story bunkhouse. The kitchen is located on the first floor, as is the large cold room used to store perishable goods and meat. The walls of the cold room were constructed of milled lumber with a space of three feet between. The inside was then filled with sawmill shavings, which acted as insulation. The sawmill shavings can still be seen slowly escaping under the wooden walls. During early spring, ice was cut and hauled to refrigerate the spacious room. Nineteenth-century ingenuity is remarkable, as the room continues to remain at a very low temperature throughout the warmer months.

The upstairs acted as sleeping quarters. Built-in window seats remain where the miners once kept their personal belongings. There is no insulation in the bunkhouse walls or ceiling. At five thousand feet, it is likely that operations ceased, and miners and mill workers left for lower elevations during the severe winter months. Several other buildings and cabins occupy the property, presumably sleeping quarters, assay office and superintendent's office.

The purity of the ore dictates the method of processing needed to separate the precious metal from the host rock. Free milling could

Golden Age Camp

not be utilized here due to the sulfides in the ore. An alternative was cyanide leaching which is a costly and time-consuming process. As a result, the Golden Age Mine did not have a long history.

A cabin that stands on the north side of White Cap Road, opposite Golden Age Camp, is considered to be the oldest structure inside the Boise Basin. This cabin predates Golden Age Camp and was constructed and used by miners who first opened the Boise Basin and endured the long Idaho winters.

The caretaker, who desires to remain anonymous, requests that you please respect private property signage.

PIONEERVILLE

Located in Boise County at an elevation of 4,439 feet, Pioneerville also goes by the names Pioneer City and Hogem. Legend has it that the first naming of Hogem came in 1862 when the first group of prospectors that arrived "hogged" all the good placer claims. As other miners arrived, they analyzed the situation and reluctantly moved down Grimes Creek and started Centerville. There are a couple dilapidated structures, as well as two or three inhabited buildings and trailers here, but other than this, very little exists.

Gold had been discovered in present-day Centerville in 1862. By the summer of 1863 Pioneerville had a population of 3,000 people, making it the third largest mining camp in the Boise Basin, behind Idaho City and Placerville. The first post office in the Boise Basin was established in Pioneerville in 1864.

Rumors suggest a smelter was established here to process silver galena ore, but this venture most likely failed. It was gold that Pioneerville was built on, both placer and lode mining. While driving along Grimes Pass Road you will see dredge tailings lining both sides of the road which is evidence of the extensive dredge activity that occurred here. The creek that parallels most of the road is Grimes Creek. Dredging didn't occur until the beginning of the 1900s. These steam-driven mechanical monsters were able to excavate placer gold which laid deep in the stream beds that prospectors from the 1800s were not able to access with mere panning and sluicing. The specific type of dredge principally used was a bucket dredge. Iron buckets or scoops were positioned along a circular rotating arm called a ladder. The bucket line of the dredge was then lowered more than thirty feet below the water line. As the buckets traveled along the rotating ladder, they scooped gold-bearing gravel up from deep within the stream bed and deposited it in a hopper and revolving screen that separated the heaver gold from the gravel. The unwanted larger river rock and sediment was then spewed out along the riverbank. These unsightly dredge tailings are what we see as we drive past them.

Pioneerville

19

George Grimes' grave site

Unfortunately, the dredge tailings didn't only scar the landscape, the process itself had tragic environmental impacts. The final process used to capture the gold particles was by flushing the gold over copper plates covered in mercury. During this process the gold was absorbed into the mercury. This gold and mercury mixture is called an amalgam. There was always a certain percentage of the toxic mercury that was washed overboard during this process which resulted in environmental issues lasting for many years. Not all forms of dredging are considered destructive to the environment. There are many examples of dredging used in construction. One example would be the Suez Canal, where dredging was used almost exclusively. Dredging ceased here in 1942, as did all gold mining in the United States, when the government shut down all non-essential mining due to World War II. Two examples of bucket dredges are outside Warren, Idaho, and on the Yankee Fork near Custer. The Yankee Fork dredge operated on two diesel engines, as opposed to steam.

From Placerville Junction travel 4.2 miles southeast (towards Idaho City) on Centerville Road to Grimes Pass Road. Turn left and drive 7.2 miles to Pioneerville. The name "Poncia" is written on a sign designating the single street entering Pioneerville. In the 1980s, two elderly brothers by the name of John and Paul Poncia lived here. John was one of the original "dredge masters." Both lived out their lives here. Their home is the smaller house with the galvanized roof facing Grimes Pass Road.

Just prior to entering Pioneerville, you will pass a road leading to the right, Arbaugh Lane. If you drive a short distance to the end, you will see Pioneer Cemetery to your right.

As already mentioned in an earlier section, George Grimes and Moses Splawn discovered gold in two creeks that flowed through the Boise Basin while leading a small party on August 2, 1862. These creeks would later be named Grimes Creek and Mores Creek. Tragically, George Grimes was killed a few days after the initial find. There is some controversy as to whether his untimely death was unjustly blamed on the Shoshoni Bannock Indians, or if he was murdered at the hands of a greedy and unfaithful partner. Historically, the death is attributed to hostile Indians, and since Mr. Splawn is not here to defend himself, we should give him the benefit of the doubt. After his death, the body of George Grimes was put into a prospect hole near present-day Grimes Pass. Later, the body was moved to an appropriate grave site. Today a granite headstone marks that grave of George Grimes in the Grimes Pass Cemetery near Grimes Pass. On George Grimes' gravestone, a bronze plaque reads, "Killed by Hostile Indians Day of Discovery."

To get to Grimes' grave site, continue on Grimes Pass Road past Pioneerville until you cross a single-lane bridge. Just past the bridge (staying on Grimes Pass Road), you will reach a junction at the summit (Grimes Pass). Park and walk up a small slope behind a wooden rail fence to see George Grime's grave. Total driving distance from Pioneerville is four miles.

From Grimes Pass, continue down Grimes Pass Road toward Garden Valley. As you enter the valley you will intersect South Fork Road. Turn left and enjoy your drive alongside the Payette River until you hit Banks Lowman Road in Garden Valley. Total driving distance from Grimes Pass to Garden Valley is nine miles.

QUARTZBURG

A quartz outcropping was discovered here in 1863 which would lead to the development of the Gold Hill Mine in 1867. The Gold Hill Mine would become one of the largest producers of gold in the Boise Basin. That same year, W.W. Raymond set up a twenty-five-stamp mill on Granite Creek. Quartzburg was far different than Placerville. It was lode mining, and following rich veins of gold quartz in the Gold Hill Mine, that earned Quartzburg its name. The Iowa Quartz Mill, Gold Hill Mill and Last Chance Mine all operated out of Quartzburg. The Gold Hill Mill processed 450,000 ounces of gold between 1863 and 1938. The Quartzburg Mining District was formed in 1860s and still exists today.

Quartzburg lays three miles west of Placerville on Granite Street/ Quartzburg Road at an elevation of 4,675 feet. However, there is a heavy gate one mile before you reach the townsite that bars the way. The current owner of the property doesn't want anyone past the gate and the formidable "No Trespassing" signs posted demonstrate his extreme sincerity. In cases like this you must respect the wishes of the property owner.

As already mentioned in another chapter, the Boise Basin encompassed an area three hundred square miles, with Idaho City in the center. Placerville, Centerville and Pioneerville competed closely in growth, with Idaho City being the largest. Within eight months of the initial strike in 1862, the Boise Basin had grown to be the largest settled area in the Pacific Northwest! Quartzburg seems to pale in recorded history next to the boomtowns of Placerville, Pioneerville, Centerville and Idaho City. This is odd, seeing as one of the largest lode mines in the Boise Basin was located in Quartzburg.

The 1931 Quartsburg Fire destroyed all the buildings in town with

This bronze plaque was once attached to the concrete piling. Due to vandalism, it was repositioned at the base.

the exception of the schoolhouse and post office. Although there are some structures today, the schoolhouse and post office were the only original structures that escaped the fire. That same fire burned much of the surrounding forest, as well as the Centerville Cemetery, and scorched treetops in the Placerville Cemetery. The Quartzburg Post Office operated between 1874 and 1940, even though large-scale mining operations ceased in 1938.

Quartzburg's history ended in 1938 with the closing of the Gold Hill Mine and Mill, which explains in part its limited chronicled history. To add to this, in 1941 a declaration issued by the federal government ordered the closing of all mines that were non-essential to the war effort. Like so many gold and silver mining towns of the time, Quartzburg never recovered.

HARRIS CREEK TOLL ROAD

Harris Creek Road is located on the southern end of Horseshoe Bend. Partially paved, it is a thoroughfare to Placerville, Centerville and Idaho City.

Felix Harris first opened the road as a toll road in 1863. Upon his death, Tom Pettingill (some sources say George Pettingill) purchased

Concrete piling alongside Harris Creek Road.

it. In 1883, Henry Hawkins purchased it and it was ultimately sold to Phillip and Lora Fry in 1904. It was the primary means of travel for traffic leading to and from Placerville and Idaho City.

Today the well-maintained road continues to be a primary route to Placerville, Centerville, Idaho City and beyond. At 7.2 miles you will see a concrete piling on the left side of the road. This is in commemoration of the Harris Creek Toll Road Gate that operated here between 1863 – 1907. The names of the proprietors who operated the station are listed: Thomas Reeves, Tom Pettingill, Felix Harris, Hank Hawkins and Phillip Fry.

At 15.7 miles after leaving Horseshoe Bend, you will come to the Star Ranch on the left. There is a historic plaque in front of the ranch house that is worth reading. Teresa Ranft Cooper, who has been a librarian at the Horseshoe Bend Library for twenty-five years, is a direct descendant. Her great grandfather settled the ranch in 1866. In addition to livestock, the Star Ranch had a racetrack where residents from Placerville would commonly enjoy horse races on weekends during summer months.

Sadly, the roof of the Ranft cabin collapsed during the winter of 2022.

BANNER CITY

Prospectors looking for less-crowded placer mining found good color in Crooked River north of Idaho City. The area became known as Rocker Diggings. A few of the prospectors concluded that, since so much silver was accompanying their placer claims on Crooked Creek, silver lode mining would be advantageous if someone could locate the source. Three miners traveled to Placerville to engage the help of two experienced miners by the names of Jess Bradford and James Carr. Together, Bradford and Carr traveled to and evaluated the new location, and discovered what would become known as the Banner Ledge above the Rocker Diggings on July 6, 1864. Interesting note here: when Bradford and Carr returned to Placerville, they learned that a strike had been made on the Payette. With this news, Bradford and a man named James H. Hawley proceeded to the new strike, leaving James Carr behind. In their absence, Carr had the samples they had brought back from the Banner Ledge assayed. The samples proved to be so rich in silver that Carr took it upon himself to return alone to Rocker Diggings and in doing so, located the Banner "Lode." A claim was immediately filed in Placerville by Carr. Out of loyalty to his absent partners, Carr included both Jess Bradford and James Hawley along with three others on the title on August 8, 1864. Upon

Banner Mine Office foundation alongside Banner Creek.

Banner Cemetery

Bradford's return the decision was made to sell the claims to the Elmira Silver Mining Company.

As two hundred miners poured into the new settlement, an astonishing fifty new ledges were discovered, although none were as rich as the first. By 1865, tunnels followed the silver veins deep into the Banner Mine. Within two weeks, the towns of Banner and Eureka were under construction. Winter snows and lack of supplies did not discourage the enthusiasm, as miners continued to blast and drill.

Although the community of Eureka started at the same time as Banner, it did not develop. There is nothing.

In the first few years, processing the ore using an arrastra was the only means available until 1874, when G.W. Craft constructed a 20-stamp mill. A cable tramway carried ore from the 5,200-foot tunnel for processing. New York capital helped develop the district even more in 1878. Gold was the prominent metal taken from the fabled Boise Basin. Of all the lode mining that took place in southern Idaho, the Banner Mine and Mill was the only large producer of silver. Its estimated yield was $3 million. The district shut down in 1921.

Evidence of an original wooden foundation can be seen off FS Road 385 next to Banner Creek. On close inspection, you will find parsnip flower and blue spruce growing inside. From the road you will see a

Processing plant foundation.

27

Banner ore dump in distance.

rooftop behind heavy brush of a more recently constructed cabin. The cabin belonged to a man who used to live here during the summer months and prospected the creek and ore dumps for gold. As he advanced in age, he ultimately gave up his yearly retreats and walked away from his cabin. It has fallen victim to rats and is in complete disrepair. As of 2022, the 150-acre property has sold. An insert on the for-sale sign that remains posted on the property estimates $22 million in silver is still available to be processed in the ore dumps alone. Directly across the road and up the hill is the Banner Cemetery with four grave sites.

A 0.7-mile drive (or walk) up a road west of 385, across Banner Creek, takes you to the Banner Mine. There is a great deal to see along the way. Do not miss this opportunity. Ore was carried from the mine by an aerial tram to two processing areas. Foundations remain from both along with machinery and debris. At the mine site above the ore dump are loose bricks suggesting a smelter site. Although there are bits of charcoal indicating a possible fuel source, there is no evidence of slag.

Mining resumed in the late 1970s but ended in 1980. Of the two concrete foundations located below the Banner Mine, only the concrete remains. Most of the equipment and structural housing was removed. The Pioneer Fire started north of Idaho City on July 18, 2016, and by August had burned 188,000 acres. Fortunately, Banner was spared.

Banner is in Boise County at 5,860 feet. From Idaho City head north on Highway 21 for thirty miles. Turn right onto FS Road 385. Bearberry grows alongside FS Road 385 and is a main food source for bears in the fall. Along with rabbit brush, several varieties of wildflowers grow along the road as well; most notable are scarlet paintbrush and lupine. If you choose the accommodations of a yurt, six are available north of Idaho City inside the Boise National Forest.

Silver City

Silver City (Dave Wilper, walking).

OWYHEES

SILVER CITY *Queen of the Idaho Ghost Towns*

Located in northwestern Owyhee County at an elevation of 6,179 feet is the historic district of Silver City. Founded in 1864 when silver was discovered on nearby War Eagle Mountain, it grew quickly to become one of the largest settlements in the Idaho Territory. Silver City has respectfully earned the title "Queen of the Idaho Ghost Towns," and if you can only visit one ghost town in southern Idaho, this is it! Surrounded by the Owyhee Mountains, it is nestled amongst Douglas fir and limber pine.

Placer claims had existed in the Owyhee Mountains since 1862, but it was the discovery of silver that earned Silver City its name and reputation. Numerous gold placer claims were being worked along Jordan Creek when a quartz lode was discovered at Whiskey Gulch on War Eagle Mountain. Between 1863 and 1865, more than 250 mines were in operation. At its height in the 1880s, Silver City had 75 businesses and 300 homes. Ten stamp mills, such as the Consolidated, Cosmos and Ainsworth, thundered throughout the daylight hours to pulverize the rich ore that came from deep shafts on War Eagle Mountain. By 1850, this southwestern district of Idaho known as the Owyhees had caught the attention of the nation! Silver City became the most important center in the Owyhees. Multiple mills, such as the Cumberland located high on War Eagle Mountain, projected an appearance of permanence, suggesting a long future in quartz mining. Freight wagons rumbled along the dirt roads delivering merchandise daily to the growing population of the isolated community.

The Poorman Mine on War Eagle Mountain, discovered in 1865, earned the standing of being the richest body of ore of its size ever discovered. One solid piece of ruby silver taken out of the mine at the 100-foot level weighed five hundred pounds and was awarded the gold medal at the Paris Exposition in 1867! The Poorman had a 10-stamp mill where ore was delivered by an elaborate tramway system one mile long. Another mine that deserves mention is the Ida Elmore Mine. It was primarily gold and was located near Silver City. Originally discovered in 1865, it was located in what was known as the French District and was situated at an elevation of 7,398 feet. Closed in 1875, its namesake is directly associated with the naming of Elmore County in southern Idaho.

Silver City had the first telegraph in Idaho and supported two newspapers. The *Idaho Avalanche* (aka *Owyhee Avalanche*) which had moved from Ruby City was the primary paper. *The Owyhee Semiweekly Tidal Wave* was also published. Silver City was the county seat from 1867 to 1934. During the 1880's, the population of Silver City soared to 2,500. Silver City contributed to the acceleration and growth of the capital of Idaho (Boise) due to a staging area and supply point that existed there. Major mining operations continued through 1912, with limited mining after the Depression in 1929. In 1934, a referendum removed county government offices, and Murphy was appointed the county seat of Owyhee County. Because of Silver City's remote location businesses declined, and the remaining population left.

There is a great deal to see in Silver City, so plan an all-day venture. I suggest a loop by driving south of Marsing on Highway 78 to the Silver City cutoff, which is a twenty-mile well-groomed dirt road. If you go in late spring, be prepared to encounter Mormon Crickets. On the return trip from Silver City, continue west through the sites of Dewey, DeLamar and Wagontown and then proceed onto Jordan Valley on Highway 95. The road to Silver City is popular with off-road vehicles. Numerous abandoned mines are peppered throughout the surrounding mountains for those seeking OHV side trips.

There are a few individuals who have the misconception that Silver City is on the order of an amusement park with an old-west town

Idaho Hotel

theme. Nothing could be further from the truth. Normally during the spring and summer months a handful of property owners escaping city life take up residence here. During the winter, the population falls to one. Residents who live in Silver City expect visitors, so feel free to explore, but at the same time please be considerate. Seventy-five original structures remain, but because Silver City is on the National Register of Historic Places, an ordinance is in place limiting exterior construction. Every dwelling in the townsite is original and owners are very strict about maintaining a flair for that look of abandonment. There are lots of opportunities for some great photographs. Little has changed here in more than a century. Some of the residents of the town are direct descendants of the original miners, others were fortunate enough to be in the right place when a piece of property went up for sale. This kind of life isn't for everyone. There are few modern amenities for those that choose to spend the spring and summer months here. One advantage is a ten-degree drop in temperature in Silver City from the valley below during the summer months.

The Idaho Hotel is open from May to the first weekend in October (Friday, Saturday and Sunday). The building is 150 years old, and its idyllic charm is as unique as the couple who manage it. In 2000, Roger and Jerri Nelson purchased the hotel and operate it today. It is like stepping through a portal back in time. The hotel is three stories with thirteen guest rooms, all on the second floor. There is no air conditioning, two flushing toilets and one community shower on the second floor. There is no running water in any of the rooms. Breakfast, lunch, and dinner are served to the guests at a specific time of the day. You can check with the hotel to see what meals will be served. I guarantee it will be robust, satisfying and filling. The downstairs dining area is more of a museum than a dining room. Roger and Jerri Nelson are authorities on the history of Silver City and Owyhee County mining and are happy to answer any questions you might have. Beer and wine are available to purchase, but I suggest bringing along an ice chest with plenty of ice and liquid refreshments to add to your enjoyment. Ice cannot be manufactured at the hotel because of solar power restrictions. Jerri and Roger bring ice with them from Boise for iced drinks and to refrigerate perishables when they open the hotel on Fridays. Meals will be served to non-guests; they just need to plan for when the hotel is serving. Cold drinks can be purchased at any time.

My wife and I stayed in room 28. The beautifully hand-carved wooden bed frame and dresser in our room was donated by descendants of the original owner, a woman who was once a resident of Silver City. A plaque on our door reads, "In Memory of Harry & Ida Reich," who were her descendants. There are common reports of paranormal activity in the hallway connecting the rooms. The story goes that

O.D. Broumbraugh, once the owner of the hotel, shot himself one night in the south wing of the hotel due to medical reasons. It is his daughter's furniture that is in room 28.

If you're lucky, Dave Wilper (The Watchman) will wander into the dining room close to closing time for a glass or two of wine, or something stronger if available. Dave is the one resident of Silver City who remains during the winter months to oversee the town and hotel after the summer residents leave. The roads are unmaintained and impassable, with snow reaching four to six feet on some years. Once the snows come to this high elevation, traveling to and from town is impossible unless by snowmobile, and even that has its limitations. Since it's a dreadful hardship to remain in Silver City during the winter months, the citizens have appointed Dave town watchman. If anyone is hearty enough to make the 20-mile trek, they are required to check in with Dave. His is the first house on your left as you enter town. Another longtime resident of Silver City is Mary O'Malley. Mary was born in Nampa. Mary's maternal grandparents, Mathew and Mary Joyce, settled in the fertile valley along Sinker Creek one year after the founding of Silver City, establishing Joyce Ranch. Today, a sign alongside the Silver City Road points out the 11,000-acre Joyce Ranch as being the oldest family-owned ranch in Idaho.

Enter Hubert (Hugh) Nettleton (Mary O'Malley's father), born to Villo and Margaret Nettleton in 1897 in Blackjack, a nearby mining camp now defunct. In 1945, Hugh married Helen Joyce. Mary was born in 1946 and is the oldest of two children. She has spent her life here and is the quintessential authority on Owyhee County's past. During the summer months, you will often find Mary at the Idaho Hotel sitting at a window table overlooking the recently restored schoolhouse while enjoying breakfast and a cup of coffee. During the winter months Mary lives in Nampa. Mary is a charter member of the Owyhee County Historical Museum in Murphy. She has been involved with the museum since she was fifteen years old and has served as vice president and president. In addition to being a volunteer, she also serves as the managing editor of the *Owyhee Outpost,* a yearly publication put out by the Owyhee County Historical Museum. Mary's parents, Hubert, and Helen Nettleton, are interned at Calgary Cemetery in Nampa.

There are three places of business that are open to the public in Silver City, one being the Idaho Hotel. There are also two gift shops directly across the street from the hotel, Pat's What Not Shop and Silver City Fire and Rescue Store. Pat Nettleton is a descendant and has owned and operated Pat's What Not Shop since 1974. She has a lovely shop which is open Friday, Saturday and Sunday during the spring and summer months. Pat specializes in unique silver jewelry, souvenirs, t-shirts and gifts. Pat also sells soft drinks, coffee, snacks and water. There is no place to purchase gasoline or groceries so be prepared.

A trip to Silver City is not complete without visiting the Silver City Cemetery. No vehicles are permitted, but it is a short walk south of town. There is a wooden marker indicating the direction. Silently walk amongst the ornate headstones and read the names and dates from Silver City's early past. You will see those of children and young women. Was it sickness, the harsh elements, or lack of medical knowledge that led to their premature deaths? This is something that you can ponder in the privacy of your own thoughts as you look upon the resting place of these individuals who called Silver City their home when this city was a vibrant mining community.

Placer mining towns and camps had a reputation for attracting single men who worked their claims independently. Because of the greater number of single men in these camps, there was a greater demand for saloons. Silver City was built on hard-rock mining and because of this the miners and mill workers were employees of a firm earning top wages. Steady income led to marriage and families. Silver City had fewer saloons than other, more raucous mining districts. This may have led to the fact that fire never ravaged the wooden structures of Silver City; often devastating fires originated in saloons.

Like all mining towns and camps of the early west, Silver City had its Chinese section. Before and after the transcontinental railroad was completed in 1869, Chinese laborers sought work in mining camps. In Idaho alone, the Chinese made up an estimated sixty percent of the mining population. They searched out every menial labor imaginable, typically that which white workers wanted no part of. They would commonly purchase old claims that had been gone over by white miners and, through painstaking detail, managed to recover minute grains of gold that had been overlooked by the previous claim holder. Although they were terribly discriminated against, the white miners eventually earned a deep respect for the Chinese because of their undaunted perseverance. As a result, friendships were formed.

Very few Chinese are buried in any of these western mining communities. The Chinese believed that their bones needed to be returned to their birthplace for the soul to rest. They would temporarily bury the deceased until the family could raise enough money to have the remains shipped to their homeland to ensure a restful afterlife.

There are a few dry camping areas north of town alongside Jordan Creek. They are first-come, first-serve and there is no charge. Just above the last campsite on Jordan Creek are the remains of a stone wall. In the early years this was used during the winter months to manufacture ice. There was a doorway in the wall which when closed created a dam. After the water froze it was harvested for the hotel.

Directly behind the Idaho Hotel is Stoddard Mansion with its decorative gingerbread trim. It was built by John Stoddard who earned the money to build it by selling a mining claim in DeLamar. Interesting fact: although the Stoddard Mansion is large, it was the advent of closets that defined it as a "mansion." Other homes of the era had no closets but used armoires. Next to the Stoddard Mansion you will see the majestic Catholic church, Our Lady of Tears. The church has a long history and still holds services once a month during summer with scheduled services. Behind the church on War Eagle Mountain the mine dump of the Morning Star Mine is clearly visible. The dump can be seen from the hotel dining room as well. The Potosi Mine dump is opposite the hotel which can be reached by car (or on foot), and provides a different vantage point of Silver City.

In 1901 the completion of the Swan Falls Dam supplied electricity to the Silver City mines. It is the oldest hydroelectric generating plant on the Snake River. In the 1990s it was replaced with a dam further upriver. Today Swan Falls Dam is on the National Register of Historic Places, and the dam itself is a museum open to the public from mid-April until Labor Day. The power poles and electrical lines leading to Silver City were removed in the early 1940s due to the war effort. As a result, the only electrical power in Silver City today comes from solar power. Water is supplied to the town from a spring-fed holding tank. As winter approaches, in late fall the water is shut off. The pipes leading to town from the tank cannot be buried deep enough to prevent their freezing, so the town has no water during the winter months, other than water carried by hand.

If you are up for a drive, you can easily make it to the top of War Eagle Mountain in a 2WD vehicle. One mile from Ruby Junction on the road you drove in on is a large dirt road to the right (Fairview Road), leading up into the Cinnabar Mountain Range. Today, War Eagle Mountain is equipped with cell towers and is one of the highest points in Owyhee County. Along the way you will pass the tiny Fairview Cemetery, established 1873. The summit is 8,051 feet and affords spectacular views.

In 1972, Silver City was listed on the National Register of Historic Places as the Silver City Historic District. Silver City is home to several fraternal organizations. The Owyhee Cattlemen's Association still meets at the Silver City schoolhouse twice a year. They have been holding continued annual meetings in Silver City for more than 143 years. There is also the Odd Fellows Hall which continues to meet in June and August. The Knights of Pythias disbanded in 1944, but used to share the I.O.O.F Hall with the Independent Order of Odd Fellows. Silver City's original Masonic Hall continues to hold periodic meetings. One thing that was essential to everyone who settled in this new frontier was mail service. In the early days, post offices were established in various places for the convenience of the settlers so long distances were not needed to be traveled to reach a main post office. At one time, Owyhee County had fifty post offices. Today five remain.

From Ruby Junction, continue on Silver City/DeLamar Road toward Jordan Valley to complete your loop. Stay on Silver City/DeLamar Road until you come to the Cow Creek Road fork. You will pass by Dewey, DeLamar and Wagontown. Take the right fork onto Cow Creek Road. Follow Cow Creek Road until you hit Old Highway 95. Total driving distance is twenty miles from Silver City. Head east towards Boise on Highway 95.

The outside world as most of us know it has not tainted this tiny community which has survived in the Owyhee Mountains for multiple generations. Most of the twisted ideals of mankind do not exist here. Instead, you will find peaceful people moving along at a slow pace, perfectly content to be living far removed from air-conditioned shopping, Wi-Fi and the throngs of people who infest our cities. Consider spending a weekend in this colorful corner of southern Idaho before it vanishes. Far removed from the light pollution of Boise, Silver City sits under a celestial blanket of spectacular stars. On a cloudless evening you can gaze into the unobstructed night sky, studying the tiny question marks that sparkle and beckon from the vastness of the universe, exactly as Silver City's first residents did a hundred years before you were born.

On your way to Silver City, I would suggest stopping at the Owyhee County Historical Society Museum in Murphy off Highway 78 behind the courthouse. Pick up a copy of Helen Nettleton's book, *Interesting Buildings in Silver City, Idaho,* for $10. A tour of the museum will provide a great deal of valuable information prior to visiting Silver City.

Idaho Hotel reservations: idahohotel@historicsilvercityidaho.com, (208) 583-4104

RUBY

Ruby City was the earliest settlement in the upper valley. The first newspaper started here, the *Owyhee Avalanche* which had its beginning in 1865. This same newspaper serviced the Owyhees throughout those early years and is still printed and circulated today. Ruby City was located about a mile north of Silver City. As a new townsite of

Silver City was being laid out, it became obvious that it was in a better location than Ruby City. It was also apparent that the primary mines were closer to the new location, so it was decided to move the buildings of Ruby City to the new location. In doing so, Silver City was born.

One thing they couldn't move was the Ruby City Cemetery. Ruby Junction is at the crossroads of Jordan Creek Road and DeLamar Road, north of Silver City. If you stand at the crossing and look west, you will see white marble headstones on the hill ahead of you. You can either walk or drive to the site. This is all that is left of Ruby City.

FLINT

Located twelve miles south of Silver City is the community of Flint, which sits at an elevation of 5,220 feet. Named after a gentleman who homesteaded here, Flint had a disappointing history. Founded in 1864, a mill was rapidly constructed, as were several framed buildings. The town consisted of several businesses with a reported population of 1,500. However, it was soon learned that the silver here was sulfide silver which presented problems. First and foremost, there was no smelting facility in Flint. Sulfide made it more difficult to extract the silver from the ore, which made it prohibitive to freight. Flint never flourished and due to the inferior ore, the residents soon moved on.

Two area deaths were reported to be at the hands of Indians. This is another indication that Flint was established in the early years of Owyhee mining. As more white settlers moved into the Owyhees, there were fewer incidents with Native Americans. The two deaths that were reported were those of William L. Black and his daughter-in-law, Emma Myers. The graves can be seen in the cemetery close to town.

Flint is located on private property that is owned by the Bonnell family, whose lineage dates back to Owyhee's early years. The remaining structures, which consist of two or three cabins and the mill, are maintained by the Bonnell family. Also left behind are beautiful rock retaining walls built by skilled craftsman when Flint was in its early development.

Although I'm told there is a way to reach Flint from Silver City, I'm doubtful. The best way I know is to take Trout Creek Road west towards Jordan Valley from DeLamar. Turn left at Juniper Mountain Road. In five miles turn left on Flint Creek Road. Follow Flint Creek Road to Flint. There may be a gate along the Flint Creek Road; if so, park off the road and walk.

FAIRVIEW

First settled in 1864 on the northeast slope of War Eagle Mountain at 7,122 feet, Fairview was one of the first settlements in the Owyhees, the primary silver/gold producing mine being the Oro Fino. A post office was established here in 1866. Being the first settlement in the Owyhees, Fairview was initially selected as the county seat but lost out to Ruby City. After Ruby, the county seat went to Silver City and eventually to Murphy.

A revolt took place in 1865 when miners took superintendent M. A. Baldwin hostage, demanding they be paid three weeks' back pay. At its peak in 1875, the town boasted a population of four hundred. In that same year, a devastating fire destroyed most of the town. The post office closed in 1878.

Other mines of Fairview were the Ida Elmore and Chariot. The Oro Fino Mine had its own community, which contained a school and post office. It operated between 1866-1899.

Nothing of Fairview's structures remain today. The tiny but maintained Fairview Cemetery is located on Fairview Road east of Silver City.

DEWEY

Originally called Booneville, the town was renamed after Colonel William Dewey purchased the mine in 1896 and rebuilt the town. In addition to the town, Dewey constructed the magnificent three-story Dewey Hotel. Along with the impressive Dewey Hotel there was a twenty-stamp mill and post office.

As the saying goes, there are two ways to make money in mining, the second being supplying the miners. William Dewey had put into motion the construction of the Boise, Nampa & Owyhee Railway in 1886, a 30-mile line beginning in Nampa to serve Silver City. For the tracks to cross the Snake River the Guffey Bridge was constructed, now located at Melba's Celebration Park. In 1899, as construction neared what is known today as Murphy, conditions in the Owyhee Mines were declining and the decision was made not to extend the tracks onto Silver City, DeLamar and Dewey, which was a crushing blow.

To further things, a fire destroyed the Dewey Hotel in 1900. With the destruction of the hotel, larger mines failing in the Owyhees and the much-anticipated railroad not continuing past Murphy, the town of Dewey was doomed.

Col. William H. Dewey was born August 1, 1823, in the state of New York. He came to San Francisco in 1852 and continued onto Virginia City, Nevada. In 1863 he arrived at the Owyhee mines and was instrumental in developing Ruby, Silver City and Dewey.

After the fire destroyed the Dewey Hotel in the city of his namesake, Dewey constructed the Dewey Palace Hotel in Nampa in 1903. He died in April of 1903, only a few weeks after the Palace Hotel opened. He was a promoter of great energy, strength and determination. In 2012, the *Idaho-Press Tribune* wrote of the Dewey Palace Hotel, "Probably Nampa's most famed and missed structure."

While freight service continued on the Boise Nampa and Owyhee (B N & O) for the farming community and local population until 1947, the tracks now terminate at Melba and the remaining tracks that once reached Murphy were torn up.

As mentioned earlier, before driving to any of the Owyhee mining sites, it is important to stop at the Owyhee County Historical Museum in Murphy.

DELAMAR

Continuing down Silver City Road, six miles west of Silver City you will start to see evidence of abandoned homes on both sides of the road. DeLamar was named after Captain Joseph DeLamar and sits at an elevation of 5,463 feet alongside Jordan Creek. In 1875, Joseph DeLamar was credited with developing the initial silver lode which eventually became Idaho's major silver mine outside of the Coeur d'Alene district. Reports of the fabulous lode brought an immediate rush.

When wives united with their husbands in these isolated camps a different tone was set. While women entering this new frontier were a heartier breed than those of the twenty-first century, they brought with them culture, schools, social gatherings, the value of church, and provided a different perspective the citizens now saw in their community.

Because DeLamar was located in the narrow Jordan Creek valley, buildings were constructed on both sides of the road and up the hillsides. By 1890, DeLamar was thriving and had the usual businesses typical of the time which included saloons, a livery, a two-story schoolhouse with bell tower, eateries, and a newspaper called the *Nugget*. By 1900, the population of DeLamar was 876. By 1910, private residences in DeLamar were comparable to other modern homes being built throughout the United States. The DeLamar

Miners had their own twenty-piece concert band that provided music at numerous annual summer banquets and holiday affairs.

Captain DeLamar was a visionary who was determined to see the town that was named for him grow and prosper. In 1890 he constructed the beautiful two-story DeLamar Hotel. By all rights the most prominent structure in town was the impressive DeLamar Mill, also credited to the captain. As you are traveling down Silver City Road you will see a gated wooden bridge spanning Jordan Creek on your left. Park and walk across the bridge. The two-story DeLamar boardinghouse for the miners and mill workers stood to your immediate left after crossing the bridge. Today there is no trace of it. However, directly behind the site of the boardinghouse and immediately in front of you is the assay office for the Delamar Mine which is still standing. If you turn right after crossing the bridge and walk a few hundred feet, you will see a debris field. This is the remains of the magnificent DeLamar Mill. Today it is only a pile of rubble, but in 1900 this was the most productive stamp mill and processing plant in the Owyhees. An estimated $8 million in silver was produced by the DeLamar mines.

Limited mining continued up to and after the Depression in 1929. DeLamar supported a post office between 1917 and 1930. Even after mining declined, the community continued to exist for several decades. There was a brief mining resurgence in the 1970s with open-pit mining.

DeLamar Mine Assay Office

Jordan Creek starts above Silver City and flows through Jordan Creek valley past Dewey and DeLamar. During the boom years the creek was used as a sewer system. Latrines were literally suspended over the creek where the human waste was swept away. Processing waste from the mills was also dumped into it to be carried out of the area. Included in the waste was mercury from the mills of Silver City, Dewey and DeLamar. Due to these toxins that were introduced over a hundred years ago, some say that they would not drink out of this creek today. I was told that fifty years ago you could retrieve one teaspoon of mercury by panning one pan of gravel from the creek. I wonder if there is any left today.

In 1976, DeLamar was listed in the National Register of Historic Places as a Historic District.

There is a cemetery up the hillside on the north side of the Silver City Road. A sign marking the cemetery can be seen showing the establishment date of 1890.

WAGONTOWN

Considered to be one of the earliest settlements on Jordan Creek, it was established in 1865 prior to DeLamar. Wagontown was a road station and stage stop on the Silas Skinner Toll Road. It was a small town and although it did not have a post office, it did have a saloon, blacksmith, mercantile and hotel. The Henrietta Stamp Mill operated on Jordan Creek above Wagontown.

Wagontown had the flattest ground on upper Jordan Creek. Due to this, a racetrack was established that featured horse racing. Wagontown was also known for weekend picnics and outings.

Other than the cemetery, nothing of Wagontown remains. To reach the cemetery, head west from DeLamar on Silver City/DeLamar Road. Turn right on the first dirt road prior to Cow Creek Road. Continue for three-quarters of a mile. The cemetery is marked with a historical sign showing the establishment date of 1866.

There are eight cemeteries that served the small communities surrounding Silver City. Thanks to efforts of volunteers like Nick and Doloras Ihli, these revered places have been spared. A primary concern is keeping adequate fencing around the sites to prevent range cattle from wandering in. The cemetery in Oreana is the only cemetery where individuals can still be buried; all others are considered historical.

Mary O'Malley's great-grandparents are interned at the Wagontown Cemetery. Mary O'Malley is currently a resident of Silver City.

Do not confuse this Wagontown with that of the Seafoam District.

MURPHY

Although not a ghost town, Murphy is significant to Idaho's history and Owyhee Mining District. At an elevation of 2,820 feet, Murphy is the county seat of Owyhee County and is considered one of the smallest county seats in the United States, with a population of ninety. Murphy is thirty-eight miles south of Nampa on Highway 78.

Murphy is home to the Owyhee County Historical Museum. It is important to visit this museum prior to driving onto Silver City, twenty-four miles to the southwest. The director of the museum is Eriks Garsvo, who is not only an authority on Silver City, but also on the vast railroad system that served Idaho in its developmental years. Highly informed docents such as Betsy Kendrick and Margret Budden are there during business hours between Tuesday and Saturday to assist visitors. There is no charge, but donations are welcomed. The museum is filled with historical documents and beautifully displayed exhibits which explain the early years of Idaho and the Owyhee Mining District. A gift shop along with literature is available to purchase or browse through during your visit.

By 1866, ten mills working twenty-four hours a day in Silver City produced $1.5 million in gold and silver, but getting that ore to market and supplies to the miners was an ordeal. Colonel William H. Dewey understood that getting supplies and equipment to the mines and the ore to market was essential to the growth of the district. Up until this point, five thousand miners relied on pack animals and freight teams to haul the ore forty miles to the train depot in Nampa.

Colonel Dewey was the visionary who developed the Boise Nampa and Owyhee Railroad (BN&O). Much of Silver City, Dewey, DeLamar and Owyhee District would not exist without his efforts. His contributions to the Owyhee Mining District were without parallel. Dewey's vision became a reality with the creation of this railroad (BN&O) which later became a subsidiary of the Union Pacific and ran a 30-mile-long track connecting Nampa with Murphy in 1903. Unfortunately, by the time the tracks reached Murphy in 1903, conditions in the Owyhee mines were declining and the plan to continue the line onto Silver City and DeLamar was abandoned. The town of Murphy developed at end of track.

Col. Dewey's vision of running track all the way to Silver City might have come true had a proposed tunnel through War Eagle Mountain come to fruition. A plan had been formulated to run a twelve-thousand-foot tunnel from the Morning Star to a point near the Oro Fino Mine. The purpose of the $5 million tunnel was to consolidate several veins and lodes, subsequently turning several independent operations into one single efficient operation. However, the venture never moved forward. This ingenious operation could have altered the history of Owyhee mining as we know it.

The much-anticipated railroad that never made it to Silver City was a psychological and financial blow to the district, although freight and ore wagons continued to commute to the railhead at Murphy.

Murphy was named for Cornelius Murphy, who was a crew boss on the construction of railroad track for the BN&O and supervised construction of the Guffey Bridge in 1897. The Guffey Bridge is a short distance (twenty-five minutes) from Murphy and worth a visit. The famous bridge was listed on the National Register of Historic Places in 1978 and is the largest historic artifact in the state of Idaho. The 70-foot-high steel, Parker-Through-Truss structure spans the Snake River in Celebration Park near Melba. Abandoned in 1947, it was saved from demolition in 1970. You are welcome to walk across the historic bridge and while looking down at the surface of the Snake River, imagine the Boise Nampa and Owyhee Railroad that once rumbled across its tracks.

On July 29, 1912, the Great Sheep Wreck took place in Guffy, three miles north of Murphy. Freight cars loaded with sheep were en route out of Murphy. As the BN&O gained speed coming down the steep grade, the locomotive and several cars jumped the track, killing the brakeman and hundreds of sheep. They incurred such a financial hardship due to this terrible accident that the Oregon Short Line Railroad took over the line. The railway operated until 1947. The tracks were scrapped between Murphy and Nampa in 1997.

Outpost Days commences the first weekend in June. An extensive list of events take place with delicious food, vintage costumes, and one-of-a-kind entries. As of this writing it was in its 54th year! Fun for all ages.

Murphy has its own asphalt airstrip which is located northeast of the community.

OREANA

Oreana is located fifteen miles from Murphy in Owyhee County. It is most known for Our Lady Queen of Heaven Catholic Church. Built is 1883, this Catholic church was added to the National Register of Historic Places in 1980. It was originally built as Oreana's general store and post office; it was converted in 1961 to a Catholic church.

The building is constructed of lava rock using cement as mortar. Although it was renovated as a church the overall construction was left intact.

Even though Oreana is near Silver City, it had no significant importance to the mining community other than as a center of ranching and agriculture. As large populations of miners poured into Silver City in 1864, there were others that foresaw the demand for food. Hash houses, restaurants and mining camps needed food for the hungry miners and grain and hay to sustain the animals that hauled the heavy loaded wagons to and from the mines. Three communities in the Owyhee's answered the call: Oreana, Jordan Valley and Bruneau. Hundreds of acres of wild hay meadows were ideal for sustaining the working animals through the long winter. Vegetables and fruit were grown in the fertile valleys as well as beef cattle, sheep, hogs, goats and chickens, which were in high demand throughout the Owyhee Mining District.

From Murphy, head east 13.3 miles on Highway 78 to Oreana Loop Road. Turn right and proceed two miles to Oreana and Our Lady Queen of Heaven Catholic Church.

If you continue on Oreana Loop Road for one-quarter mile past Our Lady Queen of Heaven Catholic Church, you will see Oreana Cemetery on your left. Mary O'Malley's parents, Hubert and Helen Nettleton, are interned here.

Catholic Mass is held once a month on a selected Saturday at Our Lady Queen of Heaven Catholic Church. For information, contact St. Paul's Parish (208-466-7031).

Root cellar behind the café, Grasmere.

GRASMERE

Grasmere is located in the southwestern sector of Owyhee County, thirty-nine miles south of Bruneau on Highway 51 at 5,089 feet.

Although listed as a ghost town, it is the location of an abandoned gas station, café and post office. It is one of the few ghost towns in Idaho's southern desert, and is still found on most Idaho road maps. Since it had a post office, it has the distinction of being a town!

This solitary group of buildings used to be the only gas between Owyhee, Nevada and Bruneau, a distance of seventy-six miles. Deciding that operating the remote location was unprofitable, the owners left, putting the service station and café up for sale in 2005. It remains abandoned today, having given up its fight to the surrounding desert. Due to vandalism and rodents, there is no hope for any renovation. Covered with graffiti, it still stands vigilant alongside this isolated section of highway.

Beware the cheatgrass and foxtails that surround the structures during late spring and summer. There is an impressive underground root cellar built behind the café. A public shower appears to be at the far north end of the property. The café is the larger structure in the center, while the post office is the southernmost building. The primary residents today are Barn Swallows that have carefully constructed their mud homes underneath the roof of the café's front porch.

Grasmere

WICKAHONEY

If you're going to be visiting Oreana or Grasmere, you might as well include this small side trip. Wickahoney was established as a stage stop between Mountain Home and Mountain City, Nevada. A small community grew up alongside the stage stop which also served as the Wickahoney post office. The stage/post office served the town from 1895 to 1911. The structure had a wooden porch that serviced both the ground level and second story. When a stage line out of Elko, Nevada replaced the stage at Wickahoney, the town slowly faded into obscurity. Today the massive stone walls are all that remain.

The partially collapsed structure is constructed of lava rock and mortar very similar to that used for Our Lady Queen of Heaven Catholic Church in Oreana. I am happy to report that, due to its isolation, the ominous structure has escaped vandalism and graffiti. The historical ruins were important enough to be added to the National Register of Historic Places in 1982.

Seven miles north of Grasmere on Highway 51 is a dirt road to the left. Take it for five miles to reach Wickahoney. You will cross over a dry section of Wickahoney Creek. The site can be seen on Google Maps. Elevation is 5,190 feet.

Located in Owyhee County, twenty miles south of Marsing and west of Highway 95, is the site of Rockville. Elevation is 3,983 feet. Very little is left today but this site is certainly worth the short drive.

In 1889 Ed Holmes and his wife operated a stage stop here. In that same year, Mrs. Holmes was killed in an Indian attack. Her grave is north of the site on a small knoll. This was the site of the Rocks Stage Station. Note the large rocks behind the grave site. In those days the stage stop operated from whatever ranch chose to be the stop. One year the stage stop might be at one place, and the next year it could be two miles down the road. The stop always stayed in close proximity to Rockville, and whoever agreed to take on the duties and responsibilities of the stage stop could be depended upon.

The Jordan Valley Stage did a 60-mile run. Stops were made near Marsing, Homedale, Jump Creek Stage Stop and Poison Creek Stage Stop. Stage stops were typically positioned every fifteen miles to acquire fresh horses and allow a welcomed break to the passengers who had to put up with the bumpy and dusty ride. Another drawback was, passengers were forced to sit close together. Cold and hot weather had disadvantages as you can imagine. Rockville was an important stop as it had a hotel.

Rockville was originally established as a stage station in 1870. Rockville had a post office that operated between 1885 and 1912. A nineteen-room stone hotel was built in 1903, as well as a saloon and other essential businesses. The hotel, which had a dance floor, was the center of activity for social gatherings. The town was abandoned in 1928 when Highway 95 bypassed it. The hotel was torn down in 1930. A rock-lined water well can be seen on the west side of the site near McBride Creek. The well is surrounded by rusting barbed wire to keep animals from accidentally falling in. This is grazing land; evidence of cattle can be seen especially in the thicket of trees and bunchgrass on the opposite side of the road adjacent to the site. The remains of a crude rock foundation remain at the site.

To get to Rockville take Highway 95 south from Marsing. At 19 miles, turn right onto McBride Road at the Leslie Gulch turnoff. Continue on this well-maintained dirt road and turn right at 2.5 miles. The Rockville site is located on the right, just after crossing the dry bed of McBride Creek. After .4 miles turn right, and drive to the top of a small knoll to visit the gravesite of Mrs. Ed Holmes and two others.

If you continue on McBride Road (Leslie Gulch Road) from the Rockville turnoff, in three miles you will come to the Rockville Cemetery. A fenced area can be seen a short distance to the left of

McBride Road before Succor Creek. Graves date from 1885 to 1905. Some stones reveal entire families buried here, where others are alone. In total, there are twenty-five grave sites, including that of Joe (Little Joe) Monahan. The first record of Joe Monahan was in Ruby City where he raised hogs and chickens but later moved to a dugout along Succor Creek near Jordan Valley. He was a small man who possessed an effeminate voice and beardless face, but he vigorously took part in men's work, so no questions were asked. Respected by his fellow miners and buckaroos, he worked menial jobs but distanced himself from social activities, keeping to himself. In 1903 while herding cattle to winter pasture, he fell ill and contracted pneumonia. He was cared for by a kindly neighbor but passed away the first week in 1904. When men came to prepare the body for burial, it was learned that Little Joe was a woman. He faced life fearlessly in this new frontier and served his community by voting during elections and serving on juries when asked. Little Joe will be remembered forever in the annals of Idaho's history.

Continuing on McBride Road past the cemetery you will come to the junction of Succor Creek Road and the Rockville Elementary School. Built in 1887, this little red schoolhouse has served the valley for 130 years. A sole teacher oversees kindergarten through 8th grade to a dozen students from surrounding ranches. Every weekday the American flag to run up the flagpole in the schoolyard by elementary students while reciting the Pledge of Allegiance. I am proud to say that patriotism is a lesson high on the list of priorities with this tiny school's curriculum.

If you continue on Leslie Gulch Road , you will come to Lake Owyhee and Leslie Gulch Recreation Area in twenty miles. It was named for Hiram Leslie who was killed here by lightning. There is another version of the story. An allegation had been filed against Hiram, charging him with cattle rustling. When questioned by the county sheriff concerning the rustling, Hiram replied, "If I was involved in any way, may the good lord strike me dead with lightning." Any way you look at it, Leslie's name is forevermore memorialized in signage of Owyhee County.

SALMON/CHALLIS CAMPS

STANLEY

Although the town of Stanley is far from a ghost, it demands mention, as it is a focal point to other mining districts close by. Stanley was established in 1890 and bordered the Stanley Mining District. It later became a supply point for outlying mines. In the years prior to having its own smelting operations, mules loaded with ore could drop their loads off here at Mose Storher Mercantile; these loads were then picked up by wagons for delivery to Ketchum smelters over Galena Summit. The miners would then load up with provisions at the mercantile in Stanley and return to the mines. Two areas became known as Upper Stanley and Lower Stanley, each with a unique and colorful past. Located in Custer County in the Sawtooth Valley and inside the Sawtooth National Recreation Area, today Stanley is at the junction of Highway 21 and 75 and has a population of 116. State Highway 75 runs the length of Sawtooth Valley (popularly known as Stanley-Sawtooth Country). It extends south of Galena Summit, from Sawtooth City and Vienna past Stanley to the north, approximately thirty miles. The Stanley Basin is an area northwest of Stanley beyond Nip-N-Tuck Mountain, including Stanley Creek and Kelly Creek. The nation's wintertime temperatures are often the lowest in Stanley.

Stanley Basin was named after Captain John Stanley, the oldest member of a group of twenty-three prospectors who entered the basin by way of Warrens in 1863 in search of gold. Gold was discovered along several tributaries but due to it remoteness, lack of provisions and threat of Indians, the men left. Gold discoveries in Custer and Bonanza as well as Wood River Valley opened the basin once again in 1879.

One-quarter mile below Lower Stanley is Joe's Gulch Jeep Road. This was primarily a placer mining area. Turn left and take the dirt road three miles up the drainage to where the road crosses the creek just before it starts a steep climb. Although deteriorated, the remains of Ora Jones' Five -Stamp Mill can be seen, proof that hard-rock mining did exist amongst the placer claims. The stamps were freighted to the site from Salt Lake City. Extensive placer and hydraulic mining took place a short distance downriver as well. In 1895, Alvah P. Challis and Henry Sturkey located several claims, considered the largest placer claims in Stanley Basin. Twelve acres of rich placer ground was staked

51

out near Kelly Creek. A series of ditches were dug to channel water into a 12-inch pipe, where a canvas hose and nozzle was attached. This hydraulic system washed the hillside down to bedrock, delivering the gold-bearing gravel into a series of sluices. Other placer areas were on Elk and Stanley Creeks, also a short distance downriver from Stanley. Several hard-rock mines existed in the Stanley Basin. The Iron Dyke (lode) Mine was developed near Stanley Lake.

Dredge mining came to the Stanley Basin on Stanley Creek with the Stanley Basin Dredging Company in 1899. Rebuilt in 1903, the steam-powered dredge continued operations on two hundred acres, including the rich placer area known as Buckley Bar (6,499 feet). In 1929, the Great Depression slowed operations. Then in 1934, President Franklin Roosevelt initiated the New Deal, which raised the price of gold from $20.67 to $35.00 per ounce, triggering new interest in gold mining across the country. In 1935, a dam was constructed on Stanley Creek. With the advent of World War II, gold mining in the Stanley Basin ceased. Some activity continued after the war, but never again on a large scale.

Fifteen miles up Valley Creek from Lower Stanley was the Valley Creek Mine which supported numerous buildings, including a twenty-stamp, steam-powered mill, assay office, mining office, lumber mill, power plant, bunkhouse and a forty-man crew. Leased by Fort Pitt Mining and Milling Company and later Western Gold Exploration Company, operations started here in 1884 and continued into the 1930s. During the winter months, supplies and mail were pulled by hand on a sled from Stanley. The Buckskin Mine is located over the next ridge from the Valley Creek Mine on Buckskin Mountain. The Buckskin Mining Company operated from 1883 to 1888.

The Valley Creek Ranger Station was going to be auctioned off in 1980 when Laurii Gadwa and others stepped forward and took possession due to its historical significance. Laurii is still involved with the museum, and is currently president of the Stanley City Council, where she has been active for sixteen years. Valley Creek Ranger Station was the first ranger station in the Stanley Basin. Built in 1909, it was rebuilt in 1933. It was built on the east side of Valley Creek, a short distance from where the creek empties into the Salmon River. Today Valley Creek Ranger Station is home to the Stanley Museum. Laurii's husband, Gary Gadwa, was the president of Sawtooth Interpretive and Historical Association (SIHA) from 2005-2019. Prior to this, Gary was a game warden for twenty-eight years with the Idaho Fish and Game (IDFG). Gary is now a board member for SIHA and also does historic walking tours of Stanley, while maintaining his position as historian for the museum. The museum and much of the incredible history surrounding Stanley owes a great deal to Gary and Laurii Gadwa for their tireless efforts in preserving this part of Idaho's past. The Stanley Museum is between Stanley and Lower Stanley on Highway 75. Its hours of operation are Memorial Day through Labor Day. It is best to call ahead. The Stanley Cemetery is located west of the Stanley Museum on Valley Creek Road (481).

An area which became known as Cape Horn was located northwest of Stanley on Bear Creek and Marsh Creek. A group of buildings here acted as a way-station to miners traveling to Bonanza, Custer and Oro Grande on Loon Creek. It owes its name to packers who said the turns in the trail leading there reminded them of rounding Cape Horn in South America. Today Cape Horn Guard Station is located here just east of Highway 21.

By the 1920s, there were greater populations in some of the surrounding mining operations than in Stanley itself. The tiny settlements of Stanley and Lower Stanley competed with one another over the years. In 1916, Lower Stanley had a schoolhouse, a general store and post office. By 1919, Leslie Niece built a general store and moved the post office from Lower to Upper Stanley. By the 1930s, Upper Stanley was seeing more businesses, while Lower Stanley was content with a quieter life along the banks of the Salmon River. While Upper Stanley has more lodging and dining opportunities, Lower Stanley has evolved into a river-rafting center with small cabin rentals. Stanley has always been a destination for outdoor enthusiasts. Automobile traffic and easy access have improved tourism, quite a difference from 1920 when the small settlement's primary function was serving the needs of settlers and miners throughout the basin and valley. Sawtooth Hotel and Restaurant in Upper Stanley has been accommodating guests since 1931. Many of the surrounding peaks and creeks bear the names of Stanley's first settlers. Owing to the fertile valley and abundant grass, settlers and cattle ranches continued to prosper after the prospectors and mining companies had moved on to other strikes and new ventures.

Today, outdoor enthusiasts come to the Sawtooth Valley every summer to take advantage of spectacular scenery, rafting, camping, hiking and fishing in the creeks and lakes that surround the valley. The Stanley-Sawtooth Chamber of Commerce sponsors the Sawtooth Festival of Arts, Crafts and Food, typically in the middle of July. Mountain Village Resort in Upper Stanley offers excellent accommodations and also features a natural hot springs, restaurant and cocktails year-round.

SEAFOAM DISTRICT

Somewhere around 1904, three mining districts formed here. The first was the Greyhound Mining and Milling Company. Located on Sulphur Creek, it boasted a forty-ton capacity smelter. In 1910, a post office was established.

The Snowstorm Mining and Milling Company formed as well, packing a smelter in by pack mules from the small settlement of Stanley.

With the advent of the Seafoam Mine on Float Creek, these operations grew into the community of Seafoam. All were equipped with boardinghouses and bunkhouses for the employees. Cabins were constructed for management. There were numerous mines throughout the Seafoam District, most of which were lead-silver and gold. In 1927, the Seafoam Mines Corporation was made up of seventeen quartz claims and six mill sites. Employees and family in the community of Seafoam numbered forty-one people. A 230-horsepower electric power plant supplied energy to the fifty-ton ball mill processing the free milling gold ore. Employees worked two shifts.

Blackhawk Mining Company also came into existence.

On the Stanley side of Vanity Mountain (east), two log cabins were constructed in 1905 by Mose Storher to accommodate miners traveling to and from the Seafoam Mining District. This became known as Wagontown. From the Seafoam District, freight wagons hauled ore to Stanley, a distance of forty miles. Those same wagons would then carry supplies on the return trip and typically spend the night here to rest the horses before continuing onto the Seafoam District the following morning. The road was constructed by the Greyhound Mining Company; a toll was charged to all travelers with the exception of company wagons.

As with most mining districts, Seafoam saw three booms, or periods of activity, the first time in 1900, another during the 1920s, and the third in the 1940s.

From Stanley, head west on Highway 21 toward Lowman. Take Marsh Creek Scenic Trail to the right, then left on Beaver Creek Road (FS 008), and continue till you get to Seafoam Guard Station. The area affords many fishing and camping opportunities.

Seafoam guard station

CLAYTON

Founded in 1880 as a smelter site, Clayton is in Custer County, thirty-four miles east of Stanley on Highway 75. Named for J.E. Clayton of Atlanta, who selected the mill site, it sits directly on the Salmon River. With a population of seven, Clayton is said to be "the town that refuses to die." Although once a mining community, it is mostly noted today for a few small cabin rentals. It appears to be an ideal spot to quietly fish alongside the Salmon River or enjoy a vast system of OHV trails.

In the 1880s it was a different story. A twenty-five-ton smelter was constructed here at the same time the Bayhorse smelter was built. Although it was common for Clayton to import four thousand tons of coal per season, kilns were also constructed here to produce charcoal. Financial capital came from the Idaho Mining and Smelter Company. The Clayton Silver Mine was southern Idaho's largest producer of silver. Unlike Bayhorse, which served multiple mines requiring a large workforce, Clayton was a smelter town. By this I mean the smelting operation only needed a small workforce. Due to Claytons small population, it didn't develop the usual businesses as other towns of the time, although it did support two general stores and a brewery. Ice was harvested during the winter months to provide residents with cold beer during the summer.

In addition to being a supply point for neighboring mines, Clayton's bullion production averaged over a million pounds each year with both lead and silver and continued for ten years after production in Bayhorse ceased. Due to the additional mines the Clayton Smelter was servicing in 1889, the smelter capacity was expanded to sixty tons. Throughout its smelting years, slag was carelessly dumped directly into the Salmon River as a means of getting rid of the waste.

In 1902 the smelter was closed. In 1926, the Idaho Mining and Smelter Company sold its interests to the Ford Motor Company. Ford continued mining lead here until 1946 for the purpose of manufacturing automobile batteries. Today the kilns and smelter are completely gone, although evidence of slag from the Clayton Smelter can still be seen alongside the shoreline of the Salmon River.

Geographically, the townsite has a total area of 0.01 square miles, making it the smallest incorporated city in Idaho and one of the smallest incorporated cities in the United States.

For such a small community there is a lot to see. The Clayton Historical Association purchased the Idaho Mining and Smelting Company Store in 2006. In 2006 and 2007, the building which was in a state of disrepair was completely renovated and is open today as a museum, located at 2 Ford Street. The museum is open from Memorial Day through Labor Day. The museum (L.B. Worthington Building) is an excellent source of information pertaining to the smelter years.

The primary business in Clayton today is the RV park and The Sawmill Station. The Sawmill Station is a country store, Bistro and RV site. The Bistro at Sawmill Station receives high marks from anyone who dines here, and if you don't believe me, check Yelp. They also have a gluten-free menu if desired. Sawmill Station is located at 21855 Highway 75. Call or check their website (208 838-2400). There are fifty RV sites with full hookups. They also provide Polaris UTV rentals equipped with GPS. Your host will program your route on GPS, or you can simply take off on your own. Historical mining sites and spectacular scenery await you. Take along your own lunch or The Sawmill will provide one for you. Cabins are also for rent. Ross and Natasha Williams are the proprietors. This is truly a wonderful way to investigate the backcountry of Bayhorse and see the remaining ruins of its principal mines, bunkhouse sites and ore dumps.

The Bistro and RV park open May 1 and close the last weekend in October. The Sawmill Station self-service gas station boasts competitive gasoline prices. This is the only gas between Stanley and Challis; propane is also available. The RV Park and Bistro are closed during the winter; the gas station is open all year. Website: www.thesawmillstation.com; email: info@thesawmillstation.com.

L.B. Worthington Building/Museum

The well-kept Clayton Cemetery is located one mile east of Clayton on the north side of Highway 75. George Washington Paul and Mary Mannix (Molly) Paul are interred here, who were early pioneers of the Stanley Basin. George and Molly built a home on Nip-and-Tuck Road that served miners, freighters and travelers going to and from the Cape Horn and Seafoam Mines. Both died within one hour of each other on October 11, 1924, both from natural causes. George Blackman, who is associated with Washington Basin, is also interred here.

The tiny community of Clayton also hosts an annual Fourth of July celebration and Clayton Heritage Day! During the Heritage Day celebration, an eighty-six-year-old man named Myron prepares doughnuts in a trailer he parks in front of the Clayton Museum. Myron has created such a reputation for these doughnuts that people bring chairs and start lining up before he even opens. They are made fresh on the spot and are considered by many to be the highlight of Clayton Heritage Day. Heritage Day combines with Labor Day and is typically the first Saturday in September.

LEESBURG

Leesburg is located in Lemhi County at an altitude of 6,653 feet in the Salmon National Forest west of Salmon. From Salmon, drive 5.1 miles south on Highway 93 and turn right on Williams Creek Road. This is the first step to reach the ghost town of Leesburg. I am not going to attempt to give directions. Whoever is reading this will no doubt have the ability to use GPS. It will take approximately one hour to reach Leesburg via a well-maintained dirt road, but it is worth the drive. You will know you are getting close when you drive across the Wade Fraser Bridge. Leesburg lies in a very remote location and is one of Idaho's true ghosts!

One interesting note is that Leesburg was different than most other "gold camps." When the gold or silver played out in other boomtowns, the residents moved on to other strikes. This wasn't the case here. Friends and families remained as a community through the 1940s. There was a school and church. A community had been established, and just because the streams no longer yielded gold didn't mean these people were going to leave their homes. Strong relationships had developed over the long winters. The community continued until the early 1940s when the town finally faded into obscurity.

It never ceases to amaze me when I see settlements as far removed as Leesburg; and I wonder what kind of individuals pushed beyond the boundaries of civilization among hostile Indians, steep terrain, and impenetrable forests? One such man was Frank Barney Sharky. In 1866 while preparing breakfast for his party of five, Sharky discovered a tree that had blown over the year before. Attached to the massive roots were chunks of quartz laden with gold! His find would set off a stampede that would become the single largest placer mining area in the history of Idaho.

The settlement was named after General Robert E. Lee. Many mining communities in Idaho and Montana at the end of the Civil War had strong Confederate ties. By spring of the year following Leesburg's founding, the population had increased to two thousand. The men who came to the new settlement weren't only men seeking gold. Two such entrepreneurs were David McNutt and Fred Phillips. They saw an urgency for supplies and set up the first mercantile. Enough supplies were packed into the fledgling community during the spring and summer months to sustain the miners throughout the harsh winter. A sawmill was constructed to supply lumber for the construction of homes and places of businesses. By summer of 1867, 140 buildings had been constructed. Businesses such as saloons, livery stables, a blacksmith, restaurants, boarding houses, feed and grain stores and even a barber shop were soon established. As the population increased, so did the people with opposing views of the recent war between the states. (The American Civil War took place between April 12, 1861 and May 26, 1865). Due to this interaction,

Main Street, Leesburg

another settlement came into existence a short distance away and was aptly named Grantsville. However, as the two towns grew together, Leesburg became the accepted name. By 1868 Leesburg's population had soared to seven thousand.

During the harsh winters, when the waters became too cold or too ice-covered to work, these miners turned their efforts to the construction of homes and businesses. Through raw courage and determination, they built a successful and thriving community with their bare hands. I salute these men as I do others from this period who opened frontiers for others to follow.

Most of the early placer mining took place along Napias Creek, Moose Creek, Arnett Creek and Daly Creek. Eventually, rich placer ground was coordinated off. Water from adjacent creeks was then channeled in to operate sluices to capture the rich gold. In the 1900s, with the advent of hard-rock mining, three processing mills were constructed: the thirty-stamp Kirkpatrick Mill, Harmony Mill and the Italian Mill. The surrounding hills echoed with the machinery processing the ore. However, local placer claims still accounted for $6.25 million in gold.

As in many mining camps, white miners sold their exhausted placer claims to eager Chinese who had more patience in extracting the elusive dust. By 1887, Leesburg's population had dwindled to 180, but small claims would continue to be worked, mostly by Chinese. Dredging superseded hard rock mining and added another chapter to Leesburg's history in the early 1900s. Mounds of river rock from the dredging years can be seen two miles outside of town before reaching the Wade Fraser Bridge.

In 1926, Leesburg saw a noticeable burst of activity with the advent of hydraulic mining. This unorthodox method was active for two seasons. Hydraulic mining uses water pressure to excavate large areas of dirt, rock and gravel, turning it into a muddy sediment. The resulting slurry is then funneled into large sluice boxes to separate the gold. It is a terribly destructive method of mining that causes devastating erosion on precious watershed, and scars the forests and land for centuries. After 1928, placer mining remained dormant until an increase in gold in 1934 prompted a brief comeback. In 1942, all gold mining shut down due to the war effort.

A new open-pit mining operation opened in 1995 called the Bear Track Meridian Mine, but mining activity ceased here in 2006. You can see the impressive installation west of Leesburg behind a chain-link fence. It is private property, and a caretaker is on the premises.

There is only one way to enter Leesburg; the road on the opposite end is blocked. As you exit town on your return trip, drive slowly

Leesburg looking north.

along the wooden fence that borders the road. Very soon you will see a path leading to a break in the fence. If you walk over the "bridge in the fence," you will enter the unmaintained cemetery. Information at the interpretive signs in town suggest that most of the graves were those of Chinese miners. Their remains were respectfully unearthed and returned to their homeland of China. There are a few markers still visible. One or two are very prominent.

As I alluded to earlier, this is an in-and-out, two-hour, round-trip drive. There is nothing of particular interest to see along the way. The advantage of Leesburg being located in such an isolated area is that the only people who make the trip possess a passion and deep love for places of this nature. This means that you will most likely be here alone! Being alone when you visit a place such as this is one of the most enriching experiences you can have. The seven thousand residents are gone, as are most of the structures along the mile-long street that used to exist. There are some interpretive signs at the entrance of town naming the buildings that are still standing. The billowing smoke from the sawmill and the thundering noise of the stamp mills and dredge has vanished. Unique to Leesburg and unlike Bayhorse, you can walk through the remaining residences and see the faded and torn wallpaper slowly giving up its battle to wind and time. In your own thoughts, you can quietly imagine who once lived here. Places such as this are vanishing due to the severe climate, and each year a percentage of these structures disappears a little bit more. If you are one of the fortunate ones to visit Leesburg, marvel at the spirit of the men and women who built it. Imagine the voices and the laughter that were once heard in the little home in which you are standing.

Leesburg was added to the National Register of Historic Places in 1975.

FORNEY

Located in Lemhi County, Forney is forty-one miles north of Challis via Morgan Creek Road at an elevation of 5,659 feet. Situated in the Salmon-Challis National Forest, Yellowjacket, Cobalt and Forney can and should be seen in the same day.

Drive north of Challis on Highway 93. In 7.6 miles turn left onto Morgan Creek Road. There is a road sign that gives Cobalt as forty miles. At thirty-plus miles, you will reach a fork. It will be a few miles past Morgan Creek Summit. Bear right onto FSR 055. In a few miles you will see the familiar steps on the left side of the road when you enter Forney.

Placer gold was discovered here on Porphyry Creek in 1890. After placer gold played out, Forney continued as a service area for

Concrete stairway leading nowhere.

Forney

ranchers and miners until 1948. Forney had a population of 150 with the usual businesses of typical small towns: post office, café, grocery, bakery, livery, saloon and school. I don't know what building was at the top of that beautiful concrete stairway. Could it have been the school? Imagine how many youngsters ran up and down those stairs shouting and laughing. Now everything is silent!

Several small structures and foundations remain today, specifically, the crumbling concrete stairs. Unfortunately, the building that they led to has completely vanished.

A short distance beyond Forney is the cutoff to Yellowjacket FS 112, which is clearly marked with a road sign.

YELLOWJACKET

Located in northern Lemhi County in the Salmon Challis National Forest, Yellowjacket sits at 6,401 feet and is fifty-seven miles and roughly two and a half hours north of Challis. Placer gold was discovered in Yellowjacket Creek in 1869 by Nathan Smith and Doc Wilson. Soon afterward, several lode mines started operating high on the hillsides surrounding the canyon, recovering gold, silver, lead and copper. Common to most newly formed mining camps of this era, Yellowjacket was in an isolated region. To get equipment and supplies into areas like this was a challenge. In 1875 a three-stamp mill was constructed. Equipment was brought in by pack animals from Mackay. The heavy iron parts were divided equally among the horses. The high yield of ore demanded more production. In the spring of 1883, a ten-stamp was packed in and assembled, which ultimately increased to a colossal sixty-stamp mill powered by water from Yellowjacket Creek. The mill was aptly named Yellowjacket Stamp Mill.

In 1892 it was determined that to better supply the mill, an aerial tramway would be constructed to deliver ore. Getting the heavy one and a quarter-inch steel cables that measured over a mile in length (8,400 feet) to Yellowjacket was a dilemma. Three trips were made with eighty mules carrying the unprecedented load. The cables needed to be strung from mule to mule. Mules were not accustomed to carrying anything such as this, which was a task. It took two men per mule, at first, to manage the confused animals. The journey from Challis to Yellowjacket took three weeks. When the tram was completed each ore bucket transported 125 pounds of ore to the mill site.

In 1895 a wagon road from Challis was completed, which helped greatly getting supplies and equipment to the remote location. By 1900, production waned but increased again in 1910 with the installation of a cyanide plant; but activity ceased again in 1914. Then in 1922, capital from outside investors once again brought prosperity to Yellowjacket. The town was now thriving with an increased population of three hundred people, with saloons, grocery stores, livery, blacksmith, restaurant and most notably the construction of a five-story hotel and boardinghouse. Construction started on the hotel in 1932. It was three stories on the north end and five stories on the opposite end where the ground sloped downward. However, soon after the completion of the hotel, another period of decline loomed over Yellowjacket. The fate of all mining towns is solely dependent on the veins of ore mined from deep within the earth. With the closing of the Yellowjacket Mine, the population declined. Multiple spurts of activity took place between 1929 and 1938.

Yellowjacket was one of the first ghost towns in Idaho to catch my attention. The name alone resonates with excitement and of a time when the concept of being politically correct wasn't the norm. The thing that most intrigued me with Yellowjacket was the magnificent five-story boardinghouse. The first photo I saw of Yellowjacket was in Wayne Sparling's Southern Idaho Ghost Towns, which was copyrighted in 1974, almost fifty years ago. Sparling's photo of the boardinghouse shows it completely intact. Bruce Raisch's Ghost Towns of Idaho shows it in 2004. The roof is missing, as is the fifth floor. At 6,400 feet, the winters are harsh here and the legacy these miners left behind is disappearing at an alarming rate. This was a big triumph for me!

Yellowjacket Stamp Mill

Yellowjacket Boardinghouse

I consider myself privileged to have seen it. As you can see from my photo, the boardinghouse is rapidly giving way to nature.

As was the case in many western mining camps, labor costs eventually exceeded profits and the colossal stamp mill was forced to shut down. An estimated $1 million was recovered, although most of that came from the late 1890s. Yellowjacket was a magnificent town and operation. Whoever makes the effort to visit Yellowjacket will see the evidence left behind which is a visual indication of the scope of things that took place here.

Drive north of Challis on Highway 93. In 7.6 miles turn left onto Morgan Creek Road (055). There is a road sign that gives Cobalt at forty miles. The road starts out lined with sage, eventually giving way to Douglas fir. At thirty-plus miles you will reach a fork. It will be a few miles past Morgan Creek Summit. Bear right onto 055. In a few miles you will pass through Forney. A short distance past Forney is the cutoff to Yellowjacket (FS 112); it is clearly marked with a road sign. You will cross Porphyry Creek at the cutoff. The distance from the cutoff to Yellowjacket is fifteen miles. Along the road you will pass patches of rabbitbrush and purple larkspur. Thickets of willow are seen all along Yellowjacket Creek.

The first structure you will see as you enter Yellowjacket is the impressive Yellowjacket Stamp Mill. Yellowjacket is shown on the Idaho Forest Service Salmon-Cobalt Ranger District Map.

Although Yellowjacket is inside the Salmon-Challis National Forest, it is on private property. The current resident lives on the property so please show respect. Yellowjacket is not part of the National Register of Historic Places.

COBALT (BLACKBIRD)

Located in Lemhi County, alongside Panther Creek at 6,890 feet, is the site of Cobalt. It was named for the mineral it mined. Cobalt had three stages of growth. Originally called Blackbird in 1892, the Blackbird Mine mined gold, but as work continued, copper was discovered, and later in 1901 a large deposit of cobalt was uncovered. Copper continued to be the prominent ore between 1913 and 1915 and then again in 1921. Then in 1939, cobalt became the primary ore under a government contract until 1960. There were slight bursts of activity in the 1980s.

In 1959 the town was moved from its original position near the Blackbird Mine to the present location. The following year Cobalt had a population of 250. Sometime in late 1959, Cobalt lost its contract with the government. The mine closed and the town became a ghost.

Idaho's Panther Creek, which is a large tributary of the Salmon River, had become decimated with heavy metals from the cobalt and copper mining years of the early 1900s. Toxic runoff had left the river lifeless and prevented salmon and steelhead from making their way to their spawning grounds . In 1990, federal agencies, mining companies and the State of Idaho began a $150 million restoration project to reclaim Panther Creek. Today, salmon and steelhead have returned, aquatic insects are thriving, and the creek has at last returned to its natural state.

The Environmental Protective Agency (EPA) carefully monitors mining operations in an effort to prevent pollution from destroying waterways and watersheds as they have in the past. The Idaho Conservation League is an environmental conservation organization closely monitoring mining operations in Idaho today. Idaho has a rich mining history and environmental agencies have learned a great deal from the carelessness of the past. Today, the EPA's primary focus is to never allow those mistakes to be repeated.

As of this writing, mining operations have resumed in Cobalt. Salmon-Challis National Forest sits on top of what is known as the Idaho Cobalt Belt, a 34-mile-long geological formation of sedimentary rock that makes up the largest cobalt deposit in the country.

Cobalt Mining Operation

67

From Challis, drive north on Highway 93. In 7.6 miles turn left onto Williams Creek Road. There will be a road sign indicating Cobalt—40 miles. You will pass through Forney and pass the Yellowjacket turnoff before reaching Cobalt. Cobalt is nine miles NE from Forney. Continuing on Panther Creek Road, you will pass the Cobalt Work Center on your left. Continue a short distance to the junction of Blackbird Creek Road. The Cobalt Mine is one mile to the left on Blackbird Creek Road. The mine is active and gated. To get to the site of Cobalt, bypass Blackbird Creek Road and continue on Panther Creek Road. It is a large grassy area with a few existing homes. There is nothing of interest to see in Cobalt. Any evidence of ruins is gone. It is a huge disappointment.

The only reason I mention Cobalt is because it had a past and is active today. It is also on the same route as Forney and Yellowjacket. If you continue past Cobalt, you will come to Deep Creek Campground. A short distance beyond the campground, turn right onto FS 076, which will lead you to Highway 93 and Salmon. You will exit onto Highway 93 five miles south of Salmon. You can drive back the same way you came but it is longer. It is important you consult the Forest Service Salmon-Cobalt Ranger District Map or have a GPS route prior to embarking.

Cobalt is used in the production of batteries. Currently, forty percent is used in rechargeable battery materials, high-performance batteries, laptops, cell phones and electric vehicles. All large-scale mining operations have the potential of injecting heavy metals into waterways, which can have devastating effects on fish, wildlife and waterfowl. Again, the EPA and other agencies carefully monitor mining operations in an effort to prevent pollution from destroying waterways and watersheds as they have in the past.

Forney and Yellowjacket are the most important locations to visit on this trip! If you have the time, you can also include Leesburg into this excursion.

MAY

May is an unincorporated farming and ranching community in Lemhi County, ten miles south of Ellis. Its elevation is 5,069 feet. Although not a ghost, May is worth the drive. The town is small, and the few residents are friendly. I had the pleasure of speaking with Jerry Wellard. Jerry is in the process of single-handedly constructing a two-story log home for his daughter and her children, which he started building in December of 2021. The beautifully and solidly built structure will be the pride of May for years to come. Jerry designed the balcony on the second floor to watch elk grazing in the pastures to the west of their home. The Wellard residence is the site of May's original post office. There was no mining in May; instead, miners from Patterson came here to reside, shop and for social activities.

May was named by the wife of Rudolph Wright who established the first post office here in 1897. There was a bank, post office, school, I.O.O.F Hall, restaurants, grange, blacksmith and saloons. Several of May's original buildings are still standing on Main Street. The most impressive are the hotel and general store. There are no services of any kind today. Most of the residents are generational.

You will pass the May cemetery on your right just prior to May Access Road leading into the townsite. There is a small airstrip east of town.

According to MapQuest, Pahsimeroi Road does eventually exit the valley and connect with Highway 33 and Highway 20 near Butte City. Or you may drive back out to Highway 93 the same way you came in. You would be wise to have four-wheel drive if you intend to continue on through to Butte City.

The community of Patterson is twelve miles south of May, continuing on Pahsimeroi Road.

Main Street, May (note the gravity-fed gasoline pump).

PATTERSON

Located in Lemhi County, Patterson is south of Ellis off of Highway 93. Silver was mined in Patterson Creek Canyon in 1880 but the veins were reported too low a grade to work. Initial discovery of the Ima Tungsten Mine by Ima Consolidated Mining and Milling was in 1881. It is associated with the Blue Wing Mining District. Production waned and started again in 1911. A mill was constructed in 1912. Limited activity continued through World War I. Production resumed again in 1934 and continued to 1958 when activity was permanently shut down. Total production is estimated at $10 million. Molybdenum was said to be mined by some of the locals, but it was tertiary, meaning third in order. Tungsten, zinc and silver were the primary ores.

From Ellis, cross Pahsimeroi River and head south on the well-paved Pahsimeroi Road. At twenty-three miles, bear left into Patterson Creek Canyon. (You will pass the town of May at 10.8 miles.) Drive one mile to the Ima Mine site. There are concrete foundations from the mill, as well as some remaining machinery. An unusual rock chimney is located directly across Patterson Creek. I was told that during spring months, orange opium poppies can be seen sprouting, a legacy from the Chinese laborers. Pahsimeroi is a Shoshone word meaning "trees along the water."

Foundations at Patterson Mine site.

There are a few abandoned structures in the townsite of Patterson itself. Today the community is mostly made up of ranches and some agriculture.

LIVINGSTON MINE

At 9,600 feet, the Livingston Mine is located at the head of Jim Creek on the south side of Railroad Ridge in the Boulder Creek Mining District of Custer County, now part of the Challis National Forest.

From Stanley, drive north thirty-seven miles on Highway 75 to East Fork Road. Turn right and drive 17.5 miles on a paved road to Big Boulder Creek Road (FS 667). Turn right and drive 3.5 miles to the mill site of the Livingston Mine. There will be a hand-painted sign on the entrance of the gateway, reading "Livingston Ball Stamp Mill Tours." You may drive into this area to look, but I caution getting out of your vehicle to investigate without permission. The owner and caretaker, Ron Swanson, is on site during the summer months. He is a wealth of information, and you will be lucky if you can get his attention. While driving into the property, pay special attention to the unusual rock cairns bordering the dirt road which are artistic works of Ron's. There are several cabins/buildings here that you may get a photograph of. Two mill sites that processed the ore for the Livingston Mine are further beyond.

The mine itself is further up the road that bypasses the mill. The road is rough and unquestionably single lane. Drive until you come to two aluminum gates, approximately three miles. Park here and walk to the mine and Livingston bunkhouse. The two-story bunkhouse is amazing. Inside you will see the different floors. Most important to me was the tin siding in the center of each room, meticulously nailed to the floor that once surrounded the wood-burning stove (now gone). This was done to prevent heat or sparks from starting an accidental fire on the wooden floor while the miners slept. There was a stove on each floor that shared a common chimney. From the outside of the bunkhouse, you can see the small chimney protruding through the galvanized roof. Please respect this historical site. It is remarkable to me that it is still standing! There are two mining sites; the obvious one is high on the cliffside opposite the bunkhouse. Another, that shows more character, is opposite the bunkhouse as well, across a small ravine.

The mine was first worked in 1902 by Albert Livingston. It wasn't until 1925 that major production commenced. From 1926 to 1930 the Livingston Mine was southern Idaho's largest mining employer. Primary ore mined was silver/lead/zinc.

Ore cart tracks leading from mine.

Livingston Mine Mill

Although I have not read it, I understand an excellent source of information concerning the Livingston Mine can be found in the book, *History of the Livingston Mine, Custer County, Idaho* by Victoria E. Mitchell. It is a ninety-page book released in 1997.

The White Clouds Wilderness Area was designated a wilderness in 2015 and consists of 276,000 acres of wilderness backcountry. Livingston Mine lies within the 756,000-acre Sawtooth National Recreation Area; however, it borders the White Clouds Wilderness. Most backpackers seeking to enter the White Clouds Wilderness do so through the Little Boulder Recreation Site off of East Fork Road. Big Boulder Trailhead, which is a few hundred feet before reaching the Livingston Mill Gateway, is another entry point to the White Cloud Wilderness. You will see cars parked at the trailhead just prior to reaching the Livingston Mill Gateway.

LAND OF THE YANKEE FORK

BONANZA

Placer gold was discovered along Jordon Creek and Yankee Fork, located in Custer County. Bonanza came into existence in 1876 after the discovery of the General Custer Mine. The actual construction of the town started in 1878 near where Jordan Creek joined the Yankee Fork. The Yankee Fork is a twenty-eight-mile-long tributary of the Salmon River that flows to its confluence in Sunbeam, Idaho, ten miles to the south. You will learn that this section of river played a highly significant role in placer mining between 1879 and 1910. Unfortunately, the role it played left devastating scars that can still be seen today and will continue to be seen for hundreds of years to come.

By 1880 the community boasted a two-story hotel, saloon, furniture store, assayer's office, boarding houses, a café, watchmaker, blacksmith/livery, a post office, the Dodge Hotel, and had the first newspaper in Custer County (*The Yankee Fork Herald,* published between 1879 -1892); with a population of six hundred. Prior to the 1880 boom, pack animals transported the heavy equipment and supplies more than eighty miles from Ketchum. By 1880, a toll road had been established from Challis. Heavy mining equipment could now be hauled into both Bonanza and Custer along this new route. The toll road brought more to the twin cities than mining equipment. It brought wives and reunited families. Women brought with them a feminine touch to the homes their husbands had carved out of the land. Lace curtains now hung in the windows, while gardens of flowers appeared in the front yards. A community was established where individuals shared their trades and skills with one another. Relationships were cultivated between neighbors. A school was built for the children, social events and dances took place. Bonanza had no mine or noisy stamp mills like Custer and conveyed a quieter atmosphere compared to its sister city. As stated in Land of the Yankee Fork Historical Area Words and Pictures, Bonanza had a croquet field, a baseball field and a small racetrack.

Unlike so many towns that sprang up in the Western United States in the middle to later part of the 1800s, Bonanza followed some strict rules of development under the guidance of Charles Franklin. Streets were carefully laid out using a grid system. Main Street was lined with majestic trees and had a public well. As the population grew, a post office was established (June 16, 1879), as were a livery, saloons, lumber mill, café, hardware, mercantile, watchmaker and blacksmith. When one blacksmith lost his teeth, the enterprising smithy fashioned a set of teeth out of metal with a working hinge. A dairy was established that delivered milk door-to-door and ladled out milk to anyone responding to his bell.

The most devastating enemy to any western town of the age was fire. Bonanza saw two major blazes that devastated the community, once in 1889 and again in 1897. After the second fire, most businesses and families moved to Custer.

Keep in mind, family ideals and values were different then. The average home was five hundred square feet. In the early morning the family gathered around the cook stove while mom prepared breakfast. Dad sipped his coffee while the children huddled close to the warmth of the wood-burning stove. The children communicated with mom and dad on when they would be home from school and what chores needed to be done. Families worked together to survive and build a future. There was no welfare, disability, government assistance or social security, only a determination to succeed.

Isolated homesteads were built after 1900 but were only occupied until 1910. Very little happened in the valley over the next few decades. Sheepherders recall using the abandoned buildings and cabins in the 1920s for a day or two to cook meals and use the utensils left by the former residents, while their sheep grazed on the natural vegetation.

In 1940 there was a new surge of prosperity as twentieth-century technology introduced an innovative new form of mining that had never before been seen—dredging. (See Yankee Fork Gold Dredge.)

Since 2005, Bonanza has been privately owned but open the public. In most cases, you are welcome to walk through the remaining cabins. If you do see a no trespassing sign, please be respectful. Signs are posted warning of the taking of artifacts of any kind. Please remember the adage here, "Take only pictures and leave only footprints."

Bonanza has not been restored like its sister town of Custer. Due to the last fire in 1897, almost all of the original structures were destroyed. The cabins you see today were constructed after 1900. If you look closely, you will notice that the nails are round. Square nails were hand-forged and indicate a date prior to 1900.

Although the Bonanza Cemetery is not very well maintained, it is a moving experience. There is a plaque posted at the cemetery entrance naming the individuals who are buried here. You will notice that several of the wooden memorials are marked "unknown." Custer did not have a cemetery in its early years, so the Bonanza Cemetery served both communities. The cemetery is west of town on FS Road 074.

Beyond the town cemetery is another cemetery with three graves. There is an unusual story behind this tiny cemetery, which is separate from the other. This cemetery holds the graves of Richard King, Agnes Elizabeth King and Robert Hawthorne. Richard and Elizabeth were married and had come to Bonanza from Bodie, California. While Richard sold real estate, Elizabeth opened and ran a billiard saloon. Elizabeth was reported to be a beautiful lady with long golden hair. In time, Elizabeth became good friends with hotel owner Charles Franklin. One night, an argument broke out between Richard and his business partner, with Richard being killed. Richard was buried in the new cemetery.

Soon afterwards Charles Franklin and Elizabeth began to openly see one another, until a handsome poker dealer named Robert Hawthorne moved into town and swept Elizabeth off her feet. In a short time, the two were married. Six days after Elizabeth and Hawthorne were married, they were found dead in their cabin. Suspicions quickly surrounded Charles Franklin, but no firm evidence could be established. Franklin oversaw the burial of the newlyweds but instead of putting the date Elizabeth died on the tombstone, he put the date that Hawthorne and Elizabeth were married. In Franklin's mind, the day Elizabeth married was the day she ceased to exist. Franklin left Bonanza, but years later was found dead, clasping a gold locket with a picture of Elizabeth inside.

To get to Bonanza, follow the same directions as that of Custer. From Stanley drive thirteen miles east and turn left at Sunbeam Village Junction. Bonanza is 8.5 miles north of Sunbeam.

CUSTER

Located in Custer County, Custer lies two miles south of Bonanza and borders Yankee Fork State Park. It is located inside Challis National Forest, which has overseen Custer since 1966. The National Registry of Historic Places listed Custer as a Historic District in 1981. If you are in the Stanley area, it is definitely worth the drive.

The story of Custer cannot be told without mentioning Bonanza, and vice versa, for they are referred to as the "twin towns or sister towns." From Stanley, head east thirteen miles on Highway 75 to Yankee Fork Road at the Sunbeam Village junction. Turn left and follow the Yankee Fork River. At three miles, the pavement ends and dirt road begins. After leaving the pavement, make note of the piles of river rock "dredge tailings" distributed alongside the Yankee Fork. This discarded river rock that has scarred the land for more than eighty years marks the beginning of a five-and-a-half-mile claim that was worked by the Yankee Fork Gold Dredge located a few miles ahead. When you consider how long these dredge piles have been here, it will give you an idea of how long it is going to take nature to recover from the thoughtlessness of man. More on that later. At 8.5 miles, you will see the remains of a few scattered cabins. Other than the Bonanza Cemetery, this is all that is left of Bonanza. You are welcome to stop and poke around if you wish. In the distance you will see the Yankee Fork Gold Dredge. You may choose to see it before proceeding on to Custer (one mile).

Custer was a mining town, where Bonanza was more residential. By 1890, the "twin towns" had almost grown together and were both governed by the town's common officials. Custer was established in 1879. In 1876, three men, James Baxter, Morton McKeim and E.K. Dodge, discovered some float rock. After careful consideration, they determined that the float had come from a ledge above the Yankee Fork. Their judgment paid off in spades, for the men had discovered the mother lode of the Yankee Fork. Due to the recent memory of the defeat of the 7th Calvary under General George Armstrong Custer (June 25, 1876), the mine took the name. Realizing that their find was far greater than their financial expectations could manage, the three men sold the claim to a firm based in England, Hagan and Grayson, creating the General Custer Mining Company. The price that Baxter, McKeim and Dodge settled on was never revealed, but a smaller claim was sold to Hagan and Grayson later for $20,000. It's even said that George Hearst (father of William Randolph Hearst) was an early investor. The magnificent, steam-operated, thirty-stamp General Custer Mill was completed in 1880. A foundation and partial ruins can still be seen just past Custer on the right. The thirty-stamp mill processed ore brought in from a 3,200-foot-long aerial tram high on the mountainside. Shipments of gold were shipped directly to England. The first leg of the journey was to the railhead at Blackfoot, 220 miles distant in Bingham County. One shipment of gold bullion alone was estimated at over $1 million.

In 1896, with a population of six hundred, Custer had a boardinghouse, several restaurants, the Nevada House Hotel, a general store, post office, school, sawmill, livery/blacksmith, and saloons, but never a church. Custer also passed a law prohibiting Chinese from living within the city limits. A small Chinese community was established southwest of town. The Chinese worked in laundries or as cooks, and prospected abandoned placer locations or claims sold to them by white miners.

An unusual feature of Custer is the fact that the past and present are in harmony with each other. Unlike Bonanza, the townsite of Custer has been completely restored. There is a museum and a gift shop that occupy two of the restored buildings. The decorative Empire Saloon is a gift shop, and the yellow-painted museum directly across the street was the Custer schoolhouse. There are ten structures you can walk into; each has an interpretive sign in front explaining its original purpose and the people who occupied the dwellings. The restoration has been done beautifully, and interpretive and numbered signage done equally well. You can pick up a free walking guide to Custer at the museum which describes each building/home. The walking guide suggests starting your tour with the schoolhouse (museum). The tour is self-conducted and well-structured. There is a volunteer at both the gift shop and museum who will answer any questions you have. Keep in mind, the buildings of Custer are open to the public during the summer months only, typically between Memorial Day and Labor Day. You may visit the town at other times of the year, but the town will be vacant. There are a few residents who live in Custer year-round. Their homes are on the north edge of town near the ruins of the General Custer Mill.

On the north end of town is the tiny Custer Cemetery, referred to as "Custer Seven Grave Site." The dirt road continues past the Custer Seven Grave Site for twenty-five miles, ending in Challis. Once a toll road that delivered provisions and equipment to the flourishing

Ed Jones Store (schoolhouse/museum seen in rear).

community of Custer and Bonanza, the well-maintained road is now called the Custer Motorway Adventure Road (FS Road # 070), and is a great way to see some interesting backcountry. If you decide to drive through, be sure to know your route. Along the road you will pass seventeen designated points of interest where the tumbled remains of various stations and liveries can be seen. You should have the Custer Motorway Adventure Road Tour Map to thoroughly appreciate the trip; the map can be picked up at Land of the Yankee Fork Historic Area Interpretive Center in Challis, or you can find it online (see following segment on the Custer Motorway Adventure Road). There are lots of first-come, first-serve camping opportunities between Sunbeam Village and Custer and beyond.

It wasn't until 1896 that Custer hit its peak population of six hundred. Low values on ore and high recovery costs forced the closure of the General Custer Mill in 1904. By 1910, both Custer and Bonanza were deserted. Thirty years would pass before twentieth-century technology revolutionized gold mining in the Yankee Fork Valley just outside the city boundaries of Custer (see Yankee Fork Gold Dredge).

At an elevation of 6,470 feet, Custer struggled in the winter months from heavy snows. Avalanches have plagued Custer throughout its entire history. The four largest mines of Custer were the General Custer, Lucky Boy, Black Mine and Fourth of July Mine.

Sporadic mining continued until 1904, which signaled the end of both Custer and Bonanza with the closing of the Lucky Boy and General Custer Mines. A few businesses remained, supplying camps at Sunbeam and the Loon Creek District (Oro Grande), but for the most part, the citizens of Custer sadly moved on to other strikes. By 1910 there were only twelve families living in Custer. The Sunbeam Mine closed in 1911, which spelled the end a magnificent era.

YANKEE FORK GOLD DREDGE

A must-see while you are visiting the towns of Custer and Bonanza is the behemoth Yankee Fork Gold Dredge. It is located along Yankee Fork Road between Bonanza and Custer. From Stanley, drive east thirteen miles on State Highway 75. Turn left on Yankee Fork Road at the Sunbeam Village Junction.

Located one mile from Custer, construction of the 988-ton, four-story dredge took place on site. Construction commenced in April of 1940 and finished four months later in August of that same year. In the three years it operated, it harvested seven miles of river bottom and took out $10 million in gold from the five-and-a-half-mile claim along the Yankee Fork. The dredge has seventy-one buckets, each weighing over two thousand pounds. The buckets (bucket line) revolved around what is called the ladder. As the ladder is lowered into the water, the buckets scooped up gold-bearing gravel and deposited it inside the dredge to be processed. Each bucket could hold up to eight cubic feet of gravel. The ladder was capable of extending thirty-seven feet below the water line. One source said the Yankee Fork Dredge looked like a Mississippi riverboat lost in the mountains!

Daily tours have been provided by the Yankee Fork Gold Dredge Association since 1980. The dredge is open for tours from the first Saturday before Memorial Day through Labor Day. There is a $5 fee and hours are 10:00 a.m. to 4:30 p.m. Highly informative volunteers are on hand to explain the operation. There is also a gift shop on site. If you tour the dredge during the summer months, pick up the book, *Gold Dredge on the Yankee Fork,* by Howard A. Packard Jr., in the gift shop. Cost is $8. If you visit the site during the off season, there are interpretive signs outside the dredge which provide essential information.

The Yankee Fork is a twenty-eight-mile-long tributary of the Salmon River. During the 1930s several companies were competing for control along this section of river. On January 15, 1940, the Bucyrus-Erie Company was given the contract and set a well-thought-out plan into motion to construct a gold dredge on a five-and-a-half-mile claim of the Yankee Fork. Machinery had to be purchased and shipped, men had to be hired and a camp needed to be constructed. The Lindburg Trucking Company carried more than sixty loads of structural steel and heavy pontoons over Galena Summit after the steel was shipped from Milwaukee by railroad to Mackay. Construction commenced in April of 1940 and finished four months later in August of that same year. Forty-six men were selected to build the dredge, along with a six-man crew to run it. Because of the isolated location from Stanley and Challis, permanent housing was built for the crew and their families. The homes were built four miles from the Sunbeam Store, north of Ramey Creek. The homes of the Yankee Fork Dredge Camp were considered modern for the time and had the first indoor plumbing and electricity in the valley. Due to the increased activity, a post office was constructed inside Mr. Howard Davis' general store at Sunbeam. One of the homes was converted into a schoolhouse for the children of the camp.

The dredge ran seven days a week, twenty-four hours a day, with the crew working three different shifts. Fresh vegetables were delivered every other week to the camp. Other staples were purchased at the

Yankee Fork gold dredge

general store in Sunbeam. Mail was delivered to the post office every three days. It became a social occasion for the wives to keep up on current events after making the four-mile walk to Mr. Davis' grocery store. The only telephone was at the general store. It was a simple and enriching life.

Every step, from harvesting the gold to manufacturing bullion, took place here. Through a complicated amalgam and heating method, gold was processed and formed into bricks not far from the dredge site. The gold bricks were wrapped in cardboard and brown paper and then taken to Mr. Davis' grocery store in a pickup truck and mailed at the post office. Never once was there a theft as the heavy bars were transported by the county mail courier from the tiny grocery store.

Steelhead and Chinook salmon migration and spawning was greatly impacted by the dredging that took place here on the Yankee Fork. Unfortunately, there were no laws prohibiting the devastation that was disrupting the ancestral waterways of the migrating salmon. Men were interested in one thing, and one thing only: to harvest as much of the yellow metal as possible! Fortunately, today multiple organizations have stepped forward to rehabilitate sections of the Yankee Fork that were impacted. For twenty-five years, the following state and federal agencies and organizations have painstakingly managed to restore much of the fish habitat: the J.R. Simplot Company, the Shoshone Bannock Tribe, Trout Unlimited, the United

States Forest Service (USFS), the Bureau of Reclamation and the State of Idaho. These all need to be recognized for their valiant efforts.

The moment you walk inside the Yankee Fork Dredge, you will smell the permeating odor of grease, oil and diesel from the two 450-horsepower engines. It was necessary to oil and grease fittings constantly throughout the enormous dredge. The Yankee Fork Dredge was donated to the United States Forest Service in 1966 by J.R. Simplot. The tour does require walking up several steps inside the dredge, but it is highly educational for young and old alike.

BAYHORSE

Bayhorse is located inside the Salmon-Challis National Forest, in Land of the Yankee Fork State Park. It sits at an elevation of 6,178 feet off Highway 75 in Custer County, south of Challis. It was the lure of gold that first brought prospectors here, but silver was to be what Bayhorse's prosperity would be built on. In 1864, prospectors panning the nearby creek saw two bay horses ridden by another group of prospectors (bay refers to the color of a horse). This led to the naming of Bayhorse Creek and later the townsite of Bayhorse.

In 1877, Tim Cooper and his partner Charlie Blackburn discovered a large lead/silver vein in their Ramshorn Mine located at 8,500 feet.

Bayhorse/Wells Fargo building on left.

Skylark Mine/bunkhouse

Inside the Ramshorn office building.

For the next five years, miners and tradesmen rushed to the isolated camp. In 1882, John T. Gilmer and O.J. Salisbury purchased the Ramshorn and built the now-famous thirty-stamp mill. The Skylark Mine was located above the Ramshorn Mine at 9,450 feet. Both mining operations were connected with a tram system in 1883. Ore was sent down the tram from the Skylark Mine to the Ramshorn. More ore was loaded into the ore buckets at the Ramshorn, where it then continued down the mountainside until it was deposited in an ore bin at the terminus building on the opposite side of Bayhorse Creek. From the bin, the ore was loaded onto horse-drawn wagons and carried to the Gilmer and Salisbury Stamp Mill (Ramshorn Mill) for processing. In 1886, the Skylark was credited with producing 130,500 ounces of silver and 3,000 pounds of copper.

The Skylark Mine is 2.75 miles northwest of Bayhorse, the Ramshorn Mine is one-quarter mile below the Skylark. Both the Skylark and Ramshorn had bunkhouses located high at their location for the convenience of the miners. Each bunkhouse had a kitchen and small staff to provide meals. Imagine what winters were like perched high on the hillside at that altitude in the 1880s. The wood-framed bunkhouses, which had no insulation, were warmed with potbellied stoves in the sleeping quarters and a wood-burning stove in the kitchen. Another mine equal in output to the Ramshorn and Skylark was the Beardsley.

Between 1877 and 1880, silver ore needed to be transported to Salt Lake City to be smelted. The round-trip journey took one month, a costly and time-consuming undertaking. In 1880 (Gilmer and Salisbury) built the thirty-ton Bayhorse Smelter to reduce shipping costs. The smelter operated on water power from Bayhorse Creek during the summer months and on steam power during the winter months. The smelter produced eighty tons of bullion per month.

Few metals are found in a pure form, gold being the exception. Silver needs to be separated from the ore and to do that it needs to be smelted. Smelting is a process which removes the unwanted elements, leaving only the purest metal—in this case silver—but an extremely high heat is needed, and mere wood cannot produce the essential heat. I'm not an authority on coal and coking coal, but I can give you an idea of what the mining engineers were facing. Coking coal had the crucial elements needed to produce the heat but was costly to import. However, charcoal could produce an equivalent heat so vitally needed. In 1882, a plan was formulated to build nine charcoal kilns (six remain today). Here, native wood from the surrounding forests could be harvested to manufacture charcoal. Charcoal was not the ideal fuel source, but it would reach the desired temperature needed. In the next five years, 180,000 bushels of charcoal were produced in the nine stone kilns by forty-eight skilled laborers. A bushel of charcoal is equal to twenty pounds. Total production from the nine kilns in the five years they operated was 3.6 million pounds of charcoal! The kilns were abandoned in 1885 when coal was brought in from Ketchum.

The kilns are in partial ruins today but are still an extremely impressive site. If you are fortunate enough to see them, take into consideration the science and engineering behind them. Also imagine that each stone you see was intricately put into place 140 years ago.

By the early 1880s, Bayhorse would reach a population of three hundred and have several boarding houses, a hotel, grocery, assay office, meat market, and blacksmith, and numerous saloons. The most impressive feature in Bayhorse is the Gilmer and Salisbury thirty-stamp mill. It was constructed in 1882 and is one of the best-preserved mills of its kind in the country. Although Bayhorse produced 6.6 million pounds of copper, 39 thousand pounds of zinc and 37 million pounds of lead, it was the 6.3 million ounces of silver that it is most recognized for. Consider that figure for a moment and you will realize the economic impact the Bayhorse Mining District had on our country. Mining continued here into the early part of the twentieth century, although the most productive years were from 1883 to 1889. The Bayhorse Mining District was one of the longest-running silver and lead producers in Idaho. The Bayhorse Smelting operation closed in 1889 and was later dismantled. Another thirty-ton smelter was built in Clayton, seventeen miles away, in the same

Bayhorse charcoal kilns

year as the Bayhorse Smelter, and operated until it closed in 1902.

When you enter Bayhorse, pay attention to the location of the Gilmer and Salisbury Stamp Mill. It is the largest and most noticeable structure in town. You will recognize it by the reddish color and the fact that it is built against the steep hillside. There was a significant reason why the mill was built here. At this stage in time, gravity was needed to transport the ore from one station to the next. Ore was deposited at the highest point in the Gilmer and Salisbury Mill. The ore then journeyed downward by gravity as it continued through the grizzly and stamps, which broke down the large pieces of rock, pulverizing it into workable gravel. As you travel to different mining towns from this era, you will see that stamp mills were commonly built in this same manner.

At the Bayhorse parking area, you will receive a self-guided tour brochure and map describing the structures you will be walking past. One particular structure is especially interesting to me. It is listed as #8—Tin Roof Building. Partially collapsed, it is the only building on the creek side of the walkway. Tin cans were flattened and used to shingle the roof and sides of the structure. Taking into consideration the harsh winters at 6,178 feet, this roof has withstood 140 years of every element mother nature has thrown at it and has held up beautifully. The building may have collapsed, but the roof is as good as the day it was built! Compare this to one of the finest composition

Ramshorn Mine

87

Gilmer and Salisbury Stamp Mill

roofs manufactured today!

Another fascinating structure is the Wells Fargo Bullion Building, constructed of native rock, where bullion was stored. This building, with its iron doors and shutters, is the only example of this kind in Idaho.

Bayhorse was added to the National Register of Historic Places in 1976. In 2006, the State of Idaho purchased Bayhorse, and in 2009, it was officially opened to the public under the direction of the Yankee Fork State Park. Other mines that fall into the Bayhorse Mining District are the Pacific Mine and the Beardsley Excelsior Mine, which was owned by Robert Beardsley and John P. Spaulding.

There is a $7 fee per car unless you have an Idaho State Parks and Recreation Pass. The Bayhorse townsite is open to the public Memorial Day to Labor Day. The hours of operation during those months are 9 a.m. to 5 p.m. Volunteers and state park employees are on hand to answer questions. Our guide was a young lady named Johndra. Your visit to Bayhorse is made more enjoyable due to docents like Johndra, who can answer frequently asked questions and give you answers to what life was like here. Because Bayhorse is under the supervision of the Yankee Fork State Park system, there is a railed walkway for self-guided tours. It is highly educational and enlightening to both children and adults. There are excellent photographic opportunities at the charcoal kilns, located further up Bayhorse Creek Road, in both the summer and winter months.

Dedicated volunteers work tirelessly to arrest the decay of (not restore) the rapidly decaying structures. One such volunteer is Ken Mason, a retired lieutenant colonel of the United States Army. Due to the efforts of Ken and other volunteers, Bayhorse is protected from both the elements and vandalism. During the smelting years, the soil around Bayhorse was saturated with carcinogens and toxins from the smelting and milling process. Arsenic is a byproduct created by rock and ore being crushed; in this case, at the Gilmer and Salisbury Mill. Over the years, dust created by the crushing of the ore accumulated throughout the area. These toxins still exist today. To protect visitors from the toxins, a heavy layer of clean dirt and gravel was trucked in by volunteers and park service employees to cover the pathways between the railings. Any dust kicked up while walking along the prescribed pathways is completely harmless.

From Challis, take Highway 75 south for eight miles to Bayhorse Creek Road; turn right. Follow the well-maintained gravel Bayhorse Creek Road for three miles to the ghost town of Bayhorse.

There is a trailhead directly across from the kilns site that leads to the Beardsley Mine and beyond. Both the Ramshorn and Skylark Mines can be reached by continuing up Bayhorse Creek Road. The Ramshorn will require a quarter-mile hike as the road is gated. You can reach the Skylark after July or August, but you will need four-wheel drive, or an ATV. Bayhorse Lake and Little Bayhorse Lake are inaccessible due to snow until July or August. There are many off-road opportunities for OHV enthusiasts beyond the townsite of Bayhorse.

There is no interpretive center at Bayhorse. However, you can visit the interpretive center in Challis, The Land of the Fork State Park. It is open daily from 9:00 a.m. to 5:00 p.m., from Memorial Day to Labor Day. It has a wonderful museum and provides a nineteen-minute video that should be seen. Books are also on sale at the gift shop. The Land of the Fork State Park is located at the corner of Highway 93 and Highway 75 in Challis.

Sunbeam Dam

SUNBEAM

Located in Custer County, Sunbeam is thirteen miles east of Stanley at the junction of State Highway 75 and Yankee Fork Road. Although it is not a mining town, it was essential to the mining activity that took place along the Yankee Fork River in the early 1900s.

Directly across Highway 75 from the Sunbeam Village Junction, alongside the Salmon River, are several historical interpretive kiosks. Before you proceed any further, stop and take advantage of what is written here. There is a great deal of beneficial information to take in. Of particular interest are the remains of the Sunbeam Dam. The Sunbeam Dam was constructed by the Sunbeam Consolidated Gold Mines Company to provide electrical power to their mill, thirteen miles up Yankee Fork on Jordan Creek. Construction of the dam commenced in 1909 and finished in 1910. The Sunbeam Mine and its mill operated for a year on the electricity provided by the dam until it was determined the ore at the mine was of insufficient value.

The Sunbeam property was sold at auction in 1911, but the power plant was never utilized again. The dam was built with a wooden fish ladder, ultimately falling into disrepair, which had devastating consequences on migrating salmon. In 1934, the Idaho Fish and Game contracted to have the bank next to the thirty-five-foot-high dam dynamited to allow sockeye salmon free passage to their spawning grounds at Redfish

Lake. The remains of the Sunbeam Dam are still visible from the fence overlooking the Salmon River at the interpretive signage site. Please take the time to see it. The Sunbeam Dam is the only dam ever constructed on the Salmon River. Excluding Alaska, the Salmon River has the distinction of being the only river inside the United States that is totally contained within a single state.

Today, Sunbeam Village has an interpretive center, a whitewater rafting business, and is home to the Sunbeam Café. I'm going to put a plug out here. The Sunbeam Café is positively in my top ten list of gourmet hamburger experiences. Check before stopping by; they are typically open from Memorial Day to Labor Day. The Sunbeam General Store was originally built here in 1881. It was owned and operated by Howard Davis at the time the Yankee Fork Dredge was in operation, but was destroyed in 1957. No general store exists today.

As mentioned in the segment on Yankee Fork Dredge, Mr. Davis' general store was the social center of the Yankee Fork Community, which was located four miles up Yankee Fork River. In 1940 a post office was added to the general store to accommodate the increase in activity from the construction of the Yankee Fork Dredge and Yankee Fork Dredge Camp.

CUSTER MOTORWAY ADVENTURE ROAD

I am adding this as a separate trip due to its beauty and importance. This 25-mile-long road trip is a must for those seeking knowledge concerning the mining years of Custer County. This road was constructed as a toll road by Alexander Toponce and a crew of ninety men from July to October, 1879. The road's primary function was to establish a wagon route from Custer/Bonanza to Challis. This road remained the only stage and wagon access for ten years. In 1933, the Civilian Conservation Corps (CCC) reconstructed the road and designated it the Custer Motorway.

Your first stop must be the interpretive center at the Land of the Yankee Fork Historic Area near Challis. While visiting the interpretive center, you will learn that the Custer Motorway Adventure Road (Forest Service Road 070) from Challis to Custer is a narrow dirt road suitable for high-clearance vehicles. Due to heavy snows, this road is typically closed from late October through May. This driving tour of Historic Yankee Fork Mining District is laid out with seventeen easy-to-find places of interest along the route. Although you can start the tour in Custer, it is easier to follow the route from Challis, since the travel guide is laid out in numerical order, beginning at the

Yankee Fork Visitor Center in Challis. When the toll road was in use, several stations were established to accommodate the freight teams, stagecoaches and travelers. Informative signs are positioned along Custer Motorway that identify these seventeen points of interest and provide information. Transporting supplies and heavy machinery to the mines was an arduous task for the horses that pulled the freight wagons. Stables, nourishment for the animals, and a change of horses was necessary for the wagons to continue onto Custer and to make the return trip loaded with gold bullion. The tumbled remains of different stage stations, stables and the original tollgate station can be seen along the route.

While visiting the interpretive center, you can pick up a free Custer Motorway Guide before starting your journey.

Again, your trip should begin by visiting the Land of the Yankee Fork Interpretive Center. Knowledgeable personnel are on hand to answer questions. While there, take the time to watch the fifteen-minute educational video. If you slow down and take the time to see the video and ask some questions, it will make your drive much more enjoyable. Also available is a quarter-mile walking tour outside the visitor center.

THUNDER MOUNTAIN

THUNDER MOUNTAIN

The following five mining camps are in the Thunder Mountain Mining District. There is no thoroughfare here to anywhere else; it is strictly an in-and-out drive.

Colonel William H. Dewey purchased the Caswell Claims on Thunder Mountain in 1900 for $100,000, setting off the last gold rush in Idaho. Dewey was well known and respected, as well as being the owner of the Boise, Nampa and Owyhee Railroad (BN&O), and building the Idaho Northern Railroad (INR). News of his purchasing the claims was immediately picked up by local newspapers. A stampede of prospectors, merchants and eager opportunists flooded the remote wilderness. Frantic to take full advantage of the much-publicized strike, a stage line was planned, a telephone line commenced being laid and the Union Pacific considered a viable route.

While other roads would eventually be completed, it was Colonel William Dewey's wagon road from Emmett to Roosevelt which first provided access for provisions and supplies to be delivered and ore to be transported to the railhead. Dewey's intention was for the Idaho Northern Railroad to follow his wagon road from Emmett to the Thunder Mountain District, but his dream never came to fruition.

In 1904, William and Annie Edwards built a post office and general store, establishing Edwardsburg. Today the site is the home of the Gillihan family in Big Creek. There is a historical marker in front of their residence as well as a private property sign which I respected. Edwardsburg became the center of commerce during the Thunder Mountain Mining Boom.

The railroad played such a vital role in the development of Idaho I feel I must make mention of it here. On April 8, 1902, the Idaho Northern Railroad was extended from Nampa to Emmett. By 1912 to 1914, it had pushed through to Smiths Ferry. Colonel Dewey's intent was for the Idaho Northern Railroad to proceed past McCall to Stanley, Challis, Salmon and finally Butte, Montana, to take full advantage of the wealthy copper mines the district of Butte was known for, but that dream never became a reality. By the beginning of the twentieth century, lumber from forested land had surpassed mining in economic importance. After the Union Pacific took over ownership of the Idaho Northern Railroad, it was renamed the Idaho Northern Pacific (INP). Track was run to Cascade and McCall. Lumber mills were established in McCall, Cascade and Horseshoe Bend, and the INP transported the virgin timber from those mills to market. In 2001, the last shipment of lumber left Cascade after eighty-seven years of continued service. Tracks were removed from McCall to Cascade in 1985.

To introduce a newer generation to the railroad, in 1998 a nonprofit group started the Thunder Mountain Line (TML), a scenic railroad out of Cascade that ran along the same tracks that were laid in the early 1900s. In 2001, Idaho Northern and Pacific Railroad took over operations, extending the ride to Horseshoe Bend following the original track alongside the Payette River and Highway 55. Tragically, due to exorbitant costs and upkeep, tours permanently shut down in 2017. The railroad cars silently sit today east of Highway 55 in Horseshoe Bend, sadly giving in to time and exposure to the elements.

To visit the Thunder Mountain locations, you will need two days. You may consider spending the night above Cascade. Located in Boise National Forest at 5,300 feet, Warm Lake offers lodging, camping, fishing, boating and hiking opportunities. Warm Lake Lodge provides a restaurant, bar and small store. Accommodations are also available at North Shore Lodge and Resort on Warm Lake. Another option

Yellow Pine

is Big Creek Lodge, which is a recreational/fly-fishing lodge set in the Payette National Forest alongside the 2.4-million-acre Frank Church River of No Return Wilderness, twenty-three miles beyond Yellow Pine. Open seasonally, it operates from May to October. It can be reached by both automobile and private aircraft. Since 1932, the Big Creek Hotel attracted outdoor enthusiasts until an electrical fire destroyed it in 2008. After extensive permits and painstaking planning, Big Creek Lodge was built ten years later. The magnificent log structure was constructed in Grangeville, then disassembled and hauled by truck to its present location.

The Thunder Mountain District of Yellow Pine, Stibnite, Big Creek, and Cinnabar is truly the best that Idaho has to offer, and worth every bumpy mile. From Cascade continue for one mile to Warm Lake Road, turn right and continue for seventy miles (consult navigation). Cell service is limited. Yellow Pine is the portal you must reach before continuing on to the other locations.

As in all mining camps and ghost towns, take only pictures and leave only footprints! Help preserve our mining heritage. Weather conditions are ravaging our remaining mining camps at an alarming rate, especially at these higher elevations. Please leave everything just as you find it for others who share our same interests to enjoy.

An interesting book that centers on Stibnite and the Thunder Mountain area is *Pans, Picks and Shovels: Mining in Valley County, Idaho.*

YELLOW PINE

Originally called Yellow Pine Basin, this was a provision stop along the trail to other mining camps. It was founded in 1902 by A. C. Behne. A post office was established here in 1906. In 1927, the general store opened. Located in Valley County at 4,802 feet, Yellow Pine is an unincorporated community bordered on the north by the Payette National Forest and on the south by the Boise National Forest. Yellow Pine is fifty miles east of McCall via Lick Creek Road (open seasonally), sixty-five miles from Cascade via Warm Lake and Johnson Creek Roads (open seasonally), and seventy miles on Warm Lake and South Fork Roads (open year-round).

The name Yellow Pine alone conjures up visions of a 1910 mining town. With a year-round population of forty-four, Yellow Pine is not a ghost and its buildings and dirt main street appear to be from a 1960 photograph. It is untouched by modernization yet offers a unique charm. In every respect, it is perfectly charming.

Yellow Pine Pit at Stibnite.

The last gold rush in Idaho was to be centered around what would be known as Thunder Mountain. The year was 1900 when Colonel William H. Dewey, owner of the Idaho Northern Railroad, purchased the Caswell Claims on Monumental Creek for $100,000. Local newspapers reported the sale, which set off a stampede to this remote wilderness. Knowing that supplies were essential, Colonel Dewey completed a wagon road. His road ran from Emmett across Payette River at Smiths Ferry and onto Thunder City before reaching Roosevelt. Today, Yellow Pine is the portal to the Thunder Mountain communities of Stibnite, Roosevelt, Big Creek and Cinnabar.

To get an early start, you may want to consider overnight accommodations on the mountain. Warm Lake is twenty-six miles east of Cascade and offers both lodging and camping. At 5,358 feet, it is the largest natural lake in Boise National Forest. Warm Lake Lodge and North Shore Lodge offer cabins, café and camping. Cell service is available.

As mentioned earlier, accommodations are available at Big Creek Lodge, which must be seen to be appreciated. It sits at 5,743 feet, twenty-three miles north of Yellow Pine. Along the road to Big Creek, you will pass Profile Gap at 7,605 feet. Although you can drive to Big Creek Lodge, many guests choose to fly and land on the private grass landing strip. The log lodge offers beautiful knotty pine interior rooms for guests. Big Creek Lodge is a nonprofit organization owned by the Idaho Aviation Association. Through generous contributions by several individuals, the lodge was built in 2018. One of those individuals is Bruce (Sparky) Parker who lives in a cabin in the community of Big Creek just down the road. Sparky often stops into the lodge for breakfast or to read. Mr. Parker and his wife donated one of the five guest rooms in the lodge. All the rooms are named after aircraft. The lodge is open June through October. Hiking opportunities abound throughout the Frank Church Wilderness. There are four campsites adjacent to the airstrip bordered by a creek and surrounded by lodgepole pine. A yurt is available in the community of Big Creek. Road travel to Big Creek Lodge is nearly impossible during the winter months due to the elevation of Profile Gap Summit.

Culturally, the annual Yellow Pine Harmonica Festival is held the first weekend in August. Upwards of two thousand people attend this event every year. Yellow Pine is a destination you want to drive to. Dave Immel is credited with originating the festival, starting in 1990. His great grandson, Jacob Immel, manages the general store. During the winter months, snowmobile rides are available from Warm Lake to Yellow Pine, with overnight accommodations. Gasoline is available at the Yellow Pine General Store and Corner Pub. Yellow Pine Lodge, located in the center of town, is available for overnight lodging. They also specialize as outfitters, catering to horse backpacking, fishing and hunting. Both the Yellow Pine Lodge and Corner Pub serve wine and beer.

A visit to Yellow Pine is not complete without visiting The Corner Pub. Tim and Jen are the proprietors. Their service, food and café accommodations were far beyond what I expected. They also possess a quality I thought was nonexistent today. I am not referring to only a smile and excellent service, but courtesy and unparalleled trust to outsiders.

The Yellow Pine Pioneer Cemetery can be found south of town. The cemetery is currently used but has headstones dating back to 1835. Among those early grave sites is that of A. C. Behne, the founder of Yellow Pine.

STIBNITE

Located fifteen miles east of Yellow Pine in Valley County, Stibnite is one of the principal towns discovered during the Thunder Mountain Gold Rush and sits inside the Meadow Creek Valley. At 6,539 feet, it wasn't just gold that the early miners discovered, but tungsten, antimony and cinnabar (mercury). Stibnite prospered throughout World War I, World War II, and well beyond the other Thunder Mountain communities. Situated at the headwaters of the East Fork of the Salmon River, it covers an area of 27,104 acres. The principal mine of Stibnite was the Meadow Creek Mine.

In 1938, the Meadow Creek Mine was the second-largest producer of gold in Idaho. In that same year, tunneling transitioned to an open pit called Yellow Pine Pit. With the onset of World War II, half of the tungsten and ninety percent of the antimony in the United States was being supplied by this operation. By 1958, total production stood at 405,000 ounces of gold, 88 million pounds of antimony, 1.5 million ounces of silver and 13.5 million pounds of tungsten.

Both tungsten and antimony were critical to the war effort. Antimony is a critical mineral used in the manufacturing of munitions, armor-piercing bullets, and hardening metal in shrapnel and is a key element in the production of tungsten steel. Some accounts say that without a supply of antimony in the United States, the outcome of World War II could have been drastically different. Prior to World War II, the United States imported all of its antimony from China. When the Japanese cut off our supply, we desperately needed to find another source. Fortunately, a small gold mine in central Idaho named Stibnite had an adequate surplus and rose to the call.

Seeing the importance of the tungsten and antimony reserves, federal assistance was granted to expedite mining during the war years. From 1941 to 1945, Stibnite was the single most productive source for tungsten and antimony in the United States, operating twenty-four hours a day. In 1943, Stibnite became the second largest producer of mercury in the United States. The Yellow Pine Pit shut down after World War II, but is still visible today. The Bureau of Mines lists Stibnite as producing $53 million in valuable metals between 1860 and 1980.

The mineral known as stibnite is used industrially for giving strength, hardness and corrosion resistance to different alloys. It is also used as a fire retardant.

With the onset of World War II, Stibnite transitioned into a family-based community. Between 1942 and 1945, Stibnite saw a four-room schoolhouse, grocery stores, a railroad bed that supported a 7.5-mile rail system, restaurant, café, hospital, bowling alley, three-story community center and a hundred homes. By the end of 1945, the population had exceeded six hundred. Lasting friendships developed and families bonded in this remote community. By 1951, the market for antimony oxide had ended. Mining declined sharply after World War II, and many of the company houses were moved to Yellow Pine and put up for sale. Mining stopped altogether in 1997. Families and businesses that had developed strong bonds were forced to go where they could find new sources of income. Family ties that developed

Did these steps lead to the hospital or a home?

Ore carts used in the early mining operation at Stibnite.

here were so strong that decades later, members still participate in a yearly picnic.

During the war years, no consideration was made regarding where the mine dumps were placed. By the 1950s more than four million cubic yards of waste rock had been discarded into the upper valley, obstructing the natural flow of Meadow Creek. In 1959, the government ordered the Bradley Mining Company to breach the waste site they had created to allow Meadow Creek to run through it. Since that time, thousands of cubic yards of rock have eroded downstream.

Stibnite has recently come under scrutiny. Beginning in 1990, the Environmental Protection Agency, the Idaho Department of Environmental Quality and the United States Forest Service joined ranks in an extensive project to clean up contaminated waste throughout the mining district. Perpetua Resources has since commenced mining but has committed to a cleanup operation as well. It will be the largest open-pit mining operation in the United States. Dubbed the "Stibnite Gold Project," the projected 14.3-year operation is estimating it will remove 4.8 million ounces of gold and 148 million pounds of antimony. Environmentalists are against the operation, stating the consequences can be devastating to the East Fork-South Fork Salmon River. The United States has no other source of antimony and currently relies on China and Russia to import this vital mineral, which has many military applications as well as being used in cell phones, semi-conductors and batteries. Stibnite remains the only source of antimony in our country. This operation above Yellow Pine is important for our energy future and national defense.

From Cascade, head west on Warm Lake Road. Do not attempt to visit the locations of Stibnite, Big Creek, Roosevelt or Cinnabar until late July.

CINNABAR

Located approximately fifteen miles west of Yellow Pine, Cinnabar is in Valley County. It sits at 7,587 feet and is rumored to be the "most intact historical mine in America."

Cinnabar is named for the ore it mined which, when refined, produces mercury. Cinnabar is a red-colored mineral from which mercury is derived. Mercury is the only metal that exists in a liquid state. Mercury fulminate was used extensively in the early and middle twentieth century in ammunition primers, but has been replaced today by more effective substances. Although highly toxic, mercury has been used for years in industries such as the manufacture of thermometers/

Cinnabar Boardinghouse

Foreground is collapsed railway cover leading to mill site.

Bear grass in the foreground of numerous abandoned cabins.

Ball mill in distance.

barometers, oil drilling, cosmetics, and Mercurochrome, and as an amalgamation process. For most of the twentieth century, mercury was a component in silver fillings.

Cinnabar operated between 1921 and 1966. It ranks as one of the most beautiful mining operations I have ever seen, but is difficult to get to. Due to the fact this operation ran until 1966, the cabins and structures are in very good condition, considering the altitude. Weathered cabins stand scattered throughout the valley, leaning in various directions from the prevailing wind. The ball mill, which was the terminus of the tracks that the ore carts once rumbled along with their loads of precious ore, stands silent, its corrugated metal siding gleaming in the afternoon sun. On closer inspection, you will see dangling electrical lines, a stairway that leads to nowhere, and different forms of rusting machinery standing exactly where it was left by the miners who abandoned them decades ago.

From Yellow Pine, drive west on Stibnite Road (FS 375). At eighteen miles you will see a rock painted pink; turn left. This is a four-wheel drive from this point forward. Continue for 3.2 miles to Cinnabar. The road consists of numerous tight switchbacks as it descends into the valley.

This is the holy grail of Idaho ghost towns and is a true ghost! The most impressive structure is the three-story bunkhouse seen just as you enter town. The town is laid out in a valley surrounded by mountains covered in Douglas fir. Cinnabar Creek runs through the center. It is easy to see how a rail system carried ore from the mine to the galvanized structure, which was the ball mill. Below the mill can be seen the mound of red tailings credited to the cinnabar ore.

Smaller cabins can be found on the south end of the camp. I am assuming they were private residences. Impressive patches of bear grass, red penstemon, sticky geranium and wild phlox can be seen growing between the cabins and along the road during the summer months.

Only the heartiest of ghost-town hunters will attempt this drive. Four-wheel is essential, and be sure to carry a length of chain or tow straps along with a saw in case you encounter a fallen tree across the road. Do not attempt this drive until late July. The ghostly remains of this unique mining camp now stand silent in this remote wilderness.

ROOSEVELT

Roosevelt was founded and settled in 1901, late in the Thunder Mountain Gold Rush. Located in Valley County at an elevation of 6,073 feet, it was named for President Theodore Roosevelt.

In 1900, stories started to spread about gold that had been discovered by the Caswell brothers on Monumental Creek, in an area that would later be known as Thunder Mountain. In 1901, Colonel William H. Dewey purchased the Caswell claims. The news of Dewey investing in Thunder Mountain set off the last gold rush in Idaho. By 1902, Roosevelt had become the leading town in the district, with a post office, restaurants, two drug stores, two butcher shops, a livery and barbershop and an unprecedented thirty-seven saloons. The townsite was laid out by the Idaho Land and Loan Company of Boise. By 1904, a wagon road built by Colonel William H. Dewey and a telephone line had reached Roosevelt, making it a prominent community. A tent community had grown into a flourishing town along with permanent structures which established the business district.

A forty-stamp mill was constructed on Marble Creek to process ore for the Belleco Mine by the Belle and Thunder Mountain Mining and Milling Company. A 1.5-mile tram system carried ore from the mine down to the mill at Roosevelt. From 1902 to 1907, Colonel Dewey's ten-stamp mill was the largest processor of gold on Thunder Mountain. In 1906, a large portion of tunnel caved in at the Dewey Mine. Lower yields of gold ore the following year caused the mine to close in 1907. Roosevelt's years were short-lived, when the last part of 1908 saw most of the mines closing.

Roosevelt's final blow came at the hand of Mother Nature. The townsite of Roosevelt was one mile long, sitting in a narrow canyon with Monumental Creek running alongside. On May 31, 1909, an enormous mudslide carrying trees and boulders in its wake flowed down the mountainside, damming up Monumental Creek south of town. With no place for the water to go, the river slowly started to back up, filling the narrow canyon that Roosevelt was located in. The mudslide became a permanent boundary, forming what is known today as Roosevelt Lake. For years afterwards, logs and pieces of wood from the submerged cabins and buildings that floated to the surface gathered along the shoreline. Nothing remains today!

The Sunnyside Mill on Marble Creek was constructed later, in 1924-1925.

Visiting Roosevelt Lake will require some footwork. There is a trailhead off of Stibnite Road west of Stibnite. A 1.8-mile meandering hike alongside Monumental Creek will deliver you to Roosevelt Lake.

A trip to Roosevelt is not complete without visiting Bill Timm's cabin off of Roosevelt Lake Trailhead. Although there have been modifications, Timm's cabin was built in 1903 and is the only remaining cabin in the Roosevelt sector. Timm was a postmaster in Roosevelt as well as a miner. The cabin is on Thunder Mountain, a few miles from the Dewey Mine. It was determined in 1992 that the cabin was not eligible to be listed on the National Register of Historic Places and was slated for destruction by the Forest Service. However, as of this writing it is still standing.

You may be able to tell I am vague with directions here. The reason is, I did not make it to Roosevelt Lake or Bill Timm's Cabin. They do exist, so hopefully your use of GPS will get you there.

DEADWOOD MINE

Located in Valley County east of Cascade on Warm Lake Road are the remnants of a fabulous mining enterprise.

Deadwood Basin attracted miners in 1863 and again in 1867. In 1868, quartz outcroppings were discovered but no appreciable mining took place. Then in 1915, the Hall Interstate Mining Company showed interest in the property. In 1927, a 2,000-foot tunnel was completed along with construction of a mill, hydroelectric plant and bunkhouse

Deadwood Mine office building

for the Deadwood Mine.

Production ceased again in the late 1930s, but in 1942, mining escalated when essential metals were needed for the war effort. Two hundred and forty tons of lead, silver and copper bullion was produced, along with five hundred and ninety tons of zinc bullion, which was in high demand. At the closing of World War II, production ceased entirely and the mine closed.

A bunkhouse, mill site and mining office offer a great deal to see. The concrete ruin below is the mill site; behind it can be seen the vast ore dump. Other structures include the bunkhouse and office building. The structures are in remarkably good condition.

There are two ways to get to the Deadwood Mine. From Cascade, head east on Warm Lake Road for twenty-six miles to Warm Lake. Continue to Landmark Stanley Road (NF 579); turn right. Drive fifteen miles (toward Deadwood Reservoir) to Deadwood Mine; it will be up the mountain to the left. Or, from Banks/Lowman Highway, you can drive to Deadwood Reservoir. Deadwood Mine is north of Deadwood Reservoir, a short distance past Deadwood Lodge, on the right.

FLORENCE

Gold was first discovered here in August of 1861 by John Healy, James Ayers, Hull Rice and Lemuel Grigsby. News of the discovery brought miners mostly from the newly established community of Elk City. Originally named Millersburg after Joseph Miller, the name was later changed to Florence. Located in Idaho County at an elevation of 6,080 feet, Florence earned a reputation unequaled by any other town in Idaho's past. The town quickly became the county seat, with the first county court taking place the same year (1862). In fact, Florence's rapid growth was the single most contributing factor to the establishment of the Idaho Territory in 1863. However, Florence was short-lived, as the rich placer gold was quickly depleted from the surrounding streams and drainage ditches. By 1884, the population had fallen to 254 residents. Even with its rapid decline, Florence remained the county seat until 1869, when it was taken over by Mount Idaho. Today, Grangeville is the county seat of Idaho County and has been since 1902.

One of the richest gulches became known as Baboon Gulch, reportedly because the man who staked the claim looked more like a baboon than a man. Another drainage area known for promising gold-bearing gravel was Summit Creek Ditch. A sign erected by the USFS marks the place

Florence Cemetery

today. A settlement as far removed from civilization as Florence had its drawbacks, primarily access to food and supplies. Provisions came in on pack animals along much the same route as Highway 95 runs today. The journey from Livingston took four and a half days. Alonzo F. Brown, a miner from Florence, wrote that, at night, one thousand campfires could be seen across the encampment. The first winter saw flour escalate to $2 per pound, bacon selling for $3 and eggs $1 each. A shovel was reported to have cost $40.

The first structures in the newly developed community consisted of five log cabins, three stores and two whiskey mills. That first winter of 1861-1862 became known as the worst on record in Idaho. It snowed for 113 days without letup! The only daylight that illuminated the cabins came from the chimneys, since the widows were blocked with ten-foot drifts of snow. Undiscouraged, the intrepid prospectors used hot water to melt the constantly accumulating ice from their rockers and dug several feet into the snow to reach the rich gravel deposits underneath. Famine set in that first winter. When a typical diet of bread dipped in syrup became exhausted, scarce provisions forced men to live on flour and pine bark boiled in snow-water, which formed a paste. By July, the sunlight's glare from the remaining snow hampered the miners with debilitating snow blindness. Then in the wake of the melting snow they dealt with mud! Although unprepared, they met the challenge and conquered it.

By summer of 1862, a new townsite had been platted and moved about a mile from the initial site so the dirt under the original townsite could be worked for gold. In total, the townsite was moved twice. Idaho's first schoolhouse was erected in Florence in 1864; it was a 12 x 14-foot, hewn-log building. Mrs. J.H. Robinson from Ohio was the first schoolteacher.

Florence was considered the wickedest mining town to ever come out of the pages of Idaho's history. One story begins with a woman by the name of Red-Headed Cynthia, who left her husband in Lewiston for Bill Mayfield, a convicted murderer who had escaped from a Nevada prison. Cynthia, Bill and another man named Cherokee Bob (H. J. Talbotte) came to Florence, where Bob fraudulently took possession of the Boomerang Saloon, which soon catered to the community's less savory element, including the notorious Henry Plummer Gang. When Cynthia left Bill for Cherokee, Bill Mayfield left town, never to be heard of again. Cherokee Bob, a habitual bully, was killed in a shootout by J. D. Williams and Orlando Robbins in 1863. Cynthia ultimately turned to a career of prostitution and faded into oblivion. Cherokee Bob's original wooden headboard has been replaced in the Florence Cemetery with the inscription:

H. J. Talbotte
Died Jan. 5, 1863
Age 29 Years
Native of Georgia

What started as a small tent city in 1861 had grown to a population of five thousand one year later and produced $7 million in gold dust. Attracted by the news of the fantastic wealth, highwaymen, gamblers, thieves and grafters descended on Florence. Lawlessness prevailed and Florence became one of the wildest towns in the west during the winter of 1862–1863. Men stumbling out of the saloons at night would carelessly fire their pistols into the sides of stores and tents. Multiple murders were reported each month. By May of 1862, the population had exploded to ten thousand people! Three months later, the placer claims were played out and six thousand residents moved on to other strikes. For the next twenty years, a mixed population of Chinese and white miners worked the abandoned claims.

The Panic of 1893 was an economic depression in the United States. When European investors started a gold run on the U. S. Treasury, gold became more valuable than paper money. Sensing opportunity with surging gold prices, miners flocked to Florence Basin and constructed New Florence. The original site of Florence was worked for gold dust that had carelessly fallen between the floorboards of the previous townsite. By the spring of 1897, the newly located townsite of Florence covered forty acres with three hotels, three general stores, a blacksmith, livery, twenty dwellings, three saloons, a Chinese laundry and a schoolhouse. During the peak years, Florence boasted the construction of the first Masonic Hall in Idaho.

The Florence Cemetery has the reputation of being one of the most interesting in Idaho. Several graves of Chinese immigrants were exhumed here so their remains could be sent to their homeland. The Chinese believed that their souls could not rest unless their remains were buried in their native soil. Between 1885 and the 1890s, two hundred Chinese worked abandoned placer claims and did menial work in Florence. A wooden marker erected by the USFS stands over the cemetery today, paying tribute to the exhumed graves of Chinese miners. Another interesting custom was that "good folks" were buried in an east-west direction, while "bad guys" were laid in a north-south direction. Bluebunch wheatgrass grows throughout the cemetery and amongst the grave markers while heavy stands of sub-alpine fir trees surround most of Florence.

Hard-rock mining brought prosperity once again to Florence between 1895 and 1900, but again, those few years of lode mining were brief. By 1940, ten people remained, and by 1950, Florence was completely deserted. Dredge ponds exist today near the townsite where dredge activity took place. Florence's history will forever lay in placer mining.

Road to Florence looking back towards Salmon River.

Unknown

As in all mining camps, abandoned buildings were typically scavenged for materials to build new structures. To add to this, in 1924 a quartz and placer mining company brought a steam shovel in to work the placer grounds, which obliterated anything that was still left in the old Florence site. In many cases the remaining abandoned structures were torn apart and used for firewood.

Florence Basin is 4,000 vertical feet above the Salmon River and is in the Summit Mining District. Other than the reconstructed cemetery, no structures remain. Over the years, scavenging, forest fire and unrelenting winters have consumed everything. Still, Florence remains one of the most iconic towns from Idaho's early years. Rich placer deposits, isolation and a wicked reputation make Florence one of Idaho's richest ghost towns!

To reach Florence, exit Highway 95 onto Salmon River Road (south of Riggins). In approximately ten miles, turn left onto Allison Creek Road (221). There are numerous signs pointing the way to Florence. Keep in mind there are at least two ways to get there along this route. Whichever sign/signs you follow will lead you there. You can also reach Florence by taking (354) Slate Creek Road (north of Lucile). For information, check with the Slate Creek District Ranger Station.

Some current gold claims still exist near Florence. Be aware of posted claim notices.

BURGDORF HOT SPRINGS

Burgdorf Hot Springs is located twenty-eight miles north of McCall on Warren Wagon Road. Ironically, the first twenty-eight miles of Warren Wagon Road are paved. Shortly after the pavement ends, Burgdorf Road will be to the left. Originally called Warm Springs by travelers, the settlement had a post office established during the Thunder Mountain Rush. Seeing the potential, Fred Burgdorf (some accounts say Fritz Burgdorf) acquired a deed here in 1870 and built a hotel. Fred and Jeanette Burgdorf operated the hotel and hot springs. Although never a mining camp, the hotel provided a gathering place and baths for the miners of Warren.

Today Burgdorf Hot Springs provides fifteen cabins to rent and enjoy the hot spring pools. The cabins have no electricity or running water. Essentially, your visit here is camping. You must bring your own bedding (sleeping bag), prepared meals and camping supplies, including lighting. The cabins are equipped with wood-burning stoves.

At 6,000 feet, Burgdorf Hot Springs is open all year, but you must make a reservation online or by phone. You cannot show up and rent a cabin without first making a reservation. Soaking in the mineral springs is available by the hour as well, but reservations are still required. Winter months (November to April), Burgdorf is accessed via snowmobile only.

The management does provide snacks, pastries, and breakfast burritos. It is a unique experience.

WARREN

Fifty-one miles northeast of McCall is the unincorporated "ghost" town of Warren. Originally called Warrens Camp, then Warrens, the name was later changed to Warren. The name is credited to James Warren, who discovered gold in what would become known as Warren Creek in 1862, making Warren one of the oldest settlements in the state of Idaho. Soon after the initial discovery, the population of the settlement swelled to two thousand. The American Civil War had commenced the year before, on April 12, 1861. Southerners named one half of the new settlement Richmond, while northern sympathizers christened their portion of camp, Washington.

As in all gold camps, rich placer mining is what first drew the enthusiastic prospectors. After the initial surface gold was harvested in the surrounding streams, lode mining took over where vertical shafts followed rich veins of gold-bearing quartz deep into the earth. In 1875, gold production dropped drastically. Then in the 1930s, dredging revolutionized Warren, bringing it to the number one gold producing community in the state. Powered by steam, the bucket dredge slowly moved back and forth along the river/stream, reaching deeper into the riverbed than the prospectors of the 1800s had ever dreamed. Multiple iron buckets or shovels were attached to a rotating belt (called a bucket line). The bucket line was attached to an arm (called a ladder). The ladder was then lowered into the stream bed below the waterline. As the buckets revolved along the ladder, they would scoop up gold-bearing gravel twenty to thirty feet into the stream bed, depositing it into the hopper where it got washed and partially separated in a revolving screen to separate the heavier gold from the lighter-weight gravel. Larger river rock was systematically spewed out of the dredge onto the side of the riverbank. These "dredge tailings" can still clearly be seen today scarring the landscape. Tragically, the discarded rock blocked the natural flow of the rivers and streams and impacted migrating salmon and other aquatic life, cutting off their ancestral waterways.

While the rest of the country was struggling economically, Warren's three dredges were working around the clock. However, with the onset of World War II, the dredges were silenced forever when the federal government instituted an order that all non-essential mining be shut down. The work force that labored in gold and silver mines across America put their skills to use mining essential metals such as the iron, lead, zinc and tungsten desperately needed in the war effort. This ended Warren's eight decades of gold production. An estimated $4 million in gold was recovered from nearby Stratton Creek and Warren River, and that is when gold was garnering $35 per ounce!

Most Chinese initially came to America seeking employment on the transcontinental railroad (Central Pacific & Union Pacific). When the railroad was completed in 1869 at Promontory Point, Utah, these Chinese laborers sought work in mining camps throughout North America. Warren became known as a law-abiding community that was strict but fair. It was one of the few communities that welcomed the Chinese, who initially purchased many of the panned-out placer claims. Reports say that in 1870, Chinese outnumbered the Caucasian community three to one. In many cases, white miners sold their played-out placer claims to the Chinese, who were willing to work harder to uncover the elusive gold that had escaped the attention of the white miners. Chinese formed their own communities and welcomed the opportunity to do work for whites, including growing vegetables that they sold. There are some Chinese artifacts on exhibit at The Baum Shelter.

The Baum Shelter

A railroad never reached Warren. The first wagon road wasn't put in until the 1890s. Prior to that, everything that came in and out of Warren was on pack animals. This is an amazing achievement, since Warren is a one-and-a-half-hour drive today from McCall by automobile. At an elevation of 5,906 feet, Warren is in a remote area of the Payette National Forest. Winters here were harsh and road travel was impossible once the snow hit. Enough supplies had to be packed in each year prior to the first snow to sustain the population.

Forest fires have threatened Warren several times, most recently in 1989, 2000, 2007 and 2017, but Warren has stood against all odds. In 1904, a fire destroyed much of Warren's business district, but it was soon rebuilt. This is testimony to the quantity of the gold that was being recovered here forty years after the initial discovery.

Today Warren boasts a whopping population of five full-time residents. Since the 1970s, the Baum family has owned and operated The Baum Shelter, which is an unusually lovely café that serves cold beer and delicious food! The café itself is actually an original building from the early years. In fact, finding a restaurant like this in a ghost town with a population of five is downright unheard of! It's a favorite stop for off-road vehicles exploring the backcountry both in the summer and winter months. They have an extensive menu that includes sandwiches, salads and burgers. It is worth the trip just to have a cheeseburger and fries, or golden-brown tater tots (my

Dredge Tailings

favorite), while enjoying the rustic decor from a century past. You can't miss it—it's the busiest place in town. There is also literature concerning the history of Warren on hand at The Baum Shelter to browse through while you are there.

During the summer and fall months a 2WD vehicle can easily make the drive to Warren. The mine dump from the Unity Mine can be seen as you enter town. Also as you enter town, you will notice signs indicating a dirt airstrip that runs parallel to the road you are driving on. This strip was originally built by the Baumhoff's Idaho Gold Dredging Company in 1931. It is still a functional airstrip and is used today by Sawtooth Aviation for delivering supplies and mail during the winter months.

North of The Baum Shelter Café is a small foot path leading up a steep hill to the town's cemetery. It is extremely unkempt but worth the walk to pay your respects and reflect back on a time when things were very different.

One of the original gold dredges remains today west of town. Just prior to the bridge (one mile from town), turn right. Follow the dirt road to the first river crossing on your right. The only time this river can be crossed in a vehicle is during the summer and fall months. The river is much too high to cross during the spring, and winter brings a whole different set of challenges. The dredge lies three-quarters

Warren

of a mile beyond the river crossing on your right. Be watchful of the single smokestack a few hundred feet from the road. The dredge itself is covered in brush as is the area to the right of the road, so be vigilant to spot the rusting smokestack towering over the brush. A short walk will bring you to the dredge. The most distinctive feature is the familiar bucket line. Each bucket weighs close to 1,000 pounds.

To get to Warren, access Warren Wagon Road off Highway 55 on the north end of McCall. A paved road provides a comfortable drive for twenty-eight miles, at which point the asphalt turns to dirt. The last sixteen miles is dirt. Winter months are accessible by snowmobile and 4WD vehicles, but not one hundred percent of the time. The biggest objective is getting over three summits along the way, either by automobile or snowmobile. One is Steamboat Summit at 6,694 feet. If you cannot get over Steamboat Summit, you cannot get to Warren. If the road is passable, The Baum Shelter Café makes a solemn pledge to be open. They are typically open seven days a week. If you are concerned about road conditions, the friendly staff at The Baum Shelter will provide answers (208-636-4393).

Many colorful characters emerged from Warren's early years. (See next section on Polly Bemis.)

Google "Warren, Idaho Walking Tour" (www.secesh.net/Walk.htm). Some of the information on this site is dated.

Ladder and iron buckets of the Warren Dredge.

POLLY BEMIS

Many colorful characters emerged out of Warren's earlier years, most notably Polly Nathoy Bemis. Although she has been mentioned already in the town of Warren, I am including a small tribute to her here as well. Lalu Nathoy was born on September 11, 1853, in a small village in China. At eighteen, she was sold into prostitution by her father, later sold to a brothel, and again sold to a slave merchant bound for the United States. In San Francisco she was auctioned to a saloonkeeper and then offered as a prize in a poker game to a wealthy Chinese man by the name of Hong King, who was the proprietor of a saloon in Warrens Camp.

Charlie Bemis was also a saloon owner and gambler in Warrens Camp. The story goes that Charlie won Polly from Hong King in a poker game, after which he granted her freedom. In the following years, Polly did a multitude of jobs in Warren. Then one day in 1890, Charlie was shot in the face during an altercation. The bullet fragmented, causing infection, and Charlie was not expected to pull through. Polly stepped forward and with a darning needle extracted the particles of lead from Charlie's cheek, saving his life. In 1894, Charlie Bemis married Polly Nathoy in Warrens Camp. It was an amicable marriage of respect, with both looking out for the other. One report specifically pointed out that Charlie "never failed her." Accompanying Charlie on a trip to the Salmon River, Polly was overwhelmed by the sound of the swift current. Soon afterwards Charlie built a cabin for Polly and himself on the bank of the Salmon River, where Polly would listen to the roar of the water for hours on end. In 1922 the cabin burned. Two months later Charlie died of tuberculosis.

Polly returned to Warren, but she missed the Salmon River. As a gesture of friendship, Peter Klinkhammer and Charlie Shepp, who were neighbors of Charlie and Polly when they lived on the Salmon River, constructed another cabin for Polly on the same spot as the original cabin. Ten years after Charlie's death in 1933, Polly was found unconscious at her Salmon River cabin from an apparent stroke. She was taken to Grangeville where she stayed in the Idaho Valley Hospital for three months before passing. During her convalescence at the hospital, Polly spoke of the many triumphs of her life. On November 5, a newspaper published her incredible story. She died the day after the publication on November 6, 1933, at eighty years of age. If it was not for that newspaper article, Polly's life story may have been lost forever.

Standing four feet, five inches, she was a true pioneer, and for her accomplishments, Polly Bemis was introduced into the Idaho Hall of Fame in 1966. In 1981 a biographical novel depicting her life was published, *Thousand Pieces of Gold,* by Ruthann Lum McCunn. Curiously, "thousand pieces of gold" was an endearing term Polly's father called her before he sold her into slavery due to a famine that struck China in 1871. In 1991, a movie of the same name was released which is loosely based on the novel. It is individuals like Polly Bemis who, when faced with insurmountable challenges, pushed onward to survive and succeed, and who have left an unprecedented legacy that today's pampered generation cannot begin to comprehend.

The Polly Bemis cabin is now located on the Polly Bemis Ranch, a twenty-six-acre nonprofit corporation. The Polly Bemis Ranch is a designated National Historic Site. It is on the Salmon River, forty-four miles east of Riggins and surrounded by 2.2 million acres of the Frank Church River of No Return Wilderness. At the time of Polly's death, she was buried in Grangeville Cemetery. One of her primary wishes in life was that she be buried next to the Salmon River. In 1987 she was exhumed and moved to the Salmon River near her beloved cabin.

There is a great deal written about the life of Polly Nathoy Bemis on the Internet. A book titled *Polly Bemis, The Life and Times of a Chinese American Pioneer, by Pricilla Wegars,* is also available. The Boise State Museum in Julia Davis Park, Boise, has an entire exhibit and video dedicated to her incredible life.

ROSEBERRY

Located two miles east of Donnelly in Valley County at an elevation of 4,870 feet is the townsite of Roseberry. Interesting side note, the name Valley County was derived for the geographical feature of the unusually long valley where Roseberry was first settled. Today, Cascade, Donnelly and McCall are the prominent cities. In 1948, the Bureau of Reclamation completed construction on Cascade Dam on the North Fork of the Payette River. Cascade Lake is the fourth largest body of water in Idaho, standing at 27,000 acres (47 sq. miles), and is located in the southern section of the valley. Located in Lake Cascade State Park, which is inside Boise National Forest, Lake Cascade has numerous camping areas along its shoreline and is an angler's paradise, with smallmouth bass, trout, kokanee and coho salmon. There is year-round fishing with a winter ice fishing season. The county seat of Valley County is Cascade with McCall being the largest city. Tamarack Resort is on the west shore of the reservoir southwest of Donnelly and Roseberry.

Roseberry was originally settled by Finnish people in the late 1800s. By 1905, Roseberry had a hotel, two blacksmiths, two grocery stores, a bakery, bank, butcher shop, dance hall, café and the largest creamery in Long Valley.

In 1915, the Pacific Idaho Northern (PIN) Railroad extended its line north into Long Valley, bypassing the growing community by two miles to the west. Homes and businesses quickly moved to the railroad crossing, which established the town of Donnelly. Some residents remained but the decision to run the railroad tracks two miles west of town doomed Roseberry to any further growth and virtually turned it into a ghost. Prior to the railroad, Roseberry was the largest town in Long Valley with a population of four hundred.

A visit to Roseberry is a must for travelers driving Highway 55 to and from McCall. From Donnelly, turn east and drive two miles on East Roseberry Road. Today the town offers a glimpse back in time with twenty-three historic buildings, including a schoolhouse, blacksmith, carriage house and a general store. Four of the buildings are original to Roseberry, while the other early turn-of-the-century structures have been donated and meticulously moved from other areas inside Long Valley. Included is a Methodist Episcopal Church. The general store is an original structure built in 1905. It is still standing in its original location and is a gift shop providing a variety of interesting items for sale. It is typically open between Memorial Day and Labor Day. Today a nineteenth-century Finnish homestead has been reconstructed of hand-hewn logs and dove-tail joints. Called "The Heritage Site," the site consists of other outbuildings reminiscent of the period. There is no post office in Roseberry.

Across the street at E. Roseberry and Farm to Market Road is the Valley County Museum. Managed by the Long Valley Preservation Committee (LVPC) since 1973, the museum provides loads of information on Roseberry's early years. You can Google historicroseberry.org for more information. On certain occasions during the summer months, local historians will spend the day at the museum and meet with guests to provide detailed accounts of Roseberry's past. Interpretive signs are posted describing the historical structures, although with the onset of the winter season they are taken down due to damage that can occur. It is not uncommon for Roseberry to receive five feet of snow during the winter months.

Much of the information I gathered was provided by Phyllis Bulgin, who is the president of the Long Valley Preservation Committee. Mrs. Bulgin is a wealth of information, as are the volunteers who work in the Valley County Museum.

Every year the McCall Folklore Society hosts the Summer Music Festival in Roseberry. The three-day event typically takes place on the third weekend in July. Well-known musicians from various parts of the county perform during the festival. During the months of July and August, the "Performing Arts Barn" hosts free concerts every Wednesday starting at 6:30 p.m., where a variety of musicians play music for anyone who wishes to listen.

Other events are Cowboy Trade Days and Antique Fair in June and the Arts and Craft Fair in July, as well as the Pioneer Picnic and the Ice Cream Social. There is a lot going on in this little town, so set aside some time to pay a visit. You won't be disappointed.

SEVEN DEVILS MOUNTAINS

CUPRUM

Located in the Payette National Forest in Adams County, thirty-nine miles northwest of Council at an altitude of 4,298 feet, Cuprum was a copper mining community. The word Cuprum is Latin for "copper." Today Cuprum is a small, modest community comprised of privately-owned log cabins that sits alongside Indian Creek. There are no commercial businesses of any kind. It is worth a visit, but be respectful of the residents, as they have gone to great lengths to lead a private and quiet existence. On the sign entering town, the population of (full-time) residents is listed as nine.

I have conflicting dates of Cuprum's founding. The sign entering town says 1909, yet another source says the first post office was established here in 1897. There were many legal issues over ownership of town lots through the years, which postponed the town's establishment until 1909.

Copper was known to exist in the Seven Devils Mountain Range at the same time gold was discovered in the Boise Basin, but because of its inaccessibility there was no technology to process it. Gold is the only metal that can be used in its natural state; all other ores containing metal found in nature must be smelted. Levi Allen first discovered copper outcroppings at Kinney Point in 1862, but it wasn't until T. J. Heath and James Ruth uncovered copper with their silver mining operation in 1874 that copper mining in the Seven Devils District was seriously considered. In 1886, Albert Kleinschmidt purchased holdings of Levi Allen's Seven Devils properties as well as property along Indian Creek. Between 1890 and 1891, to overcome the high costs of transporting the rich copper ore to be smelted, Albert Kleinschmidt and his brother Reinhold constructed a $20,000 wagon road from his Peacock Mine near Indian Creek to the bottom of the Snake River Canyon. Their plan was to transport the ore by steamboat to be smelted at Huntington and Sumpter, Oregon, and Salt Lake City, Utah. The venture was successful for a short time but unfortunately, the ship ran aground in 1891. Other land routes were built to reach the railroad in Weiser but the continuing struggle to find suitable transportation to reach a railway remained an ongoing problem. The Seven Devils District needed a railroad if a large-scale

Cuprum

Copper Cliff Mining Office

mining operation was going to be successful!

In 1897, the Northwest Copper Company built a smelter in what would become Cuprum. The new community soon had a church, hospital, grocery, livery stable, two hotels, a community hall, post office, and several saloons, and the population soared to five hundred! But the growth was short-lived. Unfortunately, assurances of a forthcoming railroad soon to reach Cuprum did not come to fruition. Construction on the railroad extending a line from Council to the Seven Devils District was started, but due to some landowners refusing to sell rights-of-way, the spur was abandoned. In addition to this, several mining companies who had invested heavily in the railroad went broke about this time. Another blow to Cuprum's success was sulfides in the copper, which could not be processed in the Cuprum smelter, leading to it being dismantled in 1898, a year after it was initially built.

Kleinschmidt Road (Kleinschmidt Grade) rises from Hells Canyon on the Snake River to Cuprum. There is a 2,200-foot elevation gain in five miles and the road is said "to test your nerves" and is not for the faint of heart if you have any fears at all concerning heights. It is dirt, rarely maintained, and is considered to be dangerous. At the same time, it affords spectacular views and is an exhilarating experience. Albert Kleinschmidt spent a great deal of money to build this road and most likely didn't benefit from the profits he had imagined. However, he was not alone.

Just above Cuprum are the remains of the Copper Cliff Mill, which was the last attempt at commercial mining in the Seven Devils Mining District, and which shut down in the 1980s. Large concrete foundation footings stand silently in the quarry above Cuprum, a testament to the massive machinery that was once used here. A galvanized structure, most likely the office of the Copper Cliff Mill which overlooked the operation, stands deserted, as the elements and rats have taken their toll from years of abandonment.

A short drive from Cuprum will take you to the site of Landore. See following segment for details.

To get to Cuprum, take Hornet Creek Road (NF 002) northwest of Council. At twenty-eight miles you will see the Cuprum cutoff exactly where the pavement ends. Hornet Creek Road will turn to Landore Road at this point, but do not attempt to drive to Landore by using this road. A much easier route is through Cuprum. Cuprum is nine miles from the Hornet Creek Road cutoff.

Before visiting any of the sites in the Seven Devils District, consider stopping by the Council Valley Museum in Council. As mentioned in the Landore segment, the address is 100 S. Galena Street. Dale Fisk is the chairman of the museum and is a historian of the area. Since 1993, Dale has written the "History Corner," a column that appears in the local *Record-Reporter* newspaper. He has also written books, Landmarks: A General History of the Council, Idaho Area, and The Story of the Pacific and Idaho Northern Railway. If you have any questions or concerns, Dale will gladly assist you. His number is posted on the museum website.

Although rich copper deposits exist in the Seven Devils District, the continued high costs of transportation remained the largest deterrent. Also, the creation of Hells Canyon Recreation Area in 1975 added legislation restrictions to mining in parts of the district. The United States Bureau of Mines estimates that in the last century, 52,800,533 pounds of copper, 11,312 pounds of silver and 412 pounds of gold were taken from the Peacock, South Peacock and Blue Jacket Mines. Although this may sound impressive, it pales in comparison to other mining ventures that have done more volume in less time. If the railroad had come through as planned, Cuprum's historical impact would have taken a much different direction. As it is, development on a grand scale bypassed this community and the wealth that lay beneath the surface will be guarded by time forever.

Today the drive northwest from Council to the Seven Devils District which includes Cuprum and Landore affords impressive views of the Payette National Forest. Most of the incredible accomplishments made by man from a century past are gone. The freight wagons and teams of horses, the smelters and the towns that once echoed with the voices of ambitious men have been forever silenced. But the allure is still there. You can feel it in the air and see it if you are willing to look close enough.

DECORAH

Located four miles northwest of Cuprum in the Payette National Forest is the site of Decorah. Established in 1897, it was situated at the confluence of Garnet and Indian Creek. C. W. Jones is credited with founding the town, which was named after Decorah, Iowa. It was known for the saloons and brothels that flourished there and operated for a longer period than the post office which operated between 1901 and 1903.

Although Decorah had a small population of 125, its primary purpose was to provide entertainment for the placer miners up and down Indian Creek, as well as to miners from the Blue Jacket Mine, Garnet Town and Landore. The stagecoach line that ran between Council and

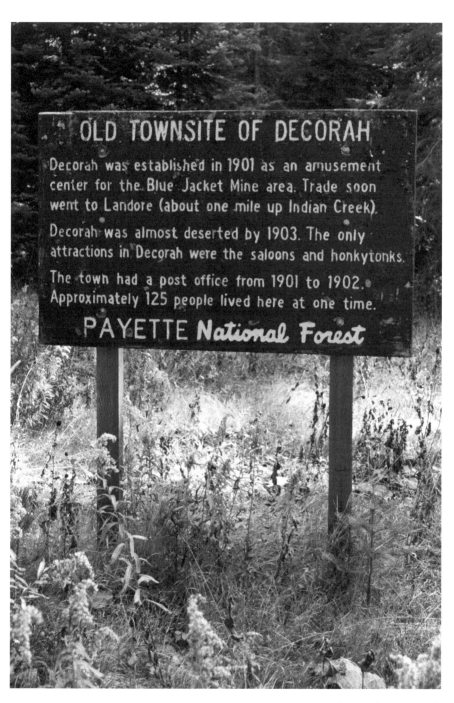

OLD TOWNSITE OF DECORAH

Decorah was established in 1901 as an amusement center for the Blue Jacket Mine area. Trade soon went to Landore (about one mile up Indian Creek).

Decorah was almost deserted by 1903. The only attractions in Decorah were the saloons and honkytonks.

The town had a post office from 1901 to 1902. Approximately 125 people lived here at one time.

PAYETTE *National Forest*

Site of Decorah

125

Landore provided additional customers to the boisterous saloons. After the post office closed in 1903, most of the businesses moved up Indian Creek to Landore.

A historical sign was placed here by the USFS which designates the site. The sign is positioned alongside the Council-Cuprum Road above Cuprum. As far as structures, nothing exists in Decorah itself. Opposite the historical sign and further up the road are the remains of a log structure. This was once a saloon.

A short distance up Garnet Creek is the three-cabin community of Garnet Town. If you look very closely, you may find some evidence of the three collapsed log structures.

LANDORE

Located in Adams County at just over one mile above sea level (5,370 feet) and west of Council, Landore was founded in 1898 and prospered quickly. It had the usual businesses, including a stage stop, saloons, a newspaper and livery. A smelter was constructed in 1909. The magnificent brick chimney from that smelter was the most prominent vestige left of Landore to be seen. Further to the south are the settlements of Decorah and Garnet Town.

Sometime after 1910, the smelter was moved to Mineral City, leaving behind the ornate red brick chimney. The magnificent brick chimney that spewed the billowing black smoke from the Landore smelter no longer stands. Several accounts report that it is standing but sadly this is not true. The story goes that as recently as 1980, the chimney stood on the property of a woman. One night the woman and her inebriated boyfriend got into an argument. To get even with the woman, the boyfriend took a D5H bulldozer and plowed into the beautifully-crafted chimney, destroying it forever. The fallen bricks are still there if you are willing to search a little. It is evident that over the years, scavengers have carted many of them away, but there are still many to be found under a forest of Douglas fir. I found them.

Continue through Cuprum up Council Cuprum Road. At 4.2 miles you will cross a bridge. Just past the bridge is an iron gate on your left; park here. Walk back over the bridge and cross into the meadow to your right that is bordering Indian Creek. On the hillside to your left are the remains of the Landore chimney. Please be respectful and leave everything as you found it.

Bricks from Landore Smelter chimney.

MINERAL CITY

Located in Washington County near the north end of Brownlee Reservoir, Mineral City is a true ghost! John James and James Peck discovered silver here in 1880. The primary mines were the Silver Bell, Black Hawk, Hancock and Black Maria. Mine dumps can be seen east of the townsite high on the mountainside.

Smelters were constructed to process the silver ore. Three small smelter sites are located east of town alongside Dennett Creek. Little evidence of the smelters exists but there are three small slag piles still visible. The largest of the smelters was located further down the canyon. You will see it as you drive along FS Road 271 when you enter the canyon. To extract the metal from the ore, a heating process called smelting is needed. It was a costly undertaking that took capital. Men did whatever was necessary to harvest, process and transport hard-rock veins of silver ore. One of these smaller smelters was moved to Landore in 1903 when it was no longer needed. A few rusting pieces of machinery are scattered in both the townsite and at the smelting site.

The first large black flow of slag seen alongside the road is especially impressive. It originated in a liquid form and as it cooled it solidified and hardened into what you see today. Winter and summer months have no effect on it. It remains exactly as it was created. At a glance, it appears like hardened tar. You will notice small chucks have been broken off that resemble obsidian. A few piles of scattered bricks remain which were once part of the furnace or smelter smokestack. Scavengers and looters have hauled away intact ones; only broken fragments remain. This enormous mound of glistening slag before you is all that remains from the Mineral City smelting years. Whether it be an oversight or intentional, it is indeed a blessing to the townsite of Mineral City. In many cases slag from smelters was hauled away to be reworked. Fortunately, this did not take place here! According to the Bureau of Mines, $800,000 in silver was produced in Mineral City, most notably from this smelter alone.

By 1890, there was a hotel, general store, blacksmith, livery, three saloons, a café and several homes. Today only two crumbling structures exist in the townsite. They are visible beside FS 271. Round-headed nails indicate the construction is from the early twentieth century. The townsite itself is located alongside Dennett Creek and surrounded by cottonwood trees, willow and Basin big sagebrush. As with most mining townsites, the buildings we see today are not among the first built. As years went on, log cabins were replaced with metal siding and hewn lumber. Corrugated metal roofing replaced hand-cut shingles. One constant was a simple design for men whose lifestyles demanded nothing else.

If you have the time, there are many interesting places to visit in Weiser. Weiser is the county seat of Washington County. Based on population, it has the highest number of historical residences in Idaho, most of which are on the National Register of Historic Places. The Chamber of Commerce at State Street and Commercial Street offers complimentary brochures showing many of the homes. The Oregon Short Line arrived in Weiser in 1884. The train depot is especially beautiful, being one of four depots in Idaho constructed in the Queen Anne style of architecture.

The annual National Old-Time Fiddlers Contest commences the third week in June each year, attracting musicians and spectators not only from all over the United States, but the world! Categories that make up the selections played range from youngsters to oldsters. Performers are required to recreate traditional songs and music played by the immigrant settlers who traveled the Oregon Trail between 1840 and 1850.

Mineral City is easy to get to but is a full-day excursion. There are a couple ways to get there; the easiest is by driving west from Weiser on Country Road 70. In four miles turn right onto Jonathan Road (dirt), and continue for twenty-two miles until you reach Brownlee Reservoir. Continue right for six miles to FS Road 271. Drive east on FS 271 for 2.9 miles.

Black slag heap at smelter site.

A few structures remain at Mineral City.

WHITE KNOB MOUNTAINS

MACKAY

Located in the southern end of Custer County at an elevation of 5,906 feet on Highway 93 is the rich mining district and town of Mackay (pronounced Mackee). With a population of 517, Mackay is no ghost. However, just a short drive from the center of town can be seen the ghostly remains of a magnificent past. Outside the town of Mackay is what locals call Mine Hill. Mackay is located inside Lost River Valley, which is between the White Knob Mountains and the Lost River Mountain Range. Both ranges make up the highest mountains in Idaho, giving Mackay the nickname of "Top of Idaho." Mt. Borah, Idaho's tallest peak (12,668 feet), is located approximately twenty miles from Mackay. Today, Mackay has transitioned into an agricultural and ranching community, but had its beginnings as a regional mining center and railroad terminus.

Copper ore had been discovered on Alder Creek in 1879. Wayne Darlington was the visionary who saw the future of mining copper here. Between 1890 and 1891, Darlington operated a fifty-ton-capacity, charcoal-fueled smelter at Cliff City as an experiment to see if he could economically recover copper by smelting the ore. Darlington's vision was to build a 600-ton capacity smelter near Big Lost River, but he needed capital. In 1900, Darlington persuaded John Mackay of Virginia City, Nevada to invest in his mining operation. History remembers John William Mackay as one of the Big Four silver kings of the Comstock Lode. Those men were John Mackay, James Fair, William O'Brian and James Flood. John Mackay would later earn the reputation of being "the richest man in the world." With Mackay's financing and Darlington overseeing production, the White Knob Mining Company was established. To properly service the venture, a spur line of the OSL (Oregon Short Line) in Blackfoot, Idaho, was constructed in 1901. A company town was laid out at end of track which would become Mackay. Most accounts state that John Mackay never set foot in the town of Mackay, but this is not true. According to the *Challis Messenger*, John Mackay did visit the town named after him, in his private railroad car in 1901.

Wayne Darlington was the state engineer between 1903 and 1904, general manager of the White Knob Mining Company, and Mackay's

131

Twelve tram towers remain standing today.

Cossack compressor building

first mayor. There is no doubt that he was the motivating force and genius behind the success of Alder Creek Mining District, but he was a failure at motivating and establishing a relationship with his employees! Darlington was a teetotaler, and he willfully forced his temperance views on the men and community. The men who worked in his mines were European and had been brought up with alcohol as an important part of their culture. Darlington insisted that no alcohol could be used anywhere in Mackay or the White Knob District, even during off hours! The miners finally revolted and formed into the Western Federation of Miners on April 4, 1902. Two days after the formation of the union, the miners organized into a strike, and Darlington's services were terminated. Wayne Darlington, who was considered to be the most successful and experienced mining engineer in America, walked off the mountain, taking his superintendent and foreman with him. Frank M. Leland took over operations of the White Knob Mining Company. With a better understanding of the miners' needs and a gift for reducing operating costs, he set to work immediately.

In 1907 the Empire Copper Company assumed the lease from the White Knob Company and took over operations. From this point, the extensive network of tunneling in this mountain sector would be called the Empire Copper Company or Empire Mine, with the Darlington Shaft as the primary entry point.

To get the copper ore down from the Empire Mine and to the smelter on the Big Lost River at Mackay, a seven-and-a-half mile narrow-gauge electric railway system had been constructed. The elevation gain of two thousand feet separates the smelter in Mackay from the Empire Mine. It was soon determined that hauling the ore by electric power was much too costly. To take the place of the electric railway, a Shay locomotive was brought in that operated at a quarter of the cost. The beauty of the Shay locomotive is it was designed to carry heavy loads up steep grades. Interesting point: today it is a three-mile drive from Mackay to the site of the (Empire Mine) and headhouse, but the Shay locomotive needed a six percent grade, which explains the length of the switchback route (seven and a half miles) needed for the locomotive. Always seeking to cut expenses and gain productivity, mine operators determined in 1917 that the locomotive was too expensive to operate so it was removed, and a gravity-operated tramway system was constructed which eliminated energy costs all together.

The smelter site was the heart of the activity, for this was also where the mining offices were that oversaw all operations. Although smelting was short-lived, everything culminated here and continued until 1940. To build a 600-ton smelter, electrical stations, compressor plant, concentrator, a locomotive railway grade, and ultimately a tramway system, hundreds of men needed to be employed. As a result, the population in the fledgling community exploded. To accommodate these men, housing was needed in both in Mackay and further up the hill. The small community of White Knob came into existence high on the mountainside close to the Empire Mine. Families of the miners moved here to be close to their husbands and fathers. The remnants of several cabins/homes can still be seen that have slowly given way to the harsh elements and high altitude.

At seven hundred feet beneath the Darlington Shaft, an "adit" was dug through to the outside. This became known as the Alberta Portal. Copper ore could then be more easily removed from the mine without hoisting it all the way to the surface. From 1918, heavy gravity-fed ore buckets traveled in a six-mile loop across thirty-six towers from the headhouse to the unloading bins below at the smelter in Mackay. One hundred and fifty tons of ore per day are reported to have been processed. Twelve of the original towers still stand today.

Several problems arose with smelting almost from the beginning. It was determined that only high-grade ore could be processed. Lower-grade ore required an addition of high sulfide ore which needed to be imported from Montana or Utah at great expense. There were also costs with importing coal to fire the blast furnaces. In 1907, smelting ended at the Mackay site. Ore was then shipped to Utah for processing. The boom years were from 1910-1920 with the

Main Street, Mackay

expansion of the community of White Knob. The end of the Great Depression in 1939, along with the exhaustion of higher-grade ore, ultimately ended mining in Mackay.

Other mines on Mine Hill that added to the total production were the Doughboy, Champion, U. S. Lead and Horseshoe. At one point, thirty-eight claims existed.

The residents of Mackay took up the cause in the 1980s to preserve their distinguished past. A contractor from out of the area was threatening to come into the old mining district to salvage the huge, distressed timbers from many of the mills, the train trestle and remaining structures. Although Alder Creek Mining District was not on the National Register of Historic Places, the residents of Mackay, under the guidance of Earl Lockie, formed the White Knob Preservation Committee and won their fight to protect their history from being stripped from the mountain and packed off. Through collections, a self-guided tour was formed with signage asking visitors to look and not touch. Today, volunteers continue to preserve their heritage. Iron donation boxes are positioned in a few areas throughout your tour. You can show your grateful support by offering whatever you can spare. Trust me when I tell you that it will be much appreciated. Extensive reparation work was done to one of the trestles that the Shay Railroad once rumbled across carrying its heavy load. The residents of Mackay realize that the existence of their community is due entirely to the vast mining operation that took place here at the beginning of the twentieth century and they intend to protect it. A million tons of ore has been excavated from the shafts and tunnels of Mine Hill over the years! After processing, this single hill has yielded sixty-two million pounds of copper, forty-two thousand ounces of gold, two million ounces of silver, fifteen million pounds of lead and five million pounds of zinc! To date, Mackay holds the title of being the largest producer of copper in the state of Idaho!

If you are truly interested in seeing for yourself the fabulous history connected with Mackay and the Copper Basin, the self-guided tour/map can be obtained from most businesses in Mackay or online. The maps are free and available at the Chamber of Commerce, local hotels, cafés and the museum. The Mackay Mine Hill Tour is skillfully laid out with colors indicating the type of terrain you will be driving on. Be aware that although a good portion of the self-guided tour can be done in 2WD vehicles, some of it requires high clearance and 4WD vehicles. The White Knob Preservation Committee and the South Custer County Historical Society have gone to great lengths to mark each point of importance with interpretive signs indicating twenty numbered points of interest along the tour. The tour takes from two to seven hours to thoroughly enjoy. There is an elevation difference from Mackay at 5,906 feet to 8,500 at the highest point along the route. Much of the road/trail you will be traveling on is the original railroad bed that once supported the seven-and-a-half-mile rail system. It is critically important to visit the Smelter Site and Hardrock Miners Exhibit (#1). Read all the interpretive signs to get a feel for the magnitude of what transpired here. Smelting ceased here in 1908. The copper ore was then shipped to Garfield, Utah for smelting. One can only marvel at the ingenuity in the construction of the headhouse, trestle, railroad and tram system. Keep in mind this was all done without cranes and modern technology. Study the large beams in the headhouse. No metal brackets were utilized; there are iron bolts, but oak pins were inserted as well to couple the massive supports.

Several structures can be seen in the old district. The engine house, smelter site, aerial tramway headhouse, Shay railroad trestle and compressor building that once pumped vital life-giving air into the maze of tunnels and shafts of the Empire Mine are highlighted on the Mackay Mine Hill Tour. The Empire Mine's name originated from the Empire Copper Company, a New York-based investment company. The most impressive structure is the headhouse (#8) where the gravity-fed aerial tram system started.

Apart from its historical mining past, Mackay is a great fisherman's destination. Mackay Reservoir, Big Lost River and Upper Cedar Creek are just a few great spots. Hundreds of miles of hiking trails are also available, as well as the famous Mackay Rodeo. Known as "Idaho's Wildest Rodeo," 2022 was the event's seventy-second year! If you are a golf enthusiast, River Park Golf Course is open to the public. Mackay also holds the designation of being the ATV Capital of Idaho. White Knob Motel, two miles south of Mackay, rents Polaris UTVs, or you may bring your own. If you prefer, kayaks are also available to rent.

In addition to the Mackay Mine Hill Tour, visit the Lost River Museum while in Mackey. It is located next to the Post Office on Main Street. It is both educational and worth the time. Along with a mining exhibit, there are other many interesting things to see. Highly-informed docents are on hand to assist you. The museum is open (weekends) from May to September. If at any time the museum is closed and you have a party of four or more, you may call (208) 588-3148, and someone will open the museum. Cheryl Benner is president of the historical society and is happy to accommodate visitors.

Konnex Resources Inc. has recently started an open-pit mining operation on Mine Hill. Gates will mark where private property boundaries exist.

Holding true to form, Mackay is one of four cities inside Custer County that has no traffic signals or fast-food restaurants. For a great breakfast and lunch try the Liar's Den on Main Street. Zan Morrell opened it as a bait and coffee shop in 2008. Then in 2020 he added a kitchen to provide meals with curbside service for locals. Today, it is a combination bait shop and café that draws customers from as far away as Arco.

For an evening dining experience, I suggest Ken's Club and Steak House, also on Main Street. Ken's specializes in large steaks, provides excellent service and has a full bar. If you are looking for a cold beer, check out Perk's Bar next door to Ken's. Perk's Bar caters to both locals and individuals just passing through wishing a drink or a game of pool. What sets it apart is it's a hundred years old and still has its original neoclassical Brunswick Bar, both front and rear. Ask for Danette (DeeDee). Enjoy anything from a cold draught to a vodka martini.

If you really want to treat yourself to a memorable night of lodging, consider Mackay Mansion. Originally built by the White Knob Mining Company to impress wealthy investors from the east with its elaborate accommodations, today it is a B&B. Your proprietress is Marie Rossi, who extends her gracious hospitality to everyone she meets. Location is the corner of Spruce and Elm (208-309-2337). Another above-average suggestion is the Wagon Wheel Motel and RV Park on W. Custer Road (208-588-3331).

I would like to extend special thanks to Earl Lockie for his vast knowledge and helpful assistance.

The Mackay Cemetery is at the far north end of Main Street.

MACKAY MANSION

I've already mentioned this home in my segment on Mackay, but due to its magnificence I am dedicating a separate writing to it alone. This is not to be confused with the Mackay Mansion in Virginia City, Nevada, although both were named for the same man.

Alice Marie Rossi is the current owner, and is operating a B&B, which is a first for the landmark residence. Rossi is the fifth owner. Many of the furnishings are original, although the interior and fixtures give the illusion that time has stood still here.

Mackay Mansion was built in 1902-1903 under the direction of the White Knob Company superintendent, Wayne Darlington. The reason for its construction was to impress potential investors from the east who were visiting the White Knob Company and Empire

Mine. In the previous chapter you learned that Darlington was the inspiration behind the success of the copper bonanza with the Empire Mine, and his concept of impressing wealthy investors with this magnificent home was right on target here as well.

The 7,400-square-foot home is three stories. It has five bedrooms and five fireplaces. As you enter the home, the first thing you see is the oak staircase with its red carpet that winds from the foyer to the second floor. At the second floor, another spiraling staircase leads to a small storage room, or crow's nest. The doors and woodwork are solid oak. The downstairs bathrooms are fashionably furnished with ball-and-claw porcelain bathtubs. The second story has been renovated for guests and has been plumbed with a walk-in shower.

The entrance to the basement is outside, where you proceed down a rock-walled flight of stone steps. It is spacious with high ceilings. Legend has it that an entrance in the basement floor connects with a maze of tunnels throughout the neighborhood. The tunnels would have been used during Prohibition. In the center of the basement is a large stone furnace which reaches through the ceiling. Long before central heat, this furnace was the heating core of the home. Wood was burned twenty-four hours a day during the winter months. The chimney exits though the roof of the home, acting as a heating

First floor, Mackay Mansion.

element to all three floors. There are two fireplaces on the first and second floor whose chimneys are cleverly coupled to the basement chimney. Originally, those fireplaces were designed to burn coal.

Although the owner says the home is not haunted, it does possess a spirit that can be aroused or remain dormant. If any construction or

Oak stairway leading from foyer to second floor.

work is being done to the house, the spirit reacts in different ways. If everything is calm, so too is the spirit. Marie admits that she never put much stock into paranormal activity until she lived in this house.

In 1983, the Borah Peak 7.0-magnitude earthquake hit Mackay. It was the largest earthquake ever recorded in Idaho. Each chimney in the home suffered damage when the bricks loosened and fell inward. Inside the home, eighty years of soot filled the house as if it were pushed through a gigantic funnel from five different directions. After the quake, each brick was meticulously recovered from the interior and reconstructed by skilled masons using historical photographs of the home's exterior.

It is truly a unique experience in history, culture and fantasy in a world long gone. Step back into time and see how it was when Idaho was young, and copper was king!

The home is located at the corner of Spruce and Elm. If you would like to make a reservation, call (208) 309-2337.

WHITE KNOB

Aside from the spectacular aerial tramway and headhouse, the collapsed remains from the community of White Knob is the most familiar feature on Mine Hill.

Contrary to what many think, there was no White Knob Mine. Many people refer to it as this because the city of White Knob was so close to the location of the Empire Mine.

The city of White Knob received its name from the White Knob Mountains which are part of the White Knob Range. White Knob Mountains tower behind the community of White Knob to the west. The townsite was established when wives and children wanted to be closer to the husbands and fathers who worked in the Empire Mine. Originally, tents were used in 1901; these later gave way to permanent structures. Soon a mercantile and other small businesses were established to supply the needs of the residents. By 1916, a boarding house, post office, movie theatre, restaurant and barber shop were servicing the community. A stage made three trips a day from Mackay.

At its peak, White Knob had a population of a thousand residents. The late 1920s saw copper prices dropping and the town's population dwindling. The Depression caused mining activity to decline even further. By 1939, White Knob was a ghost.

Collapsed structure at White Knob.

Headhouse near White Knob.

Ore tracks leading to the headhouse.

The altitude at White Knob is 7,817 feet. Tragically, every structure has collapsed or fallen into obscurity due to the horrific winters and vandalism. Although collapsed, the remaining structures are still fascinating to see. Due to winter conditions, the best time to visit White Knob is between Memorial Day and Labor Day.

CLIFF CITY

Located above Mackay on Mine Hill, Cliff City was the first emplacement to have a smelter. Once home to three hundred miners, it is located near the base of White Knob Mountain. Its name was derived from the high cliffs behind it.

There is a lot to see at Cliff City, but it takes some effort to get there. The Mackay Mine Hill map was slightly confusing to me. It is a very rough road; you will need 4WD or be willing to hike. Make sure Cliff Creek is next to you as you continue up the road. Cliff City and Cliff City Smelter site are opposite each other and will be identified with signage. The site of Wayne Darlington's fifty-ton smelter site is what was most impressive to me. The smelter ran off and on from 1884 until 1891. In 1901, Darlington received funding from John Mackay to build the 600-ton smelter closer to Mackay. The union that developed between Darlington and Mackay led to the Oregon Short Line (OSL)

Mining office in Cliff City.

Rock foundation for Darlington's fifty-ton smelter.

running a spur line to Mackay from Blackfoot. As a result, Cliff City and its smelter became obsolete, and Cliff City slowly faded into oblivion.

A few large rusting pieces of metal litter the area; one presumably is a boiler. Pay particular attention to the riveting. There was no welding in the 1880s. Rivets were needed to connect metal to metal. Two rock walls dating to before 1884 were the foundations for the smelter. Note there is no mortar between the rocks. The rock walls are as defined and solid as they were 140 years ago! You will also notice bits and pieces of charcoal scattered about the site. This 50-ton smelter was fueled with charcoal. In 1901, the 500-ton smelter built closer to Mackay was fueled with coal. However, that coal was brought in at great expense on the OSL after Cliff City had faded into oblivion.

Opposite and across the creek from the smelter site is the Cliff City townsite. One impressive log structure is all that remains of Cliff City. Evidence of a caved-in mine and its dump can be seen below the mill site. If you continue up the road you will come to the Ausich Cabin site.

Most things that are difficult to get to have greater rewards than those that are easy to find. Cliff City and Cliff City Smelter site are no exception.

DARLINGTON

Founded in 1901, Darlington is located twelve miles south of Mackay on Highway 93 in Butte County, and sits at 5,607 feet. Darlington was founded by and named after Wayne Darlington of Mackay fame. Wayne Darlington was the manager of the White Knob Mining Company (Empire Mine) who persuaded John Mackay of Virginia City, Nevada, to invest in his copper-mining operation, earning Mackay its name.

Wayne Darlington was one of the most experienced and successful mining engineers in America. He was also the visionary who saw potential in mining copper at Alder Creek, creating the Alder Creek Mining District. Among his other accomplishments he was appointed Idaho State Engineer from 1903-1904.

Although Wayne Darlington was a shrewd engineer, conflicts began developing with his miners while he was general manager at the White Knob Mining Company. On April 4, 1902, the Empire Miners reorganized as a union with the Western Federation of Miners. Overnight, the townsite of Mackay became unionized. This reorganization forced Wayne Darlington out of the White Knob

144

Truck in Darlington.

Building in Darlington.

Darlington Post Office/General Store (closed in the 1980s).

Mining Company. Being the self-governing individual he was, he left the White Knob Mining Company as well as Mackay and established Darlington. At first, Darlington was a railroad town. Today, the small community is agricultural. Most of the original buildings were torn down. As of this writing, the original post office was listed for sale.

Wayne Darlington continued operating mines on Mackay Mine Hill until 1920. He and his wife Elizabeth had eight children. He died in Pinellas, Florida in 1942 at eighty years of age.

CHILLY

I'm going to make mention of Chilly because of its history. Some sources say buildings exist, but this is not true. Chilly was established at the beginning of the twentieth century. With the Salmon Mines and Alder Creek Mining District in full swing in the early 1900s, freight lines traveled through Chilly daily. The Oregon Short Line had completed its tracks in 1901 from Blackfoot to Mackay and a daily stage line traveled through Chilly.

Robert Thalman and J. B. Hunter originally settled the area in 1898 when they brought large flocks of sheep into the Lost River Valley to graze on the plentiful grass. Its name was coined by the local

146

schoolteacher one cold morning when she said, "It is chilly!" At an elevation of 7,000 feet, temperatures are typically cold here. The lowest temperature on record was -48° F!

As homesteading and free grazing opportunities grew, so did Chilly. There was a livery, blacksmith, school and post office. J. B. Hunter opened the Chilly Mercantile Company. In 1918, Hunter moved a two-story building here from Whiskey Springs and opened the Chilly Hotel.

The end of World War I saw a definite downswing in Chilly and by 1925, it was deserted.

Although small ranches and homes are presently located in the area where Chilly once existed, it is only a memory. Nothing is left.

To get to the site of Chilly from Mackay, travel sixteen miles northwest on Highway 93. Turn left on Trail Creek Road. Proceed two miles to Old Chilly Road and turn right. The site will be in one mile.

WOOD RIVER VALLEY

KETCHUM

I must make mention of Ketchum, even though it is one of the most populated and affluent communities in Idaho. Long before it was nationally known as a recreation center and ski resort, it was a mining center. Located at 5,853 feet in Blaine County in the Wood River Valley, it sits adjacent to Sun Valley. Both communities thrive on tourism throughout the year. Outdoor enthusiasts from around the world come here to enjoy world-famous skiing and hot springs. During summer months, guests enjoy golf, fishing, hiking, tennis, upscale restaurants, boutiques, and world-class jewelry (Barry Peterson Jewelers).

Silver was discovered in areas south of Ketchum in 1879, establishing a mining district. Originally called Leadville, the name was changed when the postal service decided it was too common a name. It was renamed Ketchum after a local trapper and guide named John Ketchum, who discovered the upper Wood River Mines in May of 1880. In the spring of 1880, thousands of miners and prospectors made their way to the Wood River Valley from the Boise Basin.

Both gold and silver mining escalated here in 1880. After obtaining investment capital from the east, a smelter was established in 1881, using the most advanced methods and equipment. The Philadelphia Mining and Smelting Company, which ran on power from Wood River, revolutionized smelting in Idaho by becoming the largest smelter in the state. By 1882, the Wood River mines had produced $1 million and the Philadelphia Smelting Company was handling one-fifth of the total. The following spring, the Philadelphia Smelting Company doubled in size and was equipped with Idaho's earliest electric light system. The 1880s saw tremendous growth with the development of the Wood River Mining District. At that time, Ketchum had thirteen saloons, restaurants, a brewery, bordellos, banks, a lumberyard, a weekly newspaper, seven stage runs per day and two thousand residents!

Ten years later, in early 1890s, the Philadelphia Mining and Smelting Company shut down following the collapse of the silver market. At that same time, sheep started being herded in north of Ketchum to graze the abundant grass of the Boulder and Sawtooth Mountain

Ranges during the summer months. By the end of 1890, the sheep population had grown to 614,000. By 1919, sheep numbered 2.65 million! Due to the advent of the Union Pacific Railroad in 1920, Ketchum became the largest sheep-shipping center in the world, with sheep becoming Ketchum's primary industry, second in size only to Sidney, Australia.

Each year in October since 1997, Ketchum has held the annual "Trailing of the Sheep Festival," when 1,500 sheep are paraded down Main Street as they head south in their annual migration to lower elevations and warmer pastures. The festive parade includes sheep wagons and other local entries, and draws spectators from all over Idaho. The 2022 event was hosted by the John Faulkner family, a third-generation sheep rancher. A riderless horse sometimes accompanies the parade in tribute to family members lost the year before. Although tourism is now Ketchum's number one industry, sheep have remained a mainstay of Idaho's culture and economy.

Ever since the mining and smelting years ended and tourism started, Ketchum has been associated with celebrities, with the fashionable resorts of Sun Valley, and with recreation. Ernest Hemingway gave it even more status when he first visited Ketchum in 1939; he purchased a home here overlooking the Wood River in April of 1959. Hemingway was the recipient of a Pulitzer Prize in 1953 and a Nobel Prize in 1954. His home, The Hemingway House, still exists and is part of the National Register of Historic Places. When Hemingway's wife died in 1986, she donated the home to the Nature Conservancy. A mile north of the Sun Valley Resort there is a Hemingway memorial, a bronze bust overlooking Trail Creek near the seventh hole of the Sun Valley Golf Course. There is a beautiful verse inscribed at the base of the bust. The "Hemingway in Idaho" exhibit is on display at the Sun Valley Museum of History. However, the Ketchum that Ernest Hemingway knew has changed a great deal since his death in 1961.

Ketchum has nothing to do with the focus of this book. You won't find solitude or tranquility here. Nor will you find the ghostly remains of a hand-crafted cabin slowly giving way to a hostile environment. Instead, you will find the country's most expensive real estate, where luxurious homes, restaurants, golf courses and lavish hotels blanket the valley. Throngs of suntanned tourists have replaced the hard-working miners and mill workers. The steel tracks have been removed from the mounds of earth (called ballasts) where the Union Pacific Railroad once transported smelted silver from the mines of the Wood River Mining District. Now exercise enthusiasts wearing trendy outfits jog along those same mounds of earth, unaware and probably not giving a second thought to their origin or the men who built them. I understand progress, but this book is about towns and camps that stopped in time. Ketchum is one of the towns that marched onward with the upbeat trends of the twenty-first century. I simply want the reader to understand that in 1880, Ketchum was a formidable and imposing mining center.

The mine site of the Lucky Boy Mine is outside of Ketchum off Warm Springs Road. You will have to hike a short distance up Rooks Creek to get to the site. Very little remains; you will see remnants of cabins and a beautifully-crafted stone wall.

Thirty miles south of Sun Valley is Silver Creek, a spring-fed tributary of the Little Wood River. This 881-acre preserve is the finest example of a wildlife ecosystem in North America, hosting 150 different species of protected birds and mammals. Near Picabo, this world-renowned fly-fishing preserve attracts anglers from all parts of the globe to fish for rainbow and wild brown trout.

BELLEVUE

Hopeful prospectors who had arrived in the Boise Basin too late to file claims sought out new prospects elsewhere. One of the areas they searched was the fertile Wood River Valley of southern Idaho between 1863-1865. Some color was found but not enough to warrant the filing of placer claims. In 1875, news of a silver strike in Virginia City sent a signal to eager miners that gold was not the only precious metal to be unearthed. In 1879, a group of twenty-seven miners and prospectors spent the winter in the Wood River Valley studying what they believed to be a high-grade silver deposit.

A year later, on February 26, 1881, Warren P. Callahan filed on a Galina claim near Bellevue. The *Owyhee Avalanche* newspaper from Silver City carried an article on the same day, stating that prospects were exceedingly rich in the Wood River Valley.

Located at the southern end of the Wood River Valley, Bellevue was founded in 1880. Owen Riley built the first permanent structure here, a log cabin. In June of that same year the post office opened in the same building, making Mr. Riley the postmaster. Most settlers and miners entered the Wood River Valley along a well-travelled road from the south, making Bellevue the first settlement they encountered. By 1882, Bellevue had a population of five hundred, with seven stores, four saloons, five hotels, a livery stable, post office and a jail. News spread feverishly as the silver rush continued. As thousands of fortune seekers rushed to Wood River Valley, small towns sprang up. Jacobs City, later changed to Broadford, was one. Located one mile west of Bellevue, it was known for the Minnie Moore and Queen of the Hills

Mine, both silver mines. The Minnie Moore alone produced $8.4 million in silver ore and was considered the most important of the early Wood River mines. The Panic of 1893 ended commercial mining in the Wood River Valley. The Panic of 1893 was an economic depression that lasted from 1893 to 1897. It deeply affected every sector of the economy in the United States, including silver.

Agriculture played an important role in the early development of Bellevue. When the silver boom was over, many of the miners moved on, but just as many individuals stayed who had ties to the fertile valley and the community they had helped to build. Where other towns of the gold and silver mining booms became ghosts, Bellevue survived.

HAILEY

Named after John Hailey, a congressional delegate, Hailey is the county seat of Blaine County. The community of Hailey was founded in 1881 and is located at the foot of both the Sawtooth and Challis National Forests. Silver mining boomed here between 1881 and 1893. At first, wagons carried the silver ore to Keton, Utah where it was loaded on trains and shipped to Salt Lake City to be smelted. To offset the high cost of freighting, smelters were constructed in both Hailey and Ketchum. The first smelter, the Wood River Smelting Company, was built in Hailey in 1881. A larger, more technologically advanced smelter, The Philadelphia, was built in Ketchum a few months later.

In 1883 the Oregon Short Line completed a branch line into Hailey and production of the local mines skyrocketed now that track connected Picabo, Shoshone and Salt Lake City. The following year, the tracks of the Oregon Short Line were extended into Ketchum. A brick plant operated during the early 1880s in Hailey. Evidence of those bricks can be seen in the impressive Hailey Courthouse built in 1883. The three-story structure is located at 1st and Croy Street and was added to the National Register of Historic Places in 1978. Hailey had the first telephone service in the territory and was the first to have an electric light plant. The Federal Land Office was located here until 1925. Parcels of homesteaded land could be filed on here for Blaine and Custer Counties.

Another interesting building from Hailey's early years was the Alturas Hotel. Billed as the finest hotel between Denver and the Pacific Ocean, the magnificent three-story, eighty-two-room brick structure opened on May 25, 1886. Each room had a wood-burning stove. In 1913, the hotel was purchased by the Hiawatha Land and Water Company, who renamed it Hotel Hiawatha. After remodeling, it reopened in 1915. The elegant hotel featured a telephone in every room, along with hot running water which was piped from Hailey Hot Springs two and a half miles away. A swimming pool in the rear was heated as well with water from the hot spring. The hotel changed hands from 1928 to 1970, before closing in 1977. A fire destroyed it in 1979. Located at 93 E. Croy Street, Atkinsons' Market has occupied the space for thirty years. There is a historical plaque on the front of Atkinsons' Market, giving a history.

The silver boom of the Wood River Mining District was short-lived, lasting only ten years. Afterward, the valley focused its attention on livestock and agriculture. Then, in 1936, the lush valley would be changed forever when Sun Valley Resort opened and a whole new industry emerged though construction and tourism.

Sitting at an elevation of 5,318 feet, here the winters are cold, with snow coming as early as September. Typically, forty-four days a year never exceed 23° F. Summer temperatures rarely exceed 100° F. The lowest temperature on record was -28° F. The smelters have been silenced and the iron tracks that supported the railroad cars have been torn up. Today Hailey has a population of 9,161 and is home to Friedman Memorial Airport (SUN). However, 140 years ago it was a mining town.

I strongly suggest stopping at the Blaine County Historical Museum located at 123 N. Main Street, Hailey. Hours are Memorial Day Weekend through October 31, Monday through Saturday, 11:00 a.m. to 5:00 p.m., and Sunday 1:00 a.m. to 5:00 p.m.

BROADFORD

As mentioned in the chapter on Bellevue, Broadford was located one mile west of Bellevue in the Wood River Valley, south of Ketchum. Originally called Jacob City (named for Frank Jacob), the name was changed to Broadford when an application was filed concerning mineral rights. There is also some speculation that the name Broadford could have come from a wide fording area in the river ("broad ford"), resulting in the name.

Today, the townsite of Broadford is on private property and there is very little left of its early years. A winch house and assay office, along with some mine dumps, are all that exist from the early years. At one point in time there were numerous mines in the hills surrounding the city limits, the vast number being nothing but prospect holes. In the early days of the United States, there were various ways of fleecing unsuspecting individuals. After filing on a mine site, the property holder had one year to show proof of work before the property reverted back to the state. In that year the mine could be sold. It was a common practice for an unscrupulous property holder to travel somewhere out of state and legally sell his mine, sight unseen. In a mining district noted for its silver production and smelting abilities, selling an unseen mine could be quite simple.

The Wood River Valley boom lasted from 1880 to 1893. The towns of Bellevue, Muldoon, Doniphan, Gimlet, Hailey, Bullion City, Broadford and Galena sprang up along the well-traveled road which ran north following the Wood River, with Ketchum having the largest silver smelter in Idaho (Philadelphia Mining and Smelting Company).

There were two primary mines in Broadford, the Minnie More and Queen of the Hills. Today the 286-acre parcel of land where Broadford once stood is owned by Carl and Heather Johnston. Along with other business ventures, the Johnston family has continued to mine the Minnie More for forty-eight years. By 1893, the Minnie More was reported to have produced $8.4 million in silver. The Queen of the Hills is closed with no plans to reopen. Today, however, the 286-acre property is up for sale.

In 1888-1889, silver mining slowed considerably due to falling silver prices, which culminated into the Panic of 1893.

BOULDER CITY (BOULDER BASIN)

Located at an astonishing altitude of 10,000 feet, twenty-three miles north of Ketchum in Blaine County, are the remains of Boulder City and the Golden Glow Stamp Mill. Head north from Ketchum for thirteen miles to mile marker 141. Turn right onto FS Road 184 (Boulder Creek Road). Drive 0.9 miles to a wide parking area in a grove of aspen. If you are hiking, this is a good spot to park. Boulder City can be reached by ATV but since I appreciate and respect nature, my friend Larry Meaders and I chose to hike. It is 5.5 miles to Boulder City with a 3,000-foot elevation gain. Your hike starts at approximately 7,000 feet.

Shortly after leaving your vehicle and crossing over Boulder Creek on the worst foot bridge in Idaho, you will reach the Boulder Basin Trailhead. There is a trail register at the trailhead just past the bridge. It is always a good idea to sign in and out. There is no cell reception. At 1.75 miles from the parking area, you will pass the remains of the first log cabin. At 5.5 miles, you will reach Boulder Basin and the outskirts of Boulder City.

Due to the altitude, do not attempt this hike until July. Other than Boulder Creek, there are no other stream crossings to mention. I rate this hike at moderate to strenuous. The National Park Service lists any long steady climb with more than a 500-foot elevation gain as strenuous. This hike most certainly qualifies, with a 3,000-foot gain!

Nestled in the Boulder Mountains below Boulder Peak, Boulder City sits at just under 10,000 feet. The highlight of the hike is the Golden Glow Stamp Mill and the huge iron boiler positioned in front of it. Unfortunately, only a portion of the once-majestic Golden Glow Mill remains. Reports say that Boulder City was active between 1883 and 1893 and had a population of seven hundred. Most of the dwellings have simply been claimed by the harsh elements at this altitude. The shafts and tunnels located high on the mountainside were following veins of Galena. Galena is a lead/silver ore. Lead makes up the significant percentage of the ore which is important. However, even though the remaining percentage of silver is low in comparison, it still makes the ore extremely valuable. In many cases, even though Galena ore is being extracted, the mine may commonly be referred to as a silver mine. The mines of Boulder City were the Golden Glow, Ophir, Tip Top, Trapper, Sullivan and Bazouk.

The mining community is dwarfed by cathedrals of solid rock that surround the valley. The Boulder Mountains provide a continuous flow of scree and talus created by thousands of years of erosion, as rock slowly cascades down the mountainside toward the valley floor. Douglas fir, Western white pine and Engleman spruce give you both

Golden Glow Stamp Mill

Larry Meadors peers into the window of one of the remaining cabins in Boulder City.

cover and enjoyment along the first portion of the hike, but there are a few miles of open terrain, so be sure to have a lightweight hat. Along the hike, two impressive waterfalls can be seen in the gorge below. Patches of Western yarrow and Indian paintbrush accompany you along the trail during the summer months. After reaching Boulder City, if you look across from the Golden Glow Mill on top of the mine dump, you can see a freshwater spring bubbling from beneath the excavated rock. Evidence of a gravity-operated tramway system that hauled ore from the mines perched on the cliff side to the rock crushers of the Golden Glow Mill is clear from the cable system that is still in place.

We had our lunch in the clearing across from the stamp mill. While we were there, we left some of our trail mix in front of a freshly dug burrow of some soon-to-be-surprised ground squirrel.

A few decaying cabins in various conditions border the tiny valley. It is always interesting to me to imagine who lived here. Think of the men who built these cabins; they had no blueprints, but knew exactly what they were doing. One cabin was a two-story. Was it a family residence, or was this the remains of the hotel that was reported to have been here?

One question intrigues anyone who makes the effort to hike into places like this: How did these men get this equipment up here? The log cabins were obviously built from the surrounding forest, but the mill is constructed of hewn lumber. Then there is the heavy iron machinery that made up the working components of the mill. One thing that does not escape your attention is the gigantic iron boiler that stands in front of the Golden Glow Mill. It is obvious that it was transported here in one piece! Where did the wood-burning stoves come from that the miners cooked on and warmed their cabins with during the long winter months? Originally, pack animals carried everything into Boulder City from the settlement of Ketchum. Then a rough road was cut out, along which horses and mules laboriously pulled heavy freight wagons loaded with supplies up the steep, six-mile grade. Can you even begin to imagine what a journey in a buckboard entailed, hauling cargo and merchandise up this steep and rocky road? Man's determination and ingenuity always amazes me. There was no unemployment, no welfare, no disability! Families depended on one another to sustain their way of life, provide shelter and fuel to heat their homes and possessed a shared determination to survive. They didn't ask for or rely on handouts, or government support. They had strong family ties and a drive to see their venture succeed.

Keep in mind the diet of these miners. In these early settlements prior to supplies being freighted in, men packed in essential provisions on their horse or mule. They had to carry enough food to last them and their animals for a month's journey. Essentials were flour, bacon and coffee. Also, oats were carried to supplement natural grazing of the horses and mules. Beans were another common staple, supplemented with dried pork. Fruits and vegetables that were high in vitamin C were scarce and as a result some miners suffered from scurvy. Potatoes (which do contain vitamin C) became a staple for miners in the later years, but not initially. When game wasn't available, miners rationed a mixture of flour, sour milk and cornmeal, which was eaten as a mush or gruel.

As you enter the Boulder Basin on the outskirts of Boulder City, another road veers upward. This leads to Boulder Lake. If you are up to the additional hike, it is certainly worth it. It is a perfect example of a small alpine lake. As for us, we passed. No fish exist in the tiny lake. Most species of trout need inlet and outlet streams that flow over gravel, providing oxygen and food. This does not occur here. Winter freezing is another issue, as the shallow lake freezes solid.

It is possible to drive an ATV into the Boulder Basin; however, this writer prefers to walk. Anyone can roar up a mountain trail spewing exhaust and kicking up dust and rock on a noisy ATV. Walking provides a sense of appreciation for what miners and settlers experienced many years before us. It also gives you the privilege of saying you hiked this trail. My friend and I who did this hike together met a man on the trail who lives in Ketchum. He said he hikes this trail every ten years just for the sake of doing it. He told us that he is astonished at the deterioration that has taken place. If you are up to it, it is worth it. Every year the harsh elements claim a little bit more of what man left behind from this chapter of Idaho's mining history. I am not referring to Boulder City alone, but to all the empty mining towns across the Gem State. The thing that makes Boulder City so unique is the fact that very few people know of its existence or have the time or capability to visit it.

MULDOON

Located in Blaine County and east of Bellevue, Muldoon was founded in 1881. It is situated in Muldoon Canyon on Muldoon Creek at 7,799 feet, and is inside Challis National Forest.

From Bellevue, take W. Pine Street east off Highway 75 (Main Street). In seven blocks, Pine Street will turn into Muldoon Canyon Road. The pavement ends in one and a half miles at the familiar EE-DA-HO sign. Continue straight, passing over Muldoon Summit. In fourteen and a half miles, you will reach the Little Wood Reservoir Road and Muldoon Canyon Road junction. Continue straight on Muldoon Canyon Road to the Muldoon Sheep Company Ranch.

Another route is north of Craters of the Moon National Park. Take Little Wood Reservoir Road north of Carey (4,800 feet), which will turn into Muldoon Canyon Road. After leaving Main Street onto Little Wood Reservoir Road, you will pass Carey Pioneer Cemetery at 0.4 miles on your right. Markers here date from 1889 to 1916. After 1916 the cemetery was abandoned, and a new site was selected north of Carey. In six miles, the pavement turns to dirt. The kilns are twenty-three miles from Carey.

At the junction of Little Wood Reservoir Road and Muldoon Canyon Road are two log homes dating back to the townsite of Muldoon's beginnings. One of the log homes was the schoolhouse, the other was the post office. Today, they are privately owned and occupied. Distance from this junction to Main Street in Bellevue is sixteen miles.

Google Maps does not consider passing through private property to get to the kilns and mines. At twenty-one miles from Carey, you will see the entrance to Muldoon Sheep Company Ranch, and private property signs. Turn left here and proceed 0.3 miles. Turn right and continue 0.7 miles to kilns and smelter site. The mine is further up Muldoon Canyon. By going this route, you will avoid trespassing on Muldoon Sheep Company Ranch. Muldoon Sheep Company Ranch is owned by Guy Peterson and Kathleen Donahue. Guy is a second-generation rancher whose father started the ranch. The ranch

Two of the remaining kilns.

Entrance where wood was carried into the kiln.

originally raised sheep, eventually transitioning into cattle. Today, Mr. Peterson is retired but still resides on the ranch.

Of the twenty-three kilns, three are well-preserved; elevation is 6,555 feet. Others are in various forms of ruin. The lower portion of these kilns is constructed of native stone with the upper portion handmade brick and mortar. The brick allowed for the intricate workmanship of forming the dome on each kiln. Although the tops of the domes have collapsed, their contouring shape is still identifiable. Around the perimeter of the kilns is a heavy growth of red-twig dogwood, while bunchgrass and Idaho fescue are the primary ground cover continuing down towards Muldoon Sheep Company Ranch. The arched entrance to each kiln, which was used to carry in and stack wood prior to firing, is located on the western side facing the valley below.

The slag dump is seen a short distance north from the kilns. An irrigation ditch was dug at the time Muldoon was in full swing, presumably to supply water to the kilns and smelters. Water that feeds into the ditch came from Muldoon Creek further up Muldoon Canyon. Incredibly, the water continues to flow through this ditch today, eventually ending at the smelter site where it percolates back into the land.

The name of Muldoon Mine was derived from a prominent New York wrester of the time. William A. Muldoon (1845-1933) was a physical culturist and champion wrestler who once wrestled in a match that lasted for over seven hours. He was never defeated; his last championship match was in 1880. The mine was named after him and the town that developed adopted its name from the mine. Idaho Muldoon Mine and Muldoon Mine (7,598 feet) are located further up Muldoon Creek along with several mine dumps. Idaho Muldoon Mine is located on the east side of Muldoon Creek and Muldoon Mine is located on the west side. All the mines in this area are in the Little Wood River Mining District. The ore mined was silver/lead.

At its peak, Muldoon had a population of 1,500 people and the usual businesses—saloons, stores, livery stable, sawmill, hotel, schoolhouse and post office—but only lasted for six years (until 1887). By 1882, two forty-ton smelters were built near the mouth of Muldoon Canyon. Twenty-three charcoal kilns were constructed to fuel them. The smelters were sold and dismantled in 1887. A slag pile denotes the location of the smelter site. The townsite of Muldoon is located further down Muldoon Canyon Road near the junction of Little Wood Reservoir Road and Muldoon Canyon Road.

There was a resurgence in the Little Wood River Mining District with the onset of World War II. Lead and zinc were in high demand during the war years, resulting in the mines and earlier mine dumps being worked again. Although no smelting operations were available,

160

shipments of ore continued from 1943 to 1945. The end of World War II saw all operations cease.

GALENA

Although nothing remains of Galena, I'm going to make mention because of its importance. The name Galena is Latin for lead sulfide.

The town was located twenty-nine miles northwest of Ketchum, near what is known today as Highway 75. Galena Summit (8,701 feet) is located in the Boulder Mountains within the Sawtooth National Recreation Area of Sawtooth National Forest.

Construction of the road over Galena Summit was completed in 1881 to serve the mines at Sawtooth City, Vienna and others inside the Stanley Basin. Ore was freighted by wagon over the summit to the Philadelphia Smelter in Ketchum, but due to the elevation it was only used during the summer months. Until smelters were constructed in the Stanley Basin, this was the only way for silver ore to be processed. Today, the picturesque steep grade leading over Galena Pass is familiar to anyone driving north from Ketchum along Highway 75 towards Stanley.

Located in Blaine County, the site still appears on Idaho's state map. Galena was the oldest town inside the Wood River Valley, dating to 1879, and had four general stores, a hotel, livery, post office, saloons and a stage stop. Stage service traveled to Hailey. At its peak, population was eight hundred. The first white baby in Wood River Valley was reported to have been born in Galena.

ERA

Located in Butte County west of Arco on Champagne Creek, this settlement had a population of 1,200 at its peak. It is inside the Lave Creek Mining District and fourteen miles west of Arco. The discovery of a rich load of lead-silver ore and small amounts of gold at the Horn Silver Mine established the town in 1885.

James B. Hood had eight lead-silver veins ready for development in 1879 which were producing between –one hundred and two hundred ounces of silver to the ton. Two camps began to grow here; these finally developed into Era. In August of 1885, Frank Martin sold his Horn Silver Mine for $62,000 and Era began to flourish. The tent camp gave way to framed buildings. Era soon had a grocery, hotel, blacksmith, hardware store, restaurant, assay office, boardinghouse, two livery stables, a barber, six saloons, several brothels and an opera house. The Blackfoot-Wood Stage serviced the community. A post office operated from August 1885 to July 1894.

At first, silver ore from the Horn Silver Mine was hauled by wagon to Hailey for smelting. Then a dry crusher and twenty-stamp mill was constructed in 1886. The Horn Silver Mine drew in capital from Salt Lake City investors. Forty-eight miners were employed working two underground shifts in the Horn when an electric lighting system was installed in the mill, a year before Boise had electric power.

By 1887, Era experienced milling equipment failure. Much of the ore began to be hauled to Nicholia to be smelted. In 1889, the hoisting works of the Viola Mine at Nicholia burned. Due to low prices on lead and silver, the hoisting works was not rebuilt, and the smelter was torn down, triggering further problems for Era. With the smelter shutting down in Nicholia, the once-thriving camp of Era began to fall into obscurity.

The only visible remains of Era are the heavy stones that made up the foundation of the stamp mill, a formidable sight.

CARRIETOWN

Located in the eastern portion of Camas County on Big and Little Smokey Creeks, near Dollarhide Summit, Carrietown is twenty miles northwest of Hailey via Warm Springs Creek Road (NFD 227). From a southerly route it is twenty miles north of Fairfield, which is located on Highway 20. From Fairfield, take Soldier Creek Road north and junction with NFD 227.

Carrietown is situated in the Sawtooth National Forest at 7,440 feet. It was located inside the Rosetta Mining District, which encompassed an area of 150 square miles. In addition to gold, silver, lead and zinc were also mined.

Lode mining flourished for ten years after its discovery in 1880. Some mining shut down after 1900, while some continued from 1917 to 1942. Total production in gold is listed at ten thousand ounces. The area is littered with mining dumps from numerous mines. Some of the mines are Last Chance, Silver Star, Tyrannis, Horn Silver, King of the West and the Carrie Leonard. A cabin does exist here but appears to be of a post-dated construction.

HILL CITY

Located in Camas County at 5,090 feet, Hill City sits fourteen miles west of Fairfield along Highway 20. Hill City is a familiar site to anyone who has driven Highway 20, but most think of it is a farming community, and certainly not a city! Hill City has a fascinating past; you just need to look for it.

Hill City was born when the Oregon Short Line track ended in 1911, as it was being laid westward across the Camas Prairie, and the town grew into a major station. Mr. and Mrs. Mickelwaite laid out the townsite and would later open the first real estate office here. Hill City thrived through the 1920s and 1930s. It had a general merchandise store, a garage, three restaurants, a barber, dance hall, church, drugstore, harness shop, newspaper, the Cooper Hotel, a lumberyard, and its very own baseball team. Ice that was stored in the local ice house was harvested from the Malad River during the winter. Hill City had a grade school. High school students were transported by local agricultural trucks in the early years and later by bus to Fairfield. A post office was established in 1912. Although there were numerous post office locations over the years, postal service continued in Hill City until 1990. Today, mail is routed through Fairfield.

Hill City was named for the nearby Bennet Hills, and at one time had a population of three hundred. Throughout the 1920s, more sheep would be shipped from Hill City on the Oregon Short Line Railroad than any other place on earth! Sheep typically wintered in Buhl, Glenns Ferry and Mayfield. During early spring they were herded to Pine and Rocky Bar to fatten, before being herded to the railhead at Hill City. The Oregon Short Line served Hill City for seventy-one years. The tracks were removed in 1983.

The end of World War II signaled the end of Hill City. The last graduating class from the Hill City grade school was in 1945, when forty-nine students graduated. One of those students was Leroy Trader. Leroy now lives in Gooding and will turn ninety-two this year. There are many reasons why towns die. It could have been that many of the young men didn't return from the war, or moved onto larger cities that offered more opportunities. In some cases, businesses had no other choice but to relocate to a community with larger populations. When this happened, others followed.

Today, two large grain silos located south of Highway 20 are the most visible reminders of the past. Built in 1925, these silos were so fully packed one season that 32,000 sacks of grain had to be stacked outside. The silos stored wheat and barley, which was then transported to market by the Oregon Short Line, until 1953. On the

Farmers National Warehouse grain silo

opposite side of the highway is a small farm owned by one of the last remaining families of Hill City. A road sign marking Hill City is still standing on the westbound lane of Highway 20.

There is a photo showing the Hill City Store and Saloon floating around the internet, but the store no longer exists.

The photo I speak of is even on the wall in the downstairs hallway of the Best Western hotel in Twin Falls. The story goes that in 2012, a one-hundred-year-old building originally owned by Cass Arnold was selected to be the site of the Hill City Store and Saloon. The location of the building was on the south side of Highway 20 in front of the still-standing grain elevators. A team effort of dedicated individuals, under the guidance of a young lady named Kaylor, succeeded in opening the establishment, but its days were numbered. The roadside business provided groceries, local produce, crafts, cold beer, and even had a pool table for those in need of a friendly game. The date of the store's closing is a mystery, but in 2020 the entire building was leveled for liability reasons. Today, however, the familiar photo of the yellow, metal-sided building remains the most enduring image identifying Hill City on the internet. If you're like me and keep looking over your shoulder while driving past Hill City in hopes of catching a glimpse of the friendly landmark, know that it is only a memory.

The Hill City Cemetery is located a very short distance up 1300 W, off Highway 20. The rather large cemetery is easily identified by a wooden fence on the right side of 1300 W.

SAWTOOTH BASIN

SAWTOOTH CITY

Located twenty-five miles south of Stanley on Highway 75, in Blaine County in the Sawtooth National Recreation Area, is the site of Sawtooth City. After the Bannock War was over, Levi Smiley led the first group of prospectors into this region in 1878, discovering quartz outcroppings. Placer gold was then discovered on Beaver Creek and Lake Creek, starting a gold rush that led to a mining district being formed and Sawtooth City being established on Beaver Creek. Levi's discovery of silver outcroppings led to the discovery of the Pilgrim Lode and opening of the Pilgrim Mine. The Pilgrim Lode reported a vein of silver ore ten to twenty-five feet in width and assaying out at 3,000 to 5,000 ounces of silver per ton. Silver ore infused with gold was packed from the Pilgrim Mine to Atlanta, Idaho, in the fall of 1879. The Pilgrim Mine was Sawtooth City's principle mine. San Francisco investors purchased the Pilgrim for $30,000 in 1879 and spent another $45,000 developing the property. Investors from Wisconsin took over the Pilgrim later that same year.

Very little of the original site of Sawtooth City is left today. From Smiley Creek Lodge, drive north on Highway 75 about a half mile to the Beaver Creek Dirt Road (Forest Service Road 204) just south of the Sawtooth City Historical Marker. Turn left and follow it for 2.4 miles. You will see the ruins of a single log cabin. This is all that remains. Sawtooth City Cemetery is north of this site but unmarked and not maintained.

At an altitude of 7,342 feet, Sawtooth City suffered heavy snows during the winter months. Its peak development was between 1884-1885. The winter of 1885 saw extremely cold conditions. Temperatures dropped to -50 °F (lowest temperature ever recorded in Idaho was -60°F in 1943). Drifts of snow piled up, closing the road between Sawtooth and Vienna until the middle of July. As a result of that winter, many residents of Sawtooth City and Vienna took their families to seek refuge elsewhere the following fall. Some returned the following year, but Sawtooth and Vienna began to show a slow decline. Some mining continued on a small scale, but the boom years had ended. Some speculate that the Sawtooth Mining District was never fully developed, and a great deal of wealth still lay underneath the Sawtooth National Recreational Area; most reasons for the decline in the Sawtooth Mining District suggest mismanagement.

Sawtooth City is inside Beaver Canyon with mines on the ridgeline above Beaver Creek. By 1882, Sawtooth City had a post office, four saloons, a general store, meat market, three restaurants, two hotels, a blacksmith, Chinese laundry, assay office and a law firm—quite an accomplishment for a mining camp as far removed and isolated as Sawtooth City, yet its total production was only $250,000. Sawtooth City was added to the National Register of Historic Places as a historic district in 1975.

Smiley Creek Lodge has seventeen RV sites as well as six or seven tent sites. The lodge itself has three upstairs rooms that share a common bathroom. There are also cabins and two yurts for rent that share a bathhouse. The Smiley Creek Airport (private) is directly across Highway 75. A newer development called Sawtooth City can be seen next to Smiley Creek Lodge where residents live year-round.

Forest fire is a terribly destructive force. It travels fast, consuming everything in its path, satisfying only its destructive hunger. On August 12, 2022, lightning ignited the Ross Fork Fire in the Sawtooth National Forest, burning 37,868 acres west of Highway 75, threatening and possibly destroying the remains of the only remaining log cabin in the original site of Sawtooth City. As of this writing, I am unsure.

Cabin at Sawtooth City.

VIENNA

Vienna was the "sister town" of Sawtooth City and the larger of the two. It is in the southern portion of Sawtooth Valley and south of Sawtooth City. In 1879, E. M. Wilson discovered the Vienna Lode, or Sawtooth Mineral Belt, which was two miles wide and ten miles long. This led to the opening of the Vienna Mine and the Vienna Consolidated Mining Company. One assay report from the Vienna Mine recorded an astonishing 19,000 ounces of silver per ton in that same year. This is a statistic from *The Gold Camps and Silver Cities of Idaho.* Just stop and think about this for a moment. A silver mine today might operate on fifteen to sixteen ounces per ton. A number like 19,000 ounces per ton is incomprehensible! To take advantage of the expected wealth, a $200,000 twenty-stamp mill was constructed in 1882, with a 200-horsepower engine powered by steam, with a reducing capacity of fifty tons of ore every twenty-four hours. Other stamp mills in Vienna were the Columbia Mill and Beaver Mill. Vienna's boom continued in 1882, with the Mountain King Mine producing 1,700 tons of ore, yielding seventy-five to a hundred ounces a ton. The initial assay of 19,000 tapered off drastically. Never again was something of this order seen. Many of the mines that showed promise in 1882 could not get into major production as time went on. The following season, the Vienna Mine averaged $750 a day. By 1884, a cumulative production of $500,000 was reached. Typically, veins of ore run in straight lines or directions and can continue for many miles. Most likely, the Sawtooth Mineral Belt of silver augmented with gold that Sawtooth City was excavating was the same vein that Vienna was mining six miles to the south.

The town of Vienna, located in Smiley Canyon, consisted of two hundred buildings with six restaurants, a bank, two livery stables, meat markets, a blacksmith, a hotel, a sawmill, fourteen saloons, and a population of eight hundred. Vienna had its own newspaper, the Vienna Reporter, which consolidated with the Ketchum Keystone in 1882. The Vienna Mine was short lived; it shut down in 1886, as many of the other mines did. Total production out of the Vienna Mine was $500,000. Very little is left today. A report revealed in 1914 that of the two hundred buildings that once stood in Vienna, only a few piles of lumber remained. Consider the altitude and the fact that more than a hundred years have elapsed since that report was made.

There are some interpretive signs at the site of Vienna about six miles from Highway 75 on Smiley Creek Road. The entrance to Smiley Creek Road is located near Smiley Creek Lodge. If you are willing to look, you can find some rotting timbers and remnants of a few rock foundations. As stated earlier, when the mines played out and people moved on to the next strike, what they couldn't carry with them they left. Lumber, brick and even nails were all at a premium in this remote part of the western frontier. Other settlers and travelers took full advantage of abandoned dwellings and structures. Anything left behind was put into wagons and used elsewhere for construction or for fuel to burn. The 2022 Ross Fork Fire burned very close to the site of Vienna, possibly destroying any remaining evidence.

A Highway Historical Marker is posted on Highway 75 south of Smiley Creek Lodge, giving a brief description of Vienna. Vienna is located on the west side of Highway 75.

OBSIDIAN

Located in Custer County eleven miles south of Stanley on the east side of Highway 75 is Obsidian, at 6,660 feet. The most prominent of the buildings is the abandoned motel/café.

Obsidian originally began as a post office. In the early years it was common to have post offices scattered throughout the valley for the convenience of homeowners, so they didn't have to drive the long distance to the main post office in Stanley. The area got its name from deposits of obsidian that used to be on the hill to the east of Highway 75. Over the years, people chipped away at these, so nothing remains today. The original post office was established in 1918 in the home of Jennie Buchanan, which was located on Decker Flat, across the Salmon River from where Sessions Lodge now stands. Over the years, the location of the post office was moved several times to different residences or ranches near Obsidian, until it ultimately ended up near the Sessions Hotel.

In later years, there was a man by the name of Trigger Jim who owned the property to the west of Obsidian. Jim was a gunsmith who also had a gun shop and real estate office on his property, where he sold lots to prospective buyers.

In the late 1960s, Don and Nedra Sessions purchased the property on the east side of Highway 75 and built a café/hotel (Sessions Lodge). The café was in the main building, as were the living quarters of Mr. and Mrs. Sessions (upstairs). The hotel rooms were separate and on the south side of the main building. Adjacent to the café was a Standard gasoline station, a garage and other outbuildings. Don and Nedra had a good business. Nedra was famous for her delicious homemade pies; people made the eleven-mile drive from Stanley just to experience them. Sometime in the 1990s, Mr. and Mrs. Sessions shut the business down. Others tried to take over the location, including a bicycle shop, but failed. Abandoned buildings remain at the site today.

Sessions Lodge, Obsidian

Over the years Trigger Jim's real estate dealings led to an accumulation of unsightly trailers across the highway on the lots he had sold. In 1972, the Sawtooth National Recreation Area (SNRA) was established in the region. With federal assistance, the organization was able to buy out Trigger Jim and clean up the unappealing development that had been created. The SNRA had their fiftieth anniversary in 2022 in Stanley.

The seven-acre parcel where the abandoned hotel/café that Don and Nedra Sessions once owned has been under the ownership of Smiley Creek Lodge for several years. Smiley Creek Lodge frequently used the rooms as lodging for their employees. As of 2021, Smiley Creek sold their lodge and are considering donating the Sessions' old property. At this point nothing is definite.

Eleven miles south of Stanley on the northbound lane of Highway 75 stands a road sign identifying the town of Obsidian.

WASHINGTON BASIN

Located south of Stanley in Custer County and east of Highway 75 is Washington Basin. It was named for the Washington Lode, discovered there in September, 1879. Washington Basin is in the White Clouds Mountain Range northeast of Smiley Creek Lodge.

There is a lot to see here. Most visitors marvel at the freight teams that must have labored to haul the heavy riveted iron boilers up the steep grade in 1880. The boilers still remain, as does a cabin. Elevation is 9,098 feet.

A Black man named George Blackman is associated with the site. Blackman had come to the Washington Basin in the 1880s and operated a hard-rock mine here until mid-1930s. He lived in a small, sod-roofed cabin. Blackman said that he worked his claim during the winter months and transported the ore for shipment in early summer. He also guided hunters during the summer months.

George Blackman was born on November 8, 1854, in Kentucky. He died on April 28, 1936, at eighty-one years of age. He is interred in the Clayton Cemetery. His marker simply reads, "George Blackman died 1936." For years, George could be seen walking into Obsidian along the Fourth of July Trail to pick up mail at the post office. Blackman Peak is named for him (10,300 feet).

Washington Basin is worth the time to visit; spring, summer and fall months only.

LEADORE-BIRCH CREEK

BIRCH CREEK CHARCOAL KILNS

Twenty-nine miles south of Leadore in eastern Idaho on Highway 28 is the "well-marked" turnoff to the Birch Creek Charcoal Kilns. From the turnoff it is a five-mile drive on a nicely-graded dirt road. Information plaques are situated in and around the kilns on a groomed path. There is no ghost town here, but is a vital part of the history surrounding mining in the Lemhi Valley. This is a highly educational stop for anyone willing to invest the time. More than anything, it is a fascinating example of two men's undaunting ingenuity.

The story of the charcoal kilns cannot be told without first explaining the discovery of silver and lead at the Viola Mine. In 1881, large deposits of lead, zinc, copper and silver were discovered on the eastern side of the Lemhi Valley. It's a simple story; ore was mined but it needed to be smelted. Smelting is the process of applying a high heat to ore in order to extract the base metal. The closest smelter was in the now-defunct town of Armstead, Montana, some sixty-plus miles over Bannock Pass. Another option was to transport the ore 330 miles to Salt Lake City, an even greater distance. There was no railroad to haul the ore, so the only option was to load the ore into horse-drawn wagons and transport it, which was time consuming, expensive and an arduous undertaking. Another option was to build a smelter close to the mining activity. In 1885, two blast furnaces were constructed for a smelter at the site of Nicholia, near the Viola Mine, but to run the furnaces, fuel was needed. Our story does not end here.

To smelt ore, a high temperature must be achieved that wood cannot produce. Coal is the ideal fuel, but there was no economical way to import it. To operate the furnaces, a different source of fuel needed to be obtained. J. W. and W. C. King from Butte, Montana, rose to the challenge. Charcoal would create the heat needed, but where do you find enough charcoal to fuel two blast furnaces? The brothers patiently worked out a plan to construct sixteen beehive-shaped kilns. Clay and lime were gathered from nearby Jump Creek to manufacture brick. By 1886, sixteen kilns, each standing twenty feet tall and twenty feet in diameter were producing two thousand bushels (seventy cubic meters) of charcoal every two days. Seventy-five thousand cords of wood were cut and hauled each year from the nearby forest to load into the kilns to produce the charcoal.

However, the furnaces were ten miles west of the kilns and on the opposite side of the Lemhi Valley. The reason the kilns were not built closer to the Viola Mine and Nicholia is because there was an insufficient amount of timber on that side of the valley. The location of the kilns was carefully considered because of the plentiful supply of Douglas fir that was harvested from the adjacent forest, a short distance to the west of the kilns. For three years, the kilns provided the necessary fuel to fire the smelter at Nicholia, until fluctuating silver prices and a fire in the hoisting works of the Viola Mine forced the mine to close and the smelter to be dismantled in 1890. A short distance south of the kilns was the community of Woodland, where 150-200 kiln workers, loggers and their families lived. Another source says the name of the community was Kingville. The community was composed mostly of log cabins, but was destroyed by fire long ago. Any remaining evidence has slowly been consumed by sagebrush; nothing exists today.

These magnificently engineered and geometrically perfect creations of J. W. and W. C. King were then sadly abandoned. Over the years, twelve of the kilns were scavenged for their brick, to be used in other structures by settlers and farmers across Lemhi Valley. Only four kilns remain. Silently walk amongst them while reading the interpretive signs and consider the genius and tireless hours of labor that went into their construction. Think, too, of the vital purpose they served,

Birch Creek Charcoal Kilns

only to be left to the elements when the lead and silver mines closed, and the miners moved on to different strikes.

Kilns constructed to manufacture charcoal was not a novelty in the west. There are other examples in Idaho, as well as in California, Nevada,Montana and Wyoming. The Birch Creek Kilns are considered the best-preserved in Idaho. Twenty-three partially collapsed kilns exist in Muldoon, east of Bellevue. In 1972, the Birch Creek Charcoal Kilns were listed on the National Register of Historic Places; the site is part of the Targhee National Forest.

NICHOLIA

In 1880, the lead/silver Viola Mine was discovered in the Lemhi Range, but full-scale mining didn't commence until 1882, after ore was received in Omaha, Nebraska, to be smelted. Due to the potential value of the ore, plans were set in motion to start full-scale mining. Three years later, in 1885, to offset the transportation costs of hauling the ore to be smelted, a double furnace smelter was constructed at the foot of the mountain below the Viola Mine, and the town of Nicholia was established. By 1889, Nicholia had a population of 1,500. Nicholia took its name from Ralph Nichols, who was the manager of the Viola Mine.

As a result of the high costs to import coking coal to fuel a Nicholia Smelter, sixteen elaborate, beehive-shaped charcoal kilns were constructed on the opposite side of the valley, ten miles to the west. Today only four survive but are the best-preserved kilns in Idaho (see above).

The Viola Mine was located high on the ridge at 8,599 feet behind Nicholia, approximately three miles to the east. A tramway was constructed to carry the ore down to the smelter. Very little is left of the tram system today. In 1889, the hoisting works burned. Due to low prices on lead and silver, the hoisting works was not rebuilt, the smelter was torn down, and the community collapsed. Without the smelter, the workforce and their families took what they could carry and moved. The closing of the Nicholia Smelter affected other mining operations inside the Lemhi Valley that relied on the smelter, including Gilmore. Owing to fire and extreme weather conditions, very little is left.

Most interest today lies in the Birch Creek Charcoal Kilns (aka Nicholia Charcoal Kilns).

GILMORE

Located sixteen miles south of Leadore and one mile off Highway 28 in Lemhi Valley is the silver mining community of Gilmore. It sits at 7,200 feet and was settled in the 1880s, when a rich silver/lead ore deposit was discovered. Most mines were located along Birch Creek and Texas Creek. In the early years, ore was shipped by wagon to Nicholia and other mining ventures in the surrounding area to be smelted, but the smelter was dismantled in 1890. Gilmore struggled in the following years, until the Montana-based Gilmore & Pittsburg Railroad ran a spur into Gilmore in 1910, which saw economy and industry thrive once again. Instead of ore being hauled by horse-drawn wagons, it was speedily transported by rail to Armstead, Montana for smelting. The most productive years for Gilmore were from 1910 to 1920.

There were three primary mining operations in Gilmore: The Allie, The Latest Out and P. I. (Pittsburg-Idaho). The Latest Out and P. I. were both owned by Edgar Ross. Ross personally oversaw the production of the Pittsburg-Idaho. Just prior to the Great Depression and stock market crash of 1929, an estimated $11,520,852 in silver and lead was produced, mostly out of the P. I. Mine alone. During the Depression, Franklin D. Roosevelt set the price of precious metals so low that mining could not continue profitably. As a result, mining shut down altogether between 1929 and 1931. Gilmore relied one hundred percent on mining for its survival; without mining, residents took what they could carry and left for other regions, where men could provide for their families. Soon after 1930, the tracks were pulled up for scrap and Gilmore became a ghost.

Gilmore can easily be seen west of Highway 28 at the base of the towering Lemhi Mountain Range. Because of the years that elapsed in Gilmore, it is easy to see the transition in architecture from the construction of its buildings. The hand-cut log cabins made way for metal siding and hewn lumber as the years progressed. Today, they all blend together, reflecting a particular time in our past that was extraordinarily simple. In recent years, however, the ambiance of a preconceived ghost town has faded   through commercialization. Parcels of real estate throughout the community are being purchased by individuals who park motorhomes and trailers year-round, creating an unsavory appearance.

Gilmore was named for John T. Gilmer, but there was an error in spelling when the post office was added to the community. The name Gilmore remained, much to the dissatisfaction of Mr. Gilmer. A map of all the historical homes and places is posted at the entrance of town.

If you follow Gilmore Road (Forest Service Road 002) west beyond Gilmore, in about a mile you will see a sharp turn off to the left that leads to the town cemetery. The cemetery is in extremely poor condition, but you can walk amongst the grave sites. There has been an effort by grateful volunteers to restore portions of it. The most prominent is the grave site of Richard "Dick" Allen Molls (1930-2002). If you do some research, you will see that Mr. Molls and his brother were an enormous part of preserving and documenting Gilmore's past. Dick Molls moved to Gilmore in 1970 when he was forty years of age, and for ten years was its sole resident. Mr. Molls is the last person to be buried in this cemetery.

A century of neglect, vandalism, harsh conditions at this altitude, and exploiting what remains with current real estate sales has taken a toll on Gilmore. Fortunately, the Lemhi County Historical Society and Museum has purchased the Gilmore Mercantile and storage building behind it. The museum's goal is to stabilize and restore the mercantile and, in the process, encourage the preservation of other historical sites.

Gilmore is an authentic ghost town, where decaying buildings from the early years can be seen scattered amongst the sage brush. Every building standing represents families who established a home or business here.

Gilmore Mercantile

177

Gilmore is not listed on the National Register of Historic Places. To learn more about Gilmore, stop at the Lemhi County Historical Society and Museum at 210 Main Street, Salmon. Hours are typically June through October. Winter hours can vary; check online at www. lemhicountymuseum.org, or call (208) 756-3342.

ROCKY BAR - ATLANTA

ROCKY BAR AND ATLANTA REGION / SOUTH BOISE MINING DISTRICT

In 1863, eager prospectors searching rich claims outside the Boise Basin discovered gold forty miles east of Idaho City, along the Feather River below Soldier Mountains. Their find set off a stampede that was responsible for the building of several camps and towns and for creating the South Boise Mining District. The next few pages will try to elaborate on the frenzy that took place here in the pursuing years.

Today, the places I will detail all lay above shimmering Anderson Ranch Reservoir in Elmore County, northeast of Mountain Home. Constructed in 1941 for agricultural and hydroelectric power, Anderson Ranch Reservoir was once the tallest dam of its kind in the United States. The 4,600-acre reservoir is surrounded by the Boise National Forest and is known for camping, boating and kokanee fishing.

There is a reason why some of us are unusually attracted to these places that time forgot. We stare in wonder at the weathered wood and empty rooms. Each of us wonder what life was like in these forgotten places when the communities were new and the streets hummed with activity. There are some who simply look at the crumbling homes, rusting iron and heaps of mine dumps without seeing. There are others who, for a moment, are transported back in time and who actually feel the community when it was alive! "Anachronistic" is a term for individuals who are living in the wrong time period, or out of their chronological order. If you fall into this classification, you are like me, an anachronism. We exist in the present world, but the moment we step into one of these mining towns, we slip back in time. Was it because we were once here in another form? Why are we being pulled into these forgotten places as if some invisible force is beckoning us to come closer and to listen? I don't have the answer, at least a rational answer. If you are anything like me, then perhaps you are a dreamer; or could it be that we have an insight that others don't possess?

Atlanta and Rocky Bar, along with Featherville and Pine, are worth the drive. There were other camps along the Feather and Yuba Rivers. Evidence of some can still be found, others have vanished. I have written about a few, such as Happy Camp, Spanish Town and Yuba City. There were others.

The mining years left a fabulous legacy with much of it still intact. Prepare yourself for an adventure into the most isolated mining district in Idaho!

ATLANTA

Atlanta is located in Elmore County and sits on the Middle Fork of the Boise River at 5,383 feet. John Stanley and his party are credited with the discovery of gold in 1863, on an expedition from Warren to Idaho City. Although Stanley tried to keep his find a secret, news leaked. By 1864, a hundred miners were working placer claims along the Yuba River.

John Simmons discovered what would be named the Atlanta Lode in 1864, which transformed the sleepy placer camp into a significant lode-mining center. Due to Atlanta's remote location, lode mining had difficulty escalating. Transportation of ore out of the camp and supplies into the district remained a constant issue. The Yuba Mining District was formed, and named after the location where most of the placer mining originated, but it would take several decades before the full potential of the mining district was developed.

Initially settled by Confederate sympathizers, the town was named for a rumored victory by General John B. Hood of the Confederacy against General William T. Sherman in the Battle of Atlanta on July 22, 1864. That rumor later turned out to be incorrect. Regardless, the named remained.

Between 1868 and 1869, British capital greatly influenced the camp, making possible the construction of the Lucy Philips and Monarch Mills. Matthew Graham was responsible for much of the financial backing from British and New York investors, establishing the Lucy Phillips Gold and Silver Mining Company. Graham was an independent miner out of Rocky Bar who had worked his way from a hand arrastra to becoming an authority in milling. He was known for promotional business dealings in New York and London. Through those investments, the Lucy Phillips Mill was constructed, which at one point employed half of the male population of Atlanta. By 1869, the much-needed British capital was starting to waver. That same year, mills in Atlanta failed. By 1883, Lucy Phillips and Silver Mining Company were dissolved.

By 1876, the population had grown to five hundred. The community supported a mercantile, livery, sawmill, saloons, restaurants, hotels, a boardinghouse and a newspaper called the *Atlanta News*. In total, Atlanta had three different periods of growth. Upgraded recovery

180

Early residence.

Atlanta Club (to the right was the first and only gas station).

methods in milling, evolving mining technology, and construction of roads ushered in different chapters of Atlanta's life. In 1878, a fourteen-mile wagon road was completed from Rocky Bar to Atlanta, which allowed equipment to be more easily transported.

It wasn't until 1938 that the Middle Fork Road was completed, which connected Boise to Atlanta and allowed a direct route, as opposed to the mountainous and difficult route through Rocky Bar. The steep grade of James Creek Road was once the primary obstacle separating Atlanta from the outside world. From the beginning, the "Atlanta Lode" showed promise. In 1939 Talache Mines Inc. acquired all of the mining operations along the Atlanta Lode. The Atlanta Lode was one and a half miles in length and ranged in width from fifteen to thirty feet! A total of $18 million in gold and silver was recovered from the Yuba River District; the greatest percentage came after 1932. Atlanta remains today one of the most remote camps in the Western United States.

The discovery of the Atlanta Lode prompted the opening of other hard-rock mines. Prominent mines were the Monarch, Minerva, Last Chance, Tahoma, Buffalo, Leonora and General Pettit. Monarch Gold and Silver Mining Company operated from 1866 to 1869. The Atlanta Mines Company purchased the Monarch, Last Chance and Buffalo Mines and had an aerial tramway that carried ore to the mill at the Monarch. Other mines were south of town in what is called Quartz Gulch, where the Atlanta Lode was located. Inside the stamp mills, the ore was broken down and crushed and run through a chemical bath of cyanide to separate the gold from the matrix. The pure gold was melted and poured into molds and made ready to ship out of town. Cyanide and arsenic are sometimes both found in toxic wastes that were carelessly dumped into creeks and rivers next to stamp mills of the era. While cyanide was a chemical imported and used to leach out the gold, arsenic is a byproduct created by rock and ore being crushed. Over the years, dust created by the crushing of the ore lay in vast areas. As the wind blew, this contaminated dust would fill the air. Residents who breathed these contaminated particles over a prolonged period during this mining era could become prone to respiratory issues.

Although stamp mills began in Atlanta in 1867, the problem they faced was they were equipped to recover gold but not silver, the result being that only three-quarters of the value of the ore was being recovered. In 1869, the "Washoe Process" of recovering silver was utilized. It would, however, still be many years before significant production was seen. The Atlanta Lode was not the only lode discovery. A vein of gold in the Leonora ranged in width from one-tenth of an inch to two inches. It was said to be solid gold in the thinner portions, producing up to $10,000 in only a few hours when first discovered. Atlanta earned the reputation of being the largest underground hard-rock gold producing region in Idaho!

Two miles outside town on the Boise River can be seen the Atlanta Power Plant and Kirby Dam. Constructed in 1907, the dam utilized log cribs that were filled with rocks. The plant supplied electricity to the Monarch Mine and its 150-ton mill. Electricity from the Atlanta Dam and Power Plant was used for Atlanta and sold to neighboring mining companies. This turn-of-the-century technology still supplies electricity to Atlanta today.

Atlanta is located on the Middle Fork of the Boise River and is surrounded by the Boise National Forest, and is approximately two miles east of the Yuba River, with Idaho City approximately thirty-five miles due west. It is the northernmost mining town in the district and is at the base of Greylock Mountain, which is part of the Sawtooth Mountain Range.

Built in 1941, the Atlanta Club can be seen on Main Street. It served as a bar, restaurant and dance hall. In 2017, the roof collapsed under the weight of twenty feet of snow. The original Brunswick Bar from the Iowa-based manufacturing company still stands in the north end of the main barroom. Three bedrooms are located in the rear. A large cellar underneath was once used for food staples and supplies for the wintering population. Next to the Atlanta Club is the Veltex Gasoline Station. It was the only location for gasoline ever in town. In front, you can see the concrete footings where the pumps once stood. Directly across the street is the Whistle Stop Bar. Originally called the Blue Bird Café, it was built in 1931. Also across the street is The Hub (a bar), built in 1934; although closed, it now has the word "restaurant" printed on its side.

The story of Atlanta cannot be told without mention of Kerry Moosman. Kerry told me that he came to Atlanta when he was five days old. Today, at seventy , Kerry lives in town from July fourth to Thanksgiving. He has dedicated fifty years of his life to the preservation of the historic section of Atlanta. Although a great deal of Atlanta dates to the early 1900s, several of the structures in the center of town have been saved from oblivion by Kerry. These ten acres were added to the National Register of Historic Places in 1978. Included is the jail, Atlanta Club, and numerous structures along both Main Street and Pine Street. Another building of interest is the schoolhouse, with its deteriorating basketball court and slide, on the east end of Main Street. A short distance past the school on Main Street, you will reach a fork. A right turn onto Mine Hill Road will lead you to the mining district.

Kerry Moosman

Slide in overgrown schoolyard. How many kids slid down this?

The annual celebration of Atlanta Days is the first weekend in August, when as many as a thousand people make the drive to enjoy cold beer, festivities and past acquaintances. The year 2022 was the forty-second event and was sponsored by the Quick Response Unit (QRU) of Atlanta. Beaver Lodge is the only restaurant/saloon in town, and also has five cabins to rent. There is no cell service in Atlanta, but Beaver Lodge has Wi-Fi that customers are welcome to take advantage of. The income that Kerry earns from the sale of t-shirts at the annual Atlanta Days Celebration goes towards the continued preservation and maintenance of the Atlanta Cemetery. The cemetery is a must when visiting Atlanta. Drive east on Main Street. Turn south onto Quartz Street and then left onto Alpine Road. There is a double track leading up to the right. Follow it to the cemetery. Amongst the graves at Atlanta Cemetery are those of two mail couriers. A total of seven couriers traveling on skis between Rocky Bar and Atlanta were killed between 1870 and 1913 while attempting to deliver mail along the steep and treacherous James Creek Road.

Lazy H. Ranch and Hot Springs north of town caters weddings and special events. Originally homesteaded by Herman Coors of the Coors Brewing Company, Lazy H. Ranch provides a private landing strip and operates from spring to fall. During the winter months, a caretaker oversees the property.

There are three ways to get to Atlanta. One way is driving north from Featherville through Rocky Bar. Another is east from Idaho City. From Highway 21, turn onto Edna Creek Road near the summit and close to Whoop Em Up Park & Ski area. Signs will direct the way to Atlanta, eventually connecting with Middle Fork Road. The third way to reach Atlanta is via Middle Fork Road, which is the shortest distance from Boise. Driving distance from Highway 21 and Lucky Peak Reservoir is sixty-eight miles along the Middle Fork of the Boise River. You could churn buttermilk of the first half of the drive alongside Arrowrock Reservoir, but the washboard road improves after Twin Springs Resort. The Middle Fork Road, which traverses the Middle Fork of the Boise River, is the only road that is maintained during the winter months.

Whichever route you choose, it is going to be long, bumpy and dusty drive. Although there is always pretty country to see, there is no place of interest to visit along the way. You must want to go to Atlanta; it is strictly an in-and-out destination! It is my hope that the people reading these words have the same interests as I do. There is an allure that exists in these places that exists nowhere else! You must stop and ask yourself questions about what life was like here. More than a hundred years have passed since the streets rumbled with excitement. Walk into some of the abandoned homes, consider there was no insulation, running water or any of the conveniences most of us are accustomed to. Some of the homes that existed at the turn of 1900 are still here, although the thundering mills have vanished.

On the west end of the city limits you will see a large open area of land. This is where the Monarch Mill stood. Look closely and you will see the rusting machinery and stone wall. This is all that is left of the monstrous stamp mill that once pulverized the gold ore that traveled down the tram system from the Monarch Mine high on the opposite mountainside. Ask yourself this question: If it were somehow possible for you to go back to that time and live out your life as a superintendent of one of the large mills, would you do it? Would you trade your life today to go back to that time? If you are anything like me, you will ask yourself that question every time you set foot in a place like this!

Consider the individuals who live in these remote "living" ghost towns. Look at the way they furnish their homes. Consider the lifestyle they have chosen. Despite what the large cities have to offer, they continue to stay. Perhaps they have found something of greater value. Sit down and talk with one of them if you ever have the opportunity. The population of Atlanta stands at thirty-five; very few choose to leave their homes during the winter months. The Middle Fork Road remains open for mail delivery and grocery runs.

Dutch Em, who perished in a snowstorm trying to reach Rocky Bar.

ROCKY BAR

The discovery of gold on the Feather River in 1863 caused numerous camps to spring up throughout the district, with Rocky Bar becoming a principal settlement. Rocky Bar is located between Bear Creek and Steel Creek in the Boise National Forest, eight miles north of Featherville. By 1864, Rocky Bar had a population of 2,500, and because of its initial boom, was the county seat of Alturas County for seventeen years (1864-1882), and was a contender for the site of the territorial capital. In 1881, the city of Hailey won the election and took over the seat. At an altitude of 5,269 feet, its name was derived from large unmovable boulders that were encountered during its early mining days.

Before I go any further, let me explain the following. When Idaho was a territory, Alturas County covered an area as large as Maryland, New Jersey and Delaware combined. Rocky Bar being the county seat of such an extensive area is impressive to say the least. Alturas is derived from a Spanish word meaning "mountain summits." As time went on, Elmore County spun off of Alturas. Then in 1895, legislation created Blaine and Lincoln County, and Alturas County ceased to exist entirely. The name Elmore County was taken from the Ida Elmore Mine of Silver City, which in the 1860s was the largest producer of silver and gold in Idaho. Today, Mountain Home is the largest city of Elmore County, and the county seat.

Rocky Bar grew quickly, with mines along Bear and Steel Creeks, making it a leading settlement for South Boise miners. Placer mining in the nearby creeks and lode mining catapulted Rocky Bar's growth, establishing the South Boise Mining District. Primitive arrastras were constructed using native materials to grind the gold-bearing quartz ore. Arrastras work on the same order as a mortar and pestle. In this case, a large heavy stone is dragged in a circular motion over the tops of flat stones meticulously assembled in a circular pit. Gold-bearing quartz is then placed on the surface of the flat rocks. As the heavy top stone drags across the quartz in a circle, the ore is pulverized into workable gravel for sluicing. The arrastras were operated with either water power from a waterwheel, or were pulled by horses or mules. It was a crude device used to separate gold from mined ore until stamp mills came into use. By 1884, eighty arrastras were being utilized throughout the South Boise Mining District.

Difficulty in transporting equipment to this South Boise District impeded development. In 1864, Julius Newburg's South Boise Wagon Road Company finished construction of a toll road to Rocky Bar. As soon as Rocky Bar was accessible by road, the team of Cartee and Gates immediately set up a five-stamp mill. Stamp mills were more

Interior of Charlie Sprittles' cabin (now owned by Rick and Evy Jenkins, who moved it board by board from Rocky Bar to Atlanta).

efficient both in productivity and in the fineness of the pulverized ore. By comparison, a large arrastra could process one to one and half tons of ore per day, where a five-stamp mill could process five tons! By the fall of 1864, six more stamp mills were constructed and put into use. The most impressive was the twelve-stamp mill that arrived in November. The freight costs to ship the equipment from St. Joseph was thirty cents per pound, which calculated out to a staggering $8,400.

At its peak, Rocky Bar had the usual array of businesses, which included a mercantile, saloons, a livery, assay office, cafes, lawyers, a boardinghouse, school, hotels, a Chinese laundry and brothels. The first jail was built in 1866. Rocky Bar's first school was built in 1870. Since Rocky Bar had its beginnings during and after the Civil War (1861-1865), it had occasional conflicts between secessionists and Union sympathizers.

By 1863, "some 200 well-defined loads" had been established. Some of those were nothing more than prospect holes, some much larger. Beside the Elmore, other notable mines in Rocky Bar were the Idaho, Confederate Star, Ophir on Elk Creek and Bonaparte on Cayuse Creek. The Elmore had a celebrity associated with it by the name of H. T. P. Comstock, of the celebrated Virginia City, Nevada, "Comstock Lode." Because Comstock had an interest in the mine, he used his fame to promote it. If anyone has read about Comstock's nefarious dealings in Virginia City, they will recognize that he was on top of his game here. Typically, any mining venture is a gamble in the beginning. In the case of the Elmore, Comstock's intuition paid off in spades. The first initial reports of the Elmore yielded $347 per ton. At this point in time, the Elmore was the largest gold-producing mine in the district. By 1866, the South Boise District had more operating stamp mills than any other district in Idaho, with the Elmore surpassing them all. As rich and profitable as the hard-rock operations were, placer mining was still the most significant contribution from the South Boise District. Today, the South Boise Historic Mining District is listed on the Register of Historic Places.

Like all mining communities of the time, Rocky Bar had a Chinatown. It was located on Steel Creek north of Main Street. There were 279 registered Chinese in Rocky Bar. As mentioned in other chapters, the Chinese were persistent, hardworking and, most importantly, lived within their own community. Today, the buildings bordering Steel Creek at the cutoff to Atlanta is where the Chinese section once flourished.

Many things led to the collapse of large-scale mining in Rocky Bar and the South Boise Mining District. Inadequate pumps to lessen the perpetual flooding in the deeper mines, lack of technology, mismanagement, unwillingness to pay dividends, litigation, and even fraud led to the ultimate collapse. By the spring of 1866, Rocky Bar had a larger stamp mill capacity than any other Idaho district and eastern capitalists were frantic to continue with the construction of more mills. Unfortunately, the New York-based shareholders were unfamiliar with mining and underestimated transportation costs in the isolated camp. By the summer of 1866, companies found themselves lacking in adequate ore and insufficient capital. As a result, the larger mines failed. After the large-scale stamp operations ceased, small-scale mining efforts continued for the next few years.

A devastating fire swept through Rocky Bar on September 1, 1892, leaving most of the two to three hundred inhabitants homeless. The blaze started at 2 P. M. at the Chinese laundry of a hotel. Rocky Bar had a fire brigade that had yet to be tested. As the fire spread, the volunteers climbed aboard their horse-drawn pumper and headed for the single hydrant located in the center of town. Tragically, when the crew attempted to fasten the hose to the hydrant, they discovered the hose coupling was the wrong size for the hydrant. All the newly-formed fire brigade could do was stand and watch the fire. A bucket brigade was started, but their efforts were in vain. Reconstruction started immediately, which provided a townsite for another thirty years.

Rocky Bar

Annie Morrow's brothel/saloon

There were several attempts to reopen some of the larger mines over the next few decades, but none met with success. Between 1910-1915, a stationery dredge worked the Feather River. Between 1922-1927, a floating dredge operated. The dredge tailings for that operation can be seen north of Featherville from the Rocky Bar Road turnoff for several miles toward Rocky Bar along the Feather River. Those dredging operations yielded 33,000 ounces of gold, although the initial investment was $500,000. If gold yielded $25 per ounce at that point in time, you will see that the operation produced $825,000—not a large return on the investment. Due to low operating costs, modest mining operations took place in some of the Rocky Bar mines after 1929. In 1942, wartime restrictions forced the closing of everything.

One interesting story to come out of Rocky Bar is that of Charlie Sprittles (November 1880- November 1964). The story goes that Charlie Sprittles was born in Wakefield, England on November 25, 1880. Charlie lived in Wyoming for a few years before moving to Rocky Bar in 1932. He operated a store in Rocky Bar called White Front Store, which had one gas pump. He was also listed as the mayor of Rocky Bar. In November of 1963, he went to Boise to see a physician. He hitched a ride back to Featherville, where friends then tried to drive him up Rocky Bar Road to his cabin, but the snows were too deep, and the disadvantaged automobiles could only get him to within five miles of his cabin. In 1963, Charlie was the only wintertime resident of Rocky Bar, and much to the disapproval of his friends, he insisted on snowshoeing the remainder of the way to his cabin. Over the years, Charlie had developed a close relationship with pilots from Mountain Home Air Force Base. It was a common practice for them to fly over Charlie's cabin during the winter months to check on him. When they flew over the following day in late November and saw no smoke coming from Charlie's chimney, they radioed the sheriff in Featherville. A search party was formed, but due to heavy snows the night before no sign of Charlie was found. In April the following year, a snowshoe was spotted protruding out of the snow; it was Charlie. The cause of death was reported as being a heart attack. Charlie's wish was to be buried behind his cabin in Rocky Bar, but because Rocky Bar is inside of the Boise National Forest, it was not allowed. Charlie was buried April 24, at Mountain View Cemetery in Mountain Home. Halfway between Featherville and Rocky Bar on Rocky Bar Road is a beautifully carved wooden memorial to Charlie Sprittles. The marker is positioned close to where Charlie was found on that fateful day in April.

Charlie's cabin in Rocky Bar was purchased by Rick and Evy Jenkins when they discovered it was slowly being ripped apart and used for firewood. After purchasing the residence, Rick meticulously disassembled it, numbering each board, and reassembled the home in Atlanta. The home is now in the historical section of Atlanta on Pine Street.

Today Rocky Bar is a cluster of a few small summer residences. Some of the original buildings exist as well. Everyone you meet will be extremely friendly, and there are some great photographic opportunities. One notable structure is the two-story building at the junction of Rocky Bar Road and James Creek Road. This was Annie Morrow's Rocky Bar Brothel.

From Mountain Home, a toll road led to Dixie, Pine Grove, Junction Bar (Featherville) and eventually, Rocky Bar. The daily stage that made this run did not proceed onto Atlanta due to the steep grade of James Creek Road. Keep in mind, Rocky Bar was by far the most prominent settlement of the South Boise Mining District. Looking at it today, this doesn't seem possible. The mills are gone, as is the mercantile, fire department, numerous saloons, the boardinghouse, cafés, hotels and bordellos which once catered to the hard-working miners. During the summer months, a few property owners take up residence here, but with the first signs of winter they move on and don't return until spring. The writings in this book, as in other sources, are a legacy to the formidable community of Rocky Bar, which must be kept alive in the minds and hearts of the living.

Rocky Bar Cemetery is located on the left side of Rocky Bar Road prior to entering the townsite of Rocky Bar heading north from Featherville.

From Mountain Home, head east on Highway 20 for thirty-one miles to the Featherville/Rocky Bar Road (turnoff). Proceed 28.2 miles to Rocky Bar Road junction in Featherville. Take Rocky Bar Road for eight miles to Rocky Bar. It is fifty-nine miles from Mountain Home to Featherville. A 2WD vehicle can easily make the trip up the well-maintained Rocky Bar dirt road. The best time is during summer and early fall. Do not attempt the drive in the spring due to snow.

FEATHERVILLE

Established in the 1860s, Featherville was originally called Junction Bar. It sits at an elevation of 4,544 feet and is in Elmore County. Featherville is located alongside the South Fork of the Boise River and is inside the Boise National Forest. Featherville was originally a supply point and stage stop before continuing to Rocky Bar and Atlanta; placer deposits were discovered on the South Fork in 1900.

The most notable mining activity that took place here was dredge mining. Between 1910-1915, a stationery dredge worked the Feather River. Between 1922-1927, a floating dredge operated on both the South Fork and Feather River north of town, where 33,000 ounces of gold were recovered. In 1905, Junction Bar changed its name to Featherville.

There are several interpretive signs alongside the Rocky Bar cutoff north of town that explain the dredge history. Today, Featherville is a summer resort community that borders the north end of Anderson Ranch Reservoir. Overnight lodging is available, along with cafés, ATV opportunities, boating and fishing. Numerous camping sites exist on both sides of Anderson Ranch Reservoir. Camping opportunities exist as well along the South Fork of the Boise River between Pine and Featherville on Pine/Featherville Road.

SPANISH TOWN

Located at 5,520 feet, Spanish Town was a placer mining area on Elk Creek north of Rocky Bar. The name Spanish Town was given to the settlement, since the first prospectors to arrive found old arrastras which was evidence that Mexican—or Spanish—prospectors had worked the area prior to their arrival.

Like Happy Camp, Spanish Town was a placer mining community originating in 1863. There is still evidence of its existence despite decades of harsh elements and an unpredictable creek.

The 2012, the Trinity Ridge Fire burned the area close to Spanish Town. The trailhead leading to Spanish Town is about fifty yards past Washboard Falls on James Creek Road above Rocky Bar. Another route is to proceed through Featherville and turn left onto Cayuse Creek Road. Continue for 3.9 miles and turn left onto an unmarked double-track road. You will pass alongside massive amounts of dredge tailings expelled during the dredging years on each side of Feather River. Continue straight for 7.3 miles to a forest service sign-in box. Park here at the trailhead and continue on foot. At 1.7 miles you will cross Elk Creek and arrive at the site of Spanish Town.

Pieces of debris mark the Spanish Town site.

HAPPY CAMP

Between Rocky Bar and Featherville on the Feather River sat Happy Camp. Happy Camp was the site of the original gold discovery and became the first of the South Boise District camps. This was a placer mining camp where both sides of Feather River were sluiced and panned. It was reported that a hundred miners had settled here in 1864.

I mention Happy Camp primarily because of its significance. Wayne Sparling reported in his book, *Southern Idaho Ghost Towns,* written in 1974, that nothing remained but foundation hollows and bits of trash. Since Happy Camp was located on the banks of the Feather River, it is safe to say that decades of flooding have swept away any trace of this once flourishing camp.

GRAHAM

Located in Boise County, thirty miles northeast of Idaho City (sixteen miles southeast of Atlanta) on the North Fork of the Boise River is the site of Graham. Although there is nothing left of Graham, it possesses a fascinating history.

On January 2, 1886, Matthew Graham, who had gained credibility in Atlanta by gaining financial backing from New York and London investors, announced that he had discovered a fabulous gold and silver body on Silver Mountain. He is quoted to have said, "It is evident that the new discovery will eclipse any of the older quartz discoveries in Idaho."

He asserted that he had assay reports revealing $2,000 of free-milling gold and metallic silver. With the momentum of enthusiastic investors behind him, Matt Graham established the Idaho Gold and Silver Mining Company Ltd. Free milling is a term that means gold can be extracted from quartz by crushing without pressure leeching or chemical treatment. Further reports stated that veins of silver were ten to three hundred feet in width continuing for miles, silver that was so pure no smelting would be required.

Having faith in Matt Graham, investors were quick to respond. By the fall of 1887, a $15,000 road was completed, and a 500-foot tunnel dug. Further encouragement set into motion the employment of 150 men to build a twenty-stamp mill. By the summer of 1888, the newly formed town of Graham had six saloons, five boardinghouses, a jail, two blacksmiths, three livery stables, three hundred men, forty prostitutes and the controlling vote in Boise County. By August, a mile-long tramway went into service to haul the ore to the mill site.

By the fall of 1888 the engineers realized that the promising lode they had hoped for was nothing like what the assay reports had alluded to. English mining engineers suggested that an additional six thousand feet of tunnel be dug, but due to the lack of returns on the $600,000 of London capital that had already been invested, the project was abandoned. Sheriff's auctions were held in Idaho City, Graham and Rocky Bar, liquidating the Idaho Gold and Silver Mining Company in an attempt to recover money lost by investors. It is estimated that a million dollars was lost.

In total the mill that cost $350,000 to build ran for a total of eight to ten hours before shutting down. With winter approaching, the residents of Graham packed up what they could carry and abandoned the promising new town of Graham.

In 1995, the Rabbit Creek Forest Fire burned the area in which Graham is located. The Pioneer Fire burned the area again in 2016. Some evidence of rock retaining walls remain along with scattered debris. The site of Graham is located along NF-312 east of Deer Park Guard Station. Landmark locations near Graham are Graham Guard Station and Graham USFS landing strip (elevation 5,726 feet). Today, Deer Park and Graham Guard Stations are rented by the USFS. For information, go to Recreation.gov and search Graham or Deer Park cabins. They are in extremely isolated terrain, but can be reached by snowmobile in the winter and 4WD vehicle in summer months. Typically, the road is not clear for 4WD until late June. By working directly through the Idaho City District Ranger Station in Idaho City, keys for both cabins can be obtained. What a great way to spend a weekend! Graham is inside the Idaho City Ranger District of the Boise National Forest.

TOLL GATE

Located eleven miles east of Mountain Home on Highway 20 at mile marker 107, is the site of Toll Gate. In the asphalt pullout is historical marker #197 giving a brief history.

In 1864, Julius Newberg built a forty-mile-long wagon road from this point to Rocky Bar. An eight-mile section was constructed to avoid a steep portion of the road near Syrup Creek. Newberg chose this spot to set up his toll station, which operated for twenty years.

In 1883, Captain George Washington Hill (1820-1898) purchased Toll Gate and operated it until his death. Mr. Hill is interred at Mountain View Cemetery in Mountain Home.

Otis and Charolette Decker operated the Toll Gate Café here during the 1950s and 1960s. In addition to his role at the café, Otis had a mail route between Mountain Home, Prairie and Rocky Bar. He also did gold prospecting in the Featherville area when he wasn't delivering mail. Charlotte typically ran the café. When she wasn't performing duties in the kitchen and waiting tables, she could be seen every evening playing the piano for the guests.

Otis and Charolette's home was located up the draw behind the café. Rattlesnake Creek runs directly through the property. They had an orchard of Arkansas Black apples across the highway. Otis irrigated the orchard with water from Rattlesnake Creek. Several of those trees have survived and can be seen on the opposite side of the highway.

Otis Decker died in the late 1960s. The café was sold and sporadically operated off and on with different owners up until 2001. The buildings were eventually torn down. Today it is private property.

You can see photos taken in 2005 of the Toll Gate Café in Bruce Raisch's book, *Ghost Towns of Idaho*.

At six miles from I-84 and Mountain Home on the opposite side of Highway 20 from Toll Gate are the ruins of the Jackson School (1898 – 1925). This school was part of Rattlesnake Station, which was a major stop on the Oregon Stage Line between Salt Lake City and Walla Walla, Washington. In 1883, the Oregon Short Line Railroad ran a line ten miles east of here at a lower point in the valley. The only permanent structure other than Rattlesnake Station was the Mountain Home Post Office, which was moved to the present location of Mountain Home to be near the railroad terminus.

PINE GROVE

Although it no longer exists, Pine Grove must be mentioned primarily because of the location of the Franklin Mine. The town itself was located at a lower elevation than the Franklin Mine and Franklin Mill. Gold had been discovered on the Featherville River in the 1860s. In May of 1887, the Franklin Lode was discovered, which triggered the settling of Pine Grove. Other lode mines would come into existence near Pine Grove, but the Franklin would remain the top producer. From 1903 to 1911, the Franklin Mine produced $70 million in gold in today's money before closing.

In 1941, construction on Anderson Ranch Dam commenced. Construction ceased with the outbreak of World War II and wasn't completed until 1950. As the South Fork of the Boise River filled the reservoir in 1951, it covered the townsite of Pine Grove. Prior to the completion of the dam, some of the existing buildings of Pine Grove were moved to the present site of Pine. Most of the Franklin Stamp Mill was dismantled. What remains can still be seen today behind the Hayhurst B&B in Pine. Today, the Franklin Mine is on private property. From 1991 to 2013, Nathan Cook leased the Franklin Mine and with three partners worked its underground tunnels. During that time, they were producing seven ounces of gold per ton, which was higher than the old reports admitted to. The Franklin Mine is located south of Pine off S. Lester Creek Road. The mine dump from the Franklin can be seen high on the ridge behind the Hayhurst B&B on S. Twin Pine Drive.

When construction of Anderson Ranch Reservoir began, a small settlement was established a few miles south of the dam site on NE Anderson Ranch Dam Road. It was named Reclamation Village. A concrete stairway, foundation and garage the USFS uses for storage are all that remains.

Thomas Morrow had a mine near Pine Grove. Thomas Morrow was Annie Morrow's (Peg Leg Annie) husband. Annie raised her children in the Pine Grove residence for the fourteen years she was married to Morrow (see following section on Annie McIntyre Morrow).

To enlighten the reader, I want to point something out. In the early 1900s, Pine Grove was commonly referred to as being located between Dixie and Featherville. Dixie was a hotel and bar located close to the intersection of Highway 20 and Anderson Ranch Dam Road. It sat back off Anderson Ranch Dam Road to the left after making the turn from Highway 20. Initially it was a stage stop, and years later was the only stopover on the way to Pine Grove and beyond. Typically, stage stops were located approximately every fifteen miles to obtain fresh horses and refreshments for the passengers. After stage travel ended and automobile traffic commenced, these same spots continued as cafés, or a stop-off for refreshments and gasoline.

Marysville was another stage stop which was located above present-day Pine but was primarily tents. It was located on the South Fork of the Boise River across from where Dog Creek Campground is today on the N. Pine-Featherville Road. Nothing of it exists.

Pine is located at the mouth of the South Fork of the Boise River where it empties into Anderson Ranch Reservoir on the reservoir's north end. Pine is primarily a recreational town. Pine Cemetery is located south of Pine to the left (east) of S. Lester Creek Road. Numerous campgrounds are available surrounding Anderson Ranch Reservoir and the South Fork of the Boise River. The Pine Café is a great spot to grab a cheeseburger and cold beer!

ANNA MCINTYRE MORROW (PEG LEG ANNIE)

A mere mention of this incredible woman in the sections of Rocky Bar and Atlanta would be inexcusable, so I am dedicating a section to her alone.

Anna McIntyre was born in Jackson Township, Van Buren County, Iowa, on September 13, 1858, to Stephen and Marcella McIntyre. Her story doesn't really get interesting until 1864, when her parents embarked on the Oregon Trail en route for Rocky Bar, Idaho, where Anna's father had heard of a gold strike. The family endured the journey to Atlanta in time to build a 20 x 24-foot cabin before winter set in.

Answering to the name of Annie, she soon learned that life in a mining camp was far different to what she had remembered from Iowa, but she soon adapted to her new environment. At sixteen years of age, she married Thomas Morrow, an abusive man seventeen years her senior, a marriage that ultimately ended in divorce. She had five children with Morrow between 1875 and 1889. Like many marriages of the time, Morrow wanted Annie as a house cleaner, caregiver to his children and for his carnal needs. Annie left him in 1891 but kept in contact with Morrow for the sake of the children. Annie never remarried. Fortunately for Annie, she learned well from the lessons that life dealt her.

Annie prospered after she left Morrow and at thirty-three years of age had overcome adversity to become the proprietor of two brothels, a saloon, a boarding house and café, a remarkable accomplishment for a single woman in a frontier town in 1895. She owned businesses in both Rocky Bar and Atlanta. Aside from being a shrewd businesswoman, she had a passionate heart, and was commonly known to extend credit and a helping hand to those in need.

The episode that earned Annie her nickname started on a spring day on May 15, 1896. Annie was in Atlanta and wanted to get to Rocky Bar to oversee one of her businesses. It was fourteen miles, but she felt she could easily walk it. Atlanta sits in a valley with James Creek Road rising 2,500 feet in five miles to the crest of the road below Bald Mountain. At this time of the year, there was still snow below Bald Mountain, but the trek was doable. Knowing that Annie was about to leave, a young woman by the name of Dutch Em (Emma Von Losch) asked if she could accompany her. Annie objected at first, but Dutch Em persisted. Dutch Em was one of the prostitutes who worked for Annie, and it was important for the young girl to get to Rocky Bar to catch the stage to Boise. Not being able to dissuade Dutch Em, the two set off for Rocky Bar.

An unforeseen blizzard came up as the girls were reaching the summit of James Creek Road. At one point, Annie carried Dutch Em on her back when Em couldn't keep up. Two days later a search party was organized when Annie failed to reach Rocky Bar. A mail carrier from Rocky Bar intercepted the two girls, but it was too late for Dutch Em, who had perished from the cold. Annie was found crawling on her hands and knees; she had covered Em with some of her wool undergarments, but it wasn't enough to sustain the frail young girl. It was determined at the time of rescue that Annie's feet were frozen. After returning to Atlanta, a doctor was brought from Mountain Home whose journey took a week. By the time the doctor arrived, gangrene had set in. The result was that Annie's feet were amputated above the ankles.

How a human being could endure the pain and agony that occurred during the course of the doctor's journey, as well as the months of healing, is difficult to comprehend. Individuals who Annie had developed strong relationships with came forward to assist in the weeks that followed the operation. Considering that torn bedsheets for bandages, hot water, and whiskey ("Irish chloroform") was all there was to keep away any infection and act as anesthesia during the operation, her survival is astonishing. Keep in mind also that those bandages were washed and rewashed. A supply of bedsheets (or bandages) simply did not exist in Atlanta in 1896.

Annie Morrow's gravesite at Morris Hill Cemetery, Boise.

Annie was a remarkable woman. She not only traveled the Oregon Trail in an ox-drawn cart at four years of age, she grew up in a raucous mining camp, saw her father shot down in the streets of Rocky Bar when she was a young girl, bore five children to an abusive husband, became the madam of two brothels, owned and ran a boardinghouse, saloon and café, had both feet amputated, had her lifesavings stolen at sixty years of age by a trusted companion, opened a laundry, ran a bootlegging business during prohibition and ultimately succumbed to cancer. Only one of her daughters (Ethyl) maintained a relationship with Annie; the other children denounced her due to her choice of profession. Because of her lifelong practice of extending help to others, the grateful townspeople of Atlanta provided for her as best they could in her later years by bringing her groceries and cutting and stacking wood for her fire. No woman in the history of Idaho has faced such challenges and suffered more tragedy than this solitary woman. Her life was a struggle from beginning to end, yet through it all she triumphed and earned the respect and admiration of everyone who had the privilege of knowing her.

She was admitted to Saint Alphonsus Hospital in Boise at seventy-six years of age. Anna McIntyre Morrow died on her birthday, September 13, 1934. She was laid to rest in Morris Hill Cemetery, Boise, Idaho, next to the father of her children and to one son, William.

At 7.7 miles from Rocky Bar on the road to Atlanta a memorial plaque was erected at James Creek Summit by the Atlanta Arts Society in 2003, providing a touching eulogy to Annie Morrow. A stone marker was also erected to the memory of Dutch Em.

Dutch Em (Emma Von Losch) is buried in the Atlanta Cemetery. A marble tombstone marks her grave. Through the efforts of Kerry Moosman and generous contributions of others, the cemetery has been saved from years of abandonment.

NORTHERN IDAHO

SILVER VALLEY (COEUR D'ALENE MINING DISTRICT)

The Silver Valley must take a separate place altogether in this book. Nestled in the Coeur d'Alene Mountains, this section of Northern Idaho in Shoshone County has built such an astonishing reputation that it deserves to be in a class by itself. There are twelve towns inside the Coeur d'Alene Mining District, which is a 30 x 30-mile area, making the Silver Valley nine hundred square miles. This tiny district inside Idaho's panhandle off Interstate 90 has produced more silver than any other place on planet earth! Total production over the past 130 years is 1.4 billion ounces of silver!

Today, outdoor enthusiasts come to this alpine setting from all over the western United States to enjoy fishing, camping, bicycling, skiing and hiking, or just to relax.

It troubles me a little that only a short time ago this area was not about getting a suntan, exercising and shopping for souvenirs. Instead, it was about men and women working to support their families and building a community. It was about men braving hardships as they descended deep into the mines to establish the greatest silver empire on earth. Consider what you have today and be thankful. The men who built the towns and toiled in the mines didn't rely on government assistance. Instead, they had ambition and a drive to succeed and see that their families didn't go hungry. It was their spirit and their sacrifices that gave us what we have today.

Today things have changed drastically from the early years when miners and prospectors searched the creeks and quartz outcroppings for gold and silver. However, those men who laid aside their own comforts pursuing adventure and accomplishing miraculous achievements is what made everything before you a reality. Take the time to investigate the museums and the historical points of interest and revel in the architecture and ambiance that surrounds you.

The towns I will write about in the next few pages are not ghosts. In fact, the unprecedented amount of precious metal that lay beneath them will not permit them to be ghosts. If you look beyond the modernization, tourism and technology, you can see the extraordinary

203

and colorful history of this region's past.

The towns that make up the Silver Valley are: Wallace, Burke, Gem, Kellogg, Mullan, Silverton, Murray, Wardner, Pinehurst, Smelterville, Osburn, and Kingston. Each one has a unique history that led to its establishment, and a reason it still exists today. I wonder which you will find the most interesting and alluring. Since the mid-1800s, this region has attracted prospectors, miners, adventurers, gamblers, entrepreneurs, merchants, and even prostitutes seeking their fortune and a place in life.

You are standing in the Coeur d'Alene Mining District, the Silver Valley, the richest and most extraordinary silver deposit our planet has ever seen! It all happened right here beginning in 1881, and hasn't ended yet. Take the time now to delve into the richest part of Idaho's past that exists.

WALLACE

Named for Colonel William R. Wallace, this charming community is a must-see for anyone interested in Idaho's rich mining history. Located in Shoshone National Forest at an elevation of 2,730, it was founded in 1884. It is the county seat for Shoshone County and is in the heart of the Coeur d'Alene Mining District. It is located forty-eight miles southeast of Coeur d'Alene and sits alongside the West Fork of the Coeur d'Alene River and Interstate 90. With a production of 1.2 billion (that's billion) ounces of silver, this makes Idaho's Silver Valley, of which Wallace is the center, the largest silver-producing region on the planet! Surrounded by the Bitterroot Mountains swathed in Douglas fir and white pine, the entire town is listed on the National Register of Historic Places (only four *entire cities* in the United States are listed on the National Register of Historic Places). With twenty-one percent of the earth's silver coming from the silver mines of Wallace alone, it proclaims itself to be the "Silver Capital of the World." Four museums within its city boundaries are dedicated to its fabulous history. With a population of eight hundred, it is far from a ghost, but perhaps its enduring spirit to survive is what's kept Wallace alive and thriving. The Galena Mine near Wallace is one of three mines still in operation inside the Silver Valley. Over the past eighty years it has produced over a million ounces of silver!

The moment you drive into town you will see that you have stepped back in time. The entire business district is steeped in the rich culture reminiscent of 1900s architecture. Beautifully constructed brick buildings with decorative terracotta trim line the sidewalks, but there is an ulterior motivation behind the craftsmanship of these

204

Wallace. Photo: Historic Wallace Chamber of Commerce.

"brick" structures. Check the internet and your calendar for a list of festivals and events that take place here throughout the year. Gyro days, Oktoberfest, Huckleberry Festival, Wallace Bratfest, Statehood Parade and Celebration, Wallace Bluesfest, Under the Freeway Flea Market, Idaho Craft Beer Pub Crawl, Fall for History, Home for the Holidays and Depot Day are just a few. There is always something going on in Wallace, especially during the summer months.

With silver production escalating, the early 1900s saw even a larger population growth in Wallace along with electric lighting and paved streets. Then in mid-August of 1910 a dark cloud loomed over Wallace in the form of smoke. The largest and most destructive forest fire ever recorded in the history of the United States, burning five million acres of forest in the Northern Rocky Mountains, struck Wallace. The fire was dubbed The Big Burn and was far beyond anything the recently formed United States Forest Service had ever coped with. This wasn't merely a forest fire but a firestorm of unprecedented size and fury, with such intense heat it choked everything in its path and spewed burning ash several inches deep across every square inch of Idaho's Silver Valley. Citizens were evacuated by the railroad, leaving their homes and personal possessions behind. Soon after the trains escaped town, bridges and trestles burned and collapsed. By the afternoon of August 21, a third of Wallace was gone. The fire killed eighty-seven people, seventy-eight of whom were firefighters. Today there are interpretive signs in front of the Historic Wallace Chamber of Commerce and Visitor Center (10 River Street), describing what happened on that day in history.

Although this book is committed to Idaho's mining history, the impact this fire made cannot go without mention. Because of the large amounts of silver that still laid untapped beneath its surface,

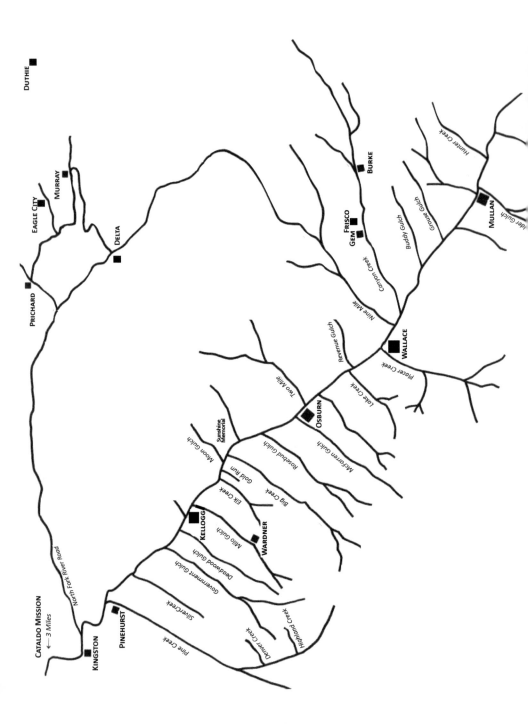

the business district of Wallace was immediately rebuilt. However, instead of using lumber, the construction would consist of fireproof brick. Like a time-capsule just opened, today this town can be seen almost exactly as it was built in 1911.

If anyone has ever held a Pulaski axe in their hands, they should know that it was designed by and named for Ed Pulaski of the United States Forest Service. Pulaski became immortalized for his heroic actions and was solely responsible for saving the lives of all but five of his forty-five-man firefighting crew by sheltering them in a mine entrance to escape the torrential flames that descended on them on August 21, 1910. Today, Pulaski Tunnel is listed on the National Register of Historic Places. Pulaski Trail is a four-mile (in-and-out,) moderately trafficked and well-maintained trail located five minutes from downtown Wallace on Moon Pass Road; it offers beautiful scenery along the way. Educational interpretive signage along the trail explains the Big Burn of 1910. I have included a separate section on Pulaski Tunnel.

While visiting Wallace, it is important to take the time to visit Nine Mile Cemetery. It is one mile north of Wallace. From Wallace, take Nine Mile Canyon Road one mile northeast. Graves here date back to the 1800s and the early mining days; there are also graves of servicemen from every conflict in American history commencing with the Civil War. Graves of the five who perished under Ed Pulaski's watch are here in a designated area. Pulaski personally tended these grave sites until his death on February 2, 1931.

Sierra Silver Mine Tour: We did this tour reluctantly, thinking it would be a farce intended primarily for children. Let me say here that I was mistaken. Small groups are taken by trolley to the Sierra Silver Mine a short distance from downtown Wallace. Once at the mine, you are given a hardhat to begin your underground walking tour. Your guide will not be a volunteer or docent but an authentic miner who has spent most of his working life laboring underground in hard-rock mines. This is a wonderful opportunity to meet and listen to an experienced professional explain every facet of hard-rock mining.

Like the Crystal Gold Mine Tour in Kellogg, this is a fabulous opportunity to listen to a man who has spent his career underground drilling, blasting, and mucking drifts and stopes. No matter what your level of experience is, I strongly suggest taking this tour. Tours are open from May to October 1. Summer hours are 10:00 a.m. to 4:00 p.m. Spring and fall are typically 10:00 a.m. to 2:00 p.m. Tours are every half hour. Temperature in the mine is a constant 50°F, so bring a light jacket. As said earlier, the tour includes a short scenic trolley car ride through town to get to the mine. For information, contact (208) 752-5151; or info@silverminetour.org.

Oasis Bordello Museum: I'm going to add this as a must-see while visiting Wallace. It's no secret that prostitution and the red-light district were significant parts of most every western community since the western migration commenced. Known as "the world's oldest profession," prostitution has been a lucrative, legitimate and essential occupation for centuries dating back to ancient Greece, Rome and the Middle Ages. Some of the beautiful young ladies earned and saved enough to eventually retire and hold a position of respectability in the towns where they lived. Regrettably, most died at an early age from drugs, opium and disease, or simply faded into obscurity. Restrictions started unfolding in the United States during the twentieth century for a myriad of reasons. With the exception of a few rural counties in Nevada, prostitution is illegal in the United States today. The Oasis Bordello Museum provides a glimpse into this fascinating life and has quite an unusual history to go with it. The story goes that although prostitution was illegal in Idaho in 1980, the Oasis Bordello continued to do business by paying handsome bribes to the local police commissioner. Then one night in 1988, word spread quickly through the brothel that federal police had been tipped off and a raid was imminent. The partially-clothed girls, madam, and customers hastily fled, leaving everything behind. No arrests were made, and the building was officially sealed. Then in 1993, a local businessman purchased the building. Seeing that everything was exactly as it had been left five years earlier, he had the foresight to open it as a museum. Today, knowledgeable guides will lead individuals through the rooms to see them as they were in 1988, down to a cigarette in an ashtray with lipstick faintly coloring the filtered tip. Nothing is fabricated. The tour is appropriate for all ages. Access the tours and gift shop at 605 Cedar Street; (208) 753-0801.

Two hotels in Wallace are The Stardust and Brooks Hotel Restaurant and Lounge. My advice is to check reviews before committing. The Brooks Hotel does have a restaurant which provides an excellent breakfast. It also has a small cocktail lounge. For lunch and dinner, I strongly recommend City Limits Brew Pub, open 11:00 a.m. to 9:00 p.m., closed on Sunday and Monday; 108 Nine Mile Road. Another option for overnight lodging is Silver Mountain Resort, Kellogg (ten miles west on Interstate 90). This is an extremely nice facility and positively worth the commute.

I would like to add this, as it is vitally important not only to Wallace but to the entire Silver Valley: a photographic partnership developed in 1893. Their names were Thomas Barnard and Nellie Stockbridge. The Barnard-Stockbridge Photography Collection is a compilation of two thousand photographs captured from 200,000 nitrocellulose and glass plate negatives taken by Nellie Stockbridge and T. N. Barnard between 1894 and 1964. The photographs specifically depict stages of life in Wallace and Kellogg. If you want to see vintage photographs of any mine, mill or city scene from the Coeur d'Alene Mining District, it is on file to view. In 2019, the Barnard-Stockbridge Museum opened its doors to the public. The director of the museum is Tammy Copelan. The museum is located at 312 4th Street, Wallace, (208) 556-5880. The museum is open May 1 to October 15. Admission is free, prints are for sale. This is a handy reference for you to obtain images I cannot provide in the following pages (www.barnardstockbridge.com). The black and white photographs are considered to be the best photographic collection in the northwest United States. I will make mention of this later but wanted to give an overview here as well.

Besides what I've already mentioned, Wallace has many other one-of-a-kind things to do:

- North Idaho Trading Company (Antiques and Oddities) at 504 Bank Street; must see to believe!

- Silver Streak Zipline Tours, located in downtown Wallace, at 523 Cedar Street; they offer ten ziplines on 250 acres of privately-owned land; (208) 556-1690

- Northern Pacific Railroad Depot Museum at 219 Sixth Street

- Wallace Brewing Company at 610 Bank Street

- Center of the Universe (marker) in the Historic District. Look for manhole cover at Bank Street and 6th Street

- Wallace District Mining Museum (Dante's Peak Mining Museum), 509 Bank Street; (208) 556-1592

- Pulaski Tunnel (see separate entry this chapter)

- Bernard-Stockbridge Photographic Museum at 312 4th Street (see separate entry, this chapter)

- Wallace Visitor Center/Chamber of Commerce, 10 River Street (www.wallaceid.fun). You can check with the visitor center concerning events and restaurants. WallaceIdahoChamber@gmail.com

- City Limits Brew Pub at 108 Nine Mile Road—best food in town!

- Johnson's Gems—jewelry, precious stones, silver—6th Street and Bank Street (Center of the Universe); www.JohnsonsGems.com

MULLAN

Mullan is the easternmost town in the Silver Valley, sitting at an elevation of 3,278 feet. Located in the Coeur d'Alene Mountains on Interstate 90, it has a population of 692 and was founded in 1884 when gold was discovered at the Gold Hunter Mine (later to mine silver). The Northern Pacific Railroad arrived in Mullan in 1889, and the city was incorporated in 1904. Two hundred miners from Mullan were involved in the much-publicized labor strike of 1899 at the Bunker Hill Mill in Wardner. The aftermath saw Mullan's sheriff and other elected officials facing disciplinary action. To read the full story, see the section on Wardner.

Mullan reached its peak population of 2,291 in 1940. Today, Mullan is home to the legendary Lucky Friday Silver Mine, owned and operated by the Hecla Mining Company. The Lucky Friday is one of the remaining operational mines in the Coeur d'Alene Mining District and, at present, the largest. Its output is 1,000 tons of ore each day, and can be seen east of town. The main shaft descends 6,200 feet and is 2,800 feet below sea level. Today the Hecla Mining Company is based in Coeur d'Alene. Hecla mines a third of all silver produced in the United States.

The tailings of the Gold Hunter Mine (now part of the Lucky Friday Mine) are still visible in town as well, at 4,012 feet. Gold Hunter's years of operation were 1901-1994. The footings of the National Copper Mill can be seen east of town. To view the National Copper Mill and Gold Hunter Mill, see the Barnard-Stockbridge Photograph Collection.

Headlines were made in 1919 when a cave-in at the Gold Hunter Mine trapped two miners for two weeks at the twenty-seventh level. In total darkness for part of their ordeal, the two miners waited while rescuers sent a diamond drill down to make an opening large enough to send them food and candles.

Mullan is named for John Mullan (1830-1909), a West Point graduate. Lieutenant Mullan was appointed to engineer to build a 624-mile military wagon route from Fort Benton, Montana to Walla Walla, Washington. Between 1859 and 1862, Mullan led the construction crew that built the road, which would be the first civilian engineered road in the Pacific Northwest, running east and west across the Idaho panhandle. Today's Interstate 90 follows much of that original wagon route. Appointed to captain after the road's completion, John Mullan is commemorated at a monument in Fourth of July Pass, a few miles east of Coeur d'Alene. Heading west on Interstate 90, take exit 28. At the top of offramp, turn right and follow the historical sign (Mullan Road Historic Site) leading down a short road to the

Lucky Friday Silver Mine in Mullan.

monument. A section of the Interstate known as Fourth of July Link is named in his honor. Due to Captain Mullan's efforts, travelers were able to access the Idaho Territory and discover the rich mineral wealth of the Silver Valley.

Another interesting highlight in Mullan is the Captain John Mullan Museum. The museum is in the old historical Liberty Theatre. The story of the township of Mullan and the fabulous Lucky Friday Mine is part of what is explained through rare photographs and interpretive notes. The museum is only open June, July and August, Monday through Friday, 10:00 a.m. to 4:00 p.m.; (208) 744-1155.

Cemeteries are important to me, for they tell a story of the individuals who lived in the young mining camps and settlements. These men and women were the first who had the adventurous spirit and courage to cross a frontier and settle in areas where no white man had been before them. Their names are now frozen in stone in these cemeteries. In some cases, towns shared a cemetery when the settlements were in close proximity to each other. Mullan has two cemeteries. Mountain View Cemetery can be reached by a short drive heading south on Copper Street up a rather steep hill. Follow the signs off of River Street to its location. The second is Fairmont Cemetery, aka Pioneer Cemetery, and is across from the Morning Mine and Mill site. You can tell at a glance that this cemetery is extremely old. My guess is it was the first cemetery in the Silver Valley. Take a moment to

Morning Mine and Mill (note large ore dump in rear).

study the names and intricate craftsmanship of the granite. In some cases, the names are almost obliterated by wind and rain, but they still silently stand watch and give a brief account of who is beneath them. "As they were, so we are, and as they are, so we shall be." To get to Fairmont Cemetery: From the center of Mullan, drive north on Second Street to Mill Road; turn left. Follow Mill Road about half a mile to Fairmont Cemetery; it will be on your left.

Directly across from Fairmont Cemetery is the Morning Mine and Mill. You will see the yellow buildings directly adjacent to Interstate 90. The Morning Mine operated from 1895 to 1980 and produced more than 18 million tons of silver ore. You will see the vast mine dump behind the mill.

The Morning Club, a three-story red brick building, was constructed by the corporate offices of the Morning Mine in 1920 as a social center for the miners and mill workers. The elaborate club was opened to the general public later, and has been the center of multiple community events for generations. It still stands today and is located at 117 Hunter Street, Mullan.

The early years of mining in Mullan, as well as in other communities throughout the Silver Valley, are available to view at The Barnard-Stockbridge Photography Collection in Wallace; or to view Barnard-Stockbridge photography, go to the University of Idaho Library Website; or to www.barnardstockbridge.com.

Mullan is accessed by exits 67, 68 and 69 from Interstate 90. From Wallace, head east on Interstate 90 and exit at exit 68.

BURKE

Located in Shoshone County, six miles northeast of Wallace on Burke Road (Burke-Canyon Creek Road, also known as State Highway 4), are the remains of Burke. For centuries prior to prospectors arriving in 1880 in search of placer gold, the Coeur d'Alene, Spokane and Flathead tribes followed the now-famous canyon from Montana to the Coeur d'Alene River. In 1884, an outcropping of galena quartz was discovered on the northern hillside of Burke Canyon by John M. Burke; this would ultimately become the Tiger Mine. At approximately the same time, another outcropping of galena was discovered on the southern hillside, which would become the Poorman Mine. These two finds were the beginning of the camp that would develop into the boomtown of Burke. S. S. Glidden later purchased a four-fifths interest from Burke in the Tiger Mine. Foreseeing the incalculable wealth that lay beneath the surface, S. S. Glidden knew that to provide for the full potential of his Tiger Mine, it was necessary to establish a concentrating plant. Also, to bring in needed machinery, a new road and a railroad were needed. By December of 1887, Glidden's vision of establishing a narrow-gauge railroad between Wallace and Burke became a reality. Silver ore shipping on the Canyon Creek Railroad became the first ore to ship from the newly-established Coeur d'Alene Mining District. Five miles west of the Montana border, Burke is located in an unusually narrow canyon at 3,700 feet. Its mining history was based on silver, zinc and lead. There is not a lot left of Burke today, but what does exist is extraordinary! Burke is without question the most alluring and haunting area inside the Silver Valley. In a glimpse you can visualize the scope of things that transpired in this tiny area. A small population exists on the north end of town.

The most prominent of the ruins that remain are those of the Hecla and Star Mines. The Hecla Sorting Plant and Compound is the large concrete structure first seen upon entering town. The Star Mine is the decorative red brick building directly behind it. The Star Mine was the last big mining operation to exist in Burke; it closed in 1981. At the time of its closing, the Star Mine was the deepest mine in North America, with a depth of 8,100 feet. When you consider that one mile is 5,280 feet, it will give you an idea of how deep this mine was, and that's not taking into account the many miles of tunnels that branched off of its main shaft. The concrete Hecla Sorting Plant and Compound was built between 1923 and 1925, after the 1923 fire destroyed the previous wooden structure. Vast mining dumps from the largest of the hard-rock mining operations can be seen as you drive through town.

By 1888, ore from the mines was being shipped to Wallace. The fact that the Canyon Creek Railroad had to share its boundaries with the Northern Pacific Railroad and Union Pacific made for an interesting set of circumstances, since the canyon that Burke was built in was a mere three hundred feet in width at its smallest point. Eventually, the Northern Pacific and the Union Pacific agreed to share the tracks. There was very little room in the canyon for both a road and railroad tracks, so wagons and later automobile traffic agreed to drive in the same direction when a train was coming. U-turns in Burke were impossible. The only way for an automobile to head in the opposite direction was to drive to the end of town and turn around.

A 150-room, three-story hotel (boarding house) named the Tiger Hotel was built in 1896 by S. S. Glidden. To comply with the widening of the railroad tracks through the narrow streets, the cooperative owners of the hotel made provisions to allow the tracks to literally run through the lobby of the hotel in 1906, which unexpectedly led to two mentions in *Ripley's Believe It or Not*. The stores and businesses were so crammed together inside the narrow canyon that legend said the shop owners had to roll up their awnings when they heard the train coming for fear of them being ripped off. During the winter months when excessive amounts of snow accumulated in the narrow canyon, railroad cars were filled with the surplus snow and transported out of town!

Burke produced something other than mineral wealth; it also produced one of the loveliest and most iconic leading ladies Hollywood ever knew. At the grand opening of the Burke Theatre and Union Hall in 1925, a four-year-old resident of the mining community made her debut by tap dancing before the jubilant audience. Her name was Julia Jean Mildred Francis Turner. Many years later, the talented youngster would shorten her name and move to California, where she would become immortalized as one of the most publicized and highly-paid leading ladies in the Golden Age of Hollywood. Married eight times and credited with playing opposite Hollywood's most celebrated leading men, her name was Lana Turner. Among her numerous awards in a career that spanned five decades and included more than fifty films, she was nominated for best actress in the 1958 motion picture, Peyton Place.

As you continue through town you will see a large two-story red brick building on the left. It will have a concrete stairway and metal railing leading up to the structure. This was the office building for the Hercules Mine. The Hercules produced 30 million ounces of silver and several hundred thousand tons of lead by the time it closed in 1924. On the right side of town past the Hecla/Star Mines is a wigwam-shaped metal structure behind a chain-link fence. This was part of the Hecla/Star Sawmill.

Burke had its share of disasters, both natural and political. The narrow canyon with its steep cliffs was known for yearly avalanches. One of many avalanches took place February 4, 1890, killing twenty-four people and burying businesses and residences in fifty to seventy feet of earth, rock and snow. Another notable calamity that took place in Burke was the Coeur d'Alene Labor Strike of 1892, with miners from Shoshone County protesting a wage cut. Tensions grew so violent that the governor of Idaho declared martial law, bringing in the National Guard and the United States Army to maintain peace.

Every year another avalanche rumbled down the mountainside and every year the necessary repairs were made. Burke also dealt with rain in the spring and fall months. Floods plagued Burke after the 1910 fire stripped the Bitterroot Mountains of precious timber and vegetation; one notable flood took place in 1913. Although Burke survived the Big Burn of 1910, it did not escape the devastating fire of 1923. Fire broke out down the canyon from Burke from the spark of a locomotive, eventually overtaking the community and

Hercules Mine office building

destroying three-fourths of the town. The entire business district along with the surface workings of the Hecla mine was wiped out. The Hecla Mine was closed for five months until mining operations could resume. That same fire caused extensive damage to the Tiger Hotel, which was soon rebuilt and enlarged. The Tiger Hotel saw a decline in the 1940s and was eventually torn down in 1954. The middle of the twentieth century saw a decline of mining in Burke. All mining ceased in 1991 with the closing of the Star Mine.

In 1903, Burke was the most developed mining community in the Coeur d'Alene Mining District. Multiple mines were producing hundreds of pounds of silver ingots a day. The Poor Man, Hecla, Standard, Sherman, Hercules and Tiger were among the top producers. Other prominent mines were the Galena, Mammoth, Anchor, Star and Custer. By 1910, Burke's population stood at 1,500, with three hundred buildings up and down the steep-walled canyon. The narrow streets of Burke roared with activity from sawmills, automobile traffic, locomotives, twenty-four-hour eateries, miners and mill workers. There were four general stores, two boarding houses, a hardware, a bakery, doctors, a fire company, lawyer's offices and seventeen saloons.

At the outbreak of World War II, non-essential mining was ordered shut down by a declaration from the United States government. The reason for this was that gold (and in some cases silver) was not considered strategic to the war effort. Also, the large labor force that toiled in the mines and mills that processed the ore could be better utilized on the war front. In many cases, entire communities that relied on gold mining as their sole stock and trade collapsed. With gold mining shut down, men had no other choice to provide for their families except to enlist in the armed forces, and at the same time fulfill their moral obligation to their country. However, the exact opposite took place in Burke. Burke and the Coeur d'Alene Mining District were considered so vital to the war effort that the government subsidized mining here to keep the mines open and operating. Where other mining operations were shutting down across the United States, Burke's mining production increased with the demand for copper, iron, zinc, lead and silver. Where other communities turned to ghosts, Burke's machinery thundered twenty-four hours a day!

Today its ghostly ruins remind curious visitors of the glory days that once reigned here. The townsite of Gem—also part of the Coeur d'Alene Mining District—just south of Burke was established in 1886. Nothing remains. There is no historical signage in Gem, although there is historical signage for the Frisco Mill just south of Burke.

From Wallace, head east on Bank Street. Drive underneath Interstate 90 onto Burke Road (Burke-Canyon Creek Road). On your short

Hecla Sorting Plant and Compound

Postcard circa 1945 showing congested conditions
typical of Burke, that contributed to its being
mentioned in Ripley's Believe or Not.

seven-mile drive to Burke, you will pass through several small communities that have existed since 1885. These towns were built around mines which bear the same name as the towns: Cornwall, Black Bear, Yellow Dog, Woodward Park, Frisco and, of course, Gem. If you visit Burke during the fall, you will see displays of autumn colors along Burke-Canyon Creek Road. The business center of Burke is three quarters of mile long. Great photography opportunities are available throughout the business section; afternoon sunlight is best.

In 2012, extensive testing conducted in the Hecla and Star Mines revealed that there is 25 million ounces of untapped silver that are still buried beneath Burke. However, due to exorbitant costs, inaccessibility and meeting current codes and standards, any future mining here would be highly unlikely.

In 2001, the Environmental Protection Agency (EPA) offered three hundred residents who live throughout Burke Canyon between Wallace and Burke a buyout program. According to the EPA, the mining years in Burke left Burke Canyon with the highest levels of contamination in the Coeur d'Alene District. The residents turned down their offer and remain to this day.

Star Mine corporate office

Located two miles south of Burke alongside Canyon Creek is the townsite of Gem. Other than a few permanent residences, very little remains of the original structures. Both the communities on Gem and Mace grew as a result of the mines that operated within their boundaries and shared the same name. The primary mines were Gem, Helena-Fresco and Big Bear.

Today, Gem is most noted for the violence that broke out here between Union Miners and company owners when several boxes of dynamite were exploded, destroying a four-story mill on July 11, 1892. There is a historical sign commemorating the violence at Frisco Mill alongside the road in Gem on the bank of Canyon Creek. The sign reads, "Overwhelmed by Union Miners, company managers surrendered. Six fatalities, half from each side, preceded four months of martial law and military occupation by a thousand soldiers."

Founded in 1886, at its height Gem supported a population of 2,500 people, and had the usual array of business associated with mining towns of this era.

I've wondered how Gem received its name. Was it named after the Gem State, or was the Gem State named after the town/mine? It seems a Shoshone Indian word was proposed to Congress in naming Idaho in 1863 which, when translated, meant "Gem of the Mountain." There is some controversy on the proposed translation, as some say the Indian word was misinterpreted. Regardless, the name stuck, and ever since, Idaho has been referred to as "the Gem State." To take this a step further, "gem" is an accurate term since Idaho produces 240 different specimens of semi-precious gems. As a matter of fact, Idaho's state gem is the star garnet, which is only found in Idaho and India. Getting back to the naming of Gem, it is possible the town was named for the state's nickname, since this controversy had taken place a few years prior to the mine's discovery.

From Wallace, head east on Bank Street. Drive underneath Interstate 90 onto Burke Road (Burke-Canyon Creek Road). Proceed approximately four miles to the site of Gem.

MACE

Located in Burke Canyon on Burke-Canyon Creek Road, between Burke and Gem, all that remains of Mace are mine dumps and a few foundations. Settled in 1884 and at an elevation of 3,921 feet, Mace was literally crammed along both sides of Canyon Creek. The Canyon Creek Railroad ran on the west side of Mace, hugging the steep mountainside, with the Northern Pacific Railroad and Union Pacific on the opposite side of the narrow canyon.

Like all the towns that lined Burke Canyon, Mace was prone to natural disaster. On February 27, 1910, an avalanche destroyed most of the town. The avalanche of 1910 affected most of the towns in Burke Canyon, but Mace received the most damage. Reports estimated that twenty people were killed and hundreds injured. One newspaper reported that houses were swept away by the slides as if they were built of cards. As with all the towns of Burke Canyon, the rich mines ensured that they were rebuilt after every natural disaster, and Mace was no exception. After the 1910 avalanche, Mace was rebuilt and continued for several more decades.

The tallest and most impressive building in Mace was the two-story schoolhouse on the north end of town. It was located between the Northern Pacific and Union Pacific tracks on one side and the Canyon Creek Railroad on the other.

Although Mace continued well into the twentieth century, natural disasters, inaccessibility, water pollution, economic challenges and young men choosing another way of life and not returning home after World War II led to its demise.

As the population of Mace continued to decline after World War ll, floods from Canyon Creek eventually swept away any remaining vestiges of the once-thriving community.

Canyon Creek has been termed the most abused river in Northern Idaho. For years, the primary method of eliminating human waste from Burke Canyon was by dumping it into the creek to be carried out of town. Up until the 1990s, raw sewage was pumped into the river directly from homes and businesses, giving it the undesirable nickname of Shit Creek. Contamination from the mining years throughout Burke Canyon have added to its continued pollution. Arsenic, mercury, and other heavy metals are just a few of the toxic wastes that have been continuously released into the natural waterway. In addition to this, water in the deep mines leaching through the rock carries with it iron sulfides, which create sulfuric acid that ultimately ends up in the same water. The creek is also littered with blast rock, sediment, concrete fragments and other hazardous debris. In 2007, the Environmental Protection Agency (EPA) initiated a project to stabilize Canyon Creek, reducing erosion and introducing a habitat for aquatic life, in order to transform the waterway back to a healthy creek.

The Bernard-Stockbridge Photographic Museum (312 4th Street in Wallace) has several photographs of Mace, as well as of the damage from the devastating avalanche of February 27, 1910.

MURRAY / EAGLE CITY / PRICHARD

I am including all three of these towns in this chapter because there is so little left of Prichard and Eagle City. Murray is the community that you will be most impressed with. The charming mining town of Murray is nestled in the Coeur d'Alene National Forest, alongside Prichard Creek, twenty miles north of Wallace on Dobson Pass Road. It is in Shoshone County and sits at an elevation of 2,772 feet. Murray has a small population of thirty-eight full-time residents and is considered a "living ghost town." Currently there is no overnight lodging available anywhere in town.

The Spragpole is a combination bar and museum. Originally advertised as having overnight accommodations, this is no longer the case. The Spragpole occupies one of the town's original buildings, built in 1884; it is only open on Saturday and Sunday. If you have the opportunity to see the museum, it is worth the trip! There is no charge to walk through the museum, but donations are welcome. This museum is a treasure trove, started by Walt Almquist in 1933, containing an astonishing amount of unique collections and educational exhibits loaded with history from an era long since passed. The only other business in town is the Bedroom Goldmine Bar, also an original building. It is both a functioning saloon and restaurant. The Bedroom Goldmine Bar is exactly what the name implies.

The building where the Bedroom Goldmine Bar is today was formerly built in 1884. Originally a bakery, it became a general store, then a gas station and a tavern. A miner and his wife, Chris and Lucille Christopherson, purchased the property, which was then a store, sometime in the 1960s. Chris had heard rumors of gold and in 1967 filed a claim and dug a thirty-six-foot shaft directly underneath his bedroom. Close to bedrock at thirty-six feet, Chris hit a vein and started tunneling for another 110 feet. Due to advancing age, Chris turned the mine over to family members, who continued working it until an aquifer was hit in 1996. Not being able to adequately pump out the water, they abandoned the mine, but not before producing

Spragpole Museum

The Bedroom Goldmine Bar

an 8½-ounce gold nugget. Reports say the nugget is the largest ever discovered in the Coeur d'Alene Mining District. Due to the unique circumstances that surrounded this enterprise, Lucille (Chris' wife) appeared on the television show *To Tell the Truth* to corroborate the existence of the unusually named mine. Chris Christopherson died in 1999. Both Chris and Lucille are buried in the Murray Cemetery.

In 2007, the building was purchased by Tammie and Barry Gleason. Seeing potential, the new owners refurbished the bar area and added a restaurant, paying particular attention to protecting the original infrastructure. Today, the vertical shaft that Chris Christopherson dug is still in the center of the saloon/restaurant for all to see. The moment you walk into this restaurant you will notice that a great deal of time and money has gone into its refurbishing. It is by far the busiest and most opulent business in Murray. It hosts a full bar, and the food that is prepared in their kitchen was by far the best cuisine we had on our entire five-day trip through the Silver Valley, including in Coeur d'Alene. Owned and operated today by Chris Littlejohn and Tammie Gleason, it is a testament to what happens when two individuals are determined to make their enterprise succeed. Open all year long, the Bedroom Goldmine Bar typically sponsors organized events that take place in Murray throughout the summer and winter months. Check your calendar or call The Bedroom Goldmine Bar (208-682-4394) to see when events are scheduled. There is usually something going on from St. Patrick's Day through Halloween, as well as on New Year's Eve. This includes the annual Molly B'Damn Days, a three-day celebration held the third week of August every year.

Originally called Murraysville, the town is named for George Murray. Mines operated here between the 1880s and the 1990s. At its peak in the 1880s, the population was ten thousand. Top producing mines were the Bear Top, Paragon and Golden Chest Mine. The Golden Chest is the only active gold mine in the Coeur d'Alene Mining District. Murray is very picturesque and offers some great photographic opportunities.

Critical to any mining camp in those early years was food. Getting supplies to these settlements was always a challenge. In 1880, A. J. Prichard (1830-1902) discovered gold on Prichard Creek in the Coeur d'Alene Mountains, setting off the Coeur d'Alene Gold Rush. The first settlement would be called Hubble's Landing (soon to be called Prichard). A well-thought-out water route was devised to transport necessary provisions. Supplies and passengers left Fort Sherman (later to be named Coeur d'Alene) by steamships on Coeur d'Alene Lake, arriving at Cataldo Mission. Cataldo Mission is the oldest building in Idaho and today is located in Old Mission State Park. From there, a smaller steamship carried the necessary supplies upriver to Kingston. There, the supplies were loaded onto flat-bottomed boats to be poled up the shallow Coeur d'Alene River to Hubble's Landing. From here the supplies were transported by mule teams three miles to Eagle City, which was the first boomtown in the Coeur d'Alene Mountains.

The Coeur d'Alene Gold Rush was one of the richest strikes in the western United States. So rich, in fact, it attracted one of the most legendary figures that ever stepped out of the pages of history. In 1885, four years after earning his reputation in Tombstone, Arizona with the gunfight at the OK Corral, Wyatt Earp and his wife, Sadie Josephine Sarah Marcus Earp, and Wyatt's brother, Jim, settled in Eagle City and opened the White Elephant Saloon. Eagle City was at the confluence of Eagle Creek and Prichard Creek. It seemed every time Wyatt came to a new town to seek a fortune, he encountered trouble, and Eagle City was no exception. In addition to running a saloon, Wyatt ended up in numerous mining claim disputes, along with being appointed deputy sheriff of Kootenai County (the northern boundary of Shoshone County) on January 30, 1885. Born in Monmouth, Illinois on March 19, 1848, Wyatt Berry Stapp Earp died January 13, 1929, in Los Angeles at eighty years of age. Sadie was never officially married to Wyatt but was his life companion for forty-eight years. She died in 1944, in the same home where Wyatt had died fifteen years earlier.

Between 1917 and 1926, the Yukon Gold Company operated a dredge on Prichard Creek. Giving no consideration to the destruction the dredge left in its path, and before any environmental laws were in place, the massive dredge dumped piles of river rock (dredge tailings) for several miles up and down Prichard Creek which can be seen today. Over a period of eight years, 63,000 ounces of gold was recovered. Ironically, it is estimated that only sixty percent of the gold taken in by the dredge was recovered from the operation, meaning the remaining forty percent never made it to the sluice and was dumped back into the stream amongst the piles of debris left in its wake.

To me, cemeteries are one of the most important things early settlers left behind, for they are rarely built over or furrowed under, and they are a testimony of people's names, dates and identities. The cemetery that served Eagle City and Murray is worth a visit. You will find it a half mile from Murray on FS Road 605 (Kings Pass Road). Although the grave markers are new, the grave sites of A. J. Prichard and Maggie Hall (aka Molly Burdan) can be found here. A native of Dublin, Ireland, Molly Burdan spent her young adult life as a prostitute, but before you judge her too harshly, understand that there were extenuating circumstances. Although her reputation earned her the nickname Molly B'Damn, she was a loving and thoughtful individual. Like Julia Bulette of Virginia City, Nevada, she earned an everlasting reputation for helping the sick and those less fortunate. During a smallpox epidemic that hit Murray in 1886, she tirelessly cared for dozens of miners suffering from the deadly disease. There is much written about Molly Burdan, along with an entire exhibit (and her original grave marker) inside the museum at the Spragpole. She died of tuberculosis on January 17, 1888, at the age of thirty-five. Every year her memory is honored with the Molly B'Damn Days event!

After visiting the Murray Cemetery, head back to the Prichard Creek Road (a paved road) and continue three miles. You will see a road to your right, Eagle City Road. You can drive up this road, but nothing remains of Eagle City. There is a grove of cedar trees here worth seeing. Drive back to Prichard Creek Road and continue for two miles to Prichard Tavern. You will cross a small bridge on your left to reach the tavern. Established in 1890, this is the only original building left in Prichard. Today, Prichard is a bedroom community with a population of one hundred. Prichard Tavern is open seven days a week until January, at which time it is open four days, Thursday through Sunday. It is located at 183 Prichard Street. To continue onto Wallace, head west on Prichard Street.

There are a couple of ways of getting to Murray. One is from Wallace on Dobson Pass Road/Beaver Creek Road. Another is from Kingston, a thirty-mile drive.

Comment: If you are driving to Murray from Wallace, at approximately thirteen miles you will see a road sign pointing out Murray, six miles to the right. This route will take you on a dirt road, Delta Murray Road (Kings Pass Road). While it will get you to Murray, it is a bumpy dirt road; if you continue straight through Prichard, you can follow a paved road all the way to Murray. Your choice.

WARDNER

Located in Shoshone County at 2,657 feet in the Coeur D'Alene Mining District, Wardner was the original site of the Bunker Hill Mine and in 1885 was named for Jim Wardner, who was an early promoter of the Bunker Hill and Sullivan Mine Concentrating Company (BHS). Ore was originally transported from the Bunker Hill Mine in Wardner by way of a tramway system to the Bunker Hill Mill in Kellogg, where it was processed. The distance from the original Bunker Hill Mine in Wardner to the Bunker Hill Mill in Kellogg was two miles.

Wardner was the center of the much-publicized labor strike between union and non-union employees. Protests broke out in 1892 and again in 1899 when union miners invaded non-union miners at Bunker Hill Mill. An estimated eight hundred union miners, fortified with a significant amount of Periwinkle whiskey, commandeered a Northern Pacific train at the Gem Mine in Burke, and at gunpoint, ordered the engineer to take them to Wardner Junction. After arriving at Wardner Junction, the enraged miners headed for the Bunker Hill Mill. Seeing the horde of advancing union miners, the non-union miners fled the mill. Union miners then made use of the sixty cases of dynamite they had stolen from the Fresco powder house. The inebriated mob strategically placed the three thousand pounds of dynamite inside the Bunker Hill and Sullivan Ore Concentrator and office building and blew it to splinters. The time was 2:26 p.m. Fragments of wood and iron shrapnel rained down on the town of Kellogg one mile away and made newspaper headlines across the United States!

On May 3, the governor of Idaho declared martial law in Shoshone County, and federal troops moved into the district. The government set up a work permit system that dissolved the union in the Coeur d'Alene District until World War I. Bunker Hill Mill was rebuilt within three months and continued operating with non-union labor.

In 1902, the two-mile-long Kellogg Tunnel was completed near the town of Kellogg, which provided a new entrance to the Bunker Hill Mine. The new adit eliminated the need for the tramway system that carried ore buckets from Wardner to the Bunker Hill Mill, and as a result, the ten-thousand-foot tramway system was shut down. Wardner saw an immediate decline in population when most of the miners and families moved to Kellogg to be near the new entrance. The Kellogg Tunnel came at a huge cost. The nine-year project (from 1893 to 1902) met with numerous difficulties, including flooding, ventilation problems, legal complications, wage negotiations and exorbitant costs. Close to the tunnel's completion in 1901, miners fortuitously cut into what would be called the Andrews Stope, a massive vein of silver rich ore. Unknown at the time of discovery, this was the top of the legendary silver vein that would later be christened the March Ore Body, and would set in motion twenty years of silver production that led to 180 miles of underground tunnels reaching 3,600 feet below sea level. Because of this accidental find, the Bunker Hill Mine became the richest silver lode in the world!

My wife has a good friend whose grandfather was a lode miner in Wardner during the boom years. His name was Emmanuel Ernest Jennings. He was the eighth of thirteen siblings born in Cornwall, England, to William R. Jennings and Ann Marie Pope Jennings. Born in 1879 into a family of Cornish miners, Emmanuel immigrated to the United States and arrived in New York in 1899, along with two of his brothers. Emmanuel was the only brother to travel to Idaho. He was naturalized in Wardner on August 31, 1910. He married Minerva Smith on November 12, 1911. They had three children. A hard-rock miner all his life (several of those years in Wardner), Emmanuel died July 6, 1919, in Golden, Colorado at thirty-nine years of age, from pneumoconiosis. Up until 1870, underground mining was done with a hammer and hand drill, which did not create high levels of dust. In 1870, the pneumatic air-compressed drill was introduced, which revolutionized mining. The compression drill created quartz dust that led to a chronic lung disease called pneumoconiosis. A more common name is "miner's consumption," or silicosis, which is associated with prolonged inhalation of inorganic dust particles such as those generated with underground drilling. It is a terrible death where the lungs are literally shredded by breathing in the dry dust created from drilling in the confines of underground tunnels where there is little or no ventilation, resulting in a slow suffocation. This was the destiny of many young men who chose underground mining as an occupation. The compression drills soon earned the nickname, "widowmaker." Even if miners didn't succumb to pneumoconiosis, they became prone to pneumonia and tuberculosis. In 1897, John G. Leyner introduced a water-cooled drill that forced water through the drill bit, eliminating the deadly dust in underground drilling. However, it took time for the revolutionary technology to be put to use.

Today, Wardner is strictly a small residential hamlet with a steady

Chuck's Memorabilia Museum

228

population of 188. No evidence remains of the tumultuous mining activity that once existed here. There are a few original buildings from the early years still standing in the center of Wardner that make for a great photo. One original structure, with faded and peeling paint, is Chuck's Memorabilia Museum. Unfortunately, we were not able to get inside Chuck's as it was closed for the day. Both the exterior and interior looked highly interesting as we peered through a downstairs window. I wish we could have been able to go inside! A mannequin dressed in sexy lingerie in the upstairs window behind lace curtains appeared to be looking down towards the street in search of a paying customer! Directly across the street from Chuck's Memorabilia Museum is a bronze plaque commemorating Noah S. Kellogg and his faithful burro, who are credited with the founding of the Bunker Hill Mine near this spot, on August 26, 1885. To get to Wardner from Kellogg, take McKinley Avenue east to S. Division Street; turn right.

KELLOGG

Kellogg is located in the Silver Valley about thirty-six miles southeast of Coeur d'Alene on Interstate 90, at 2,303 feet. With a population of 2,282, it is the most populated city inside the Coeur d'Alene Mining District.

For all of you mining enthusiasts, Kellogg is a must-see. It claims to be "the Center of the Coeur d'Alene Mine District." The romanticized tale of how silver was discovered here is a familiar one, but unlike some narratives, this has a great deal of validity to it. Noah Kellogg was a down-and-out prospector who had received a grubstake from two businessmen by the names of Cooper and Peck. After purchasing provisions in Murray, he set out, down the North Fork of the Coeur d'Alene River to Milo Gulch, and made camp approximately where the city of Wardner is today. The following morning, while searching for his burro that had wandered off, he spotted an outcropping of galena silver glistening in the morning sun high on the hilltop from where he had camped. It was September, 1885, and this accidental find would become the Bunker Hill and Sullivan Mine. The Bunker Hill Mine was named for the 1775 Revolutionary War battle in Charlestown, Massachusetts. Little did Noah Kellogg realize at the time that, not only would his name be synonymous with the town of Kellogg for ever more, but his accidental find would set into motion a mining operation that would account for more than fifteen percent of the silver production in the Coeur d'Alene Mining District. When the mine closed ninety-five years after its discovery, 165 million ounces of silver, 3 million tons of lead and 1.3 million tons of zinc had been produced!

On September 4, 1885, Phillip O'Rourke would file the original claim, with Noah Kellogg as a witness. Other mining claims were made by Noah Kellogg. A court awarded O. O. Peck and J. D. Cooper a one-quarter interest in the Bunker Hill Mine for their original grubstake to Noah Kellogg. Noah Kellogg later leased his claim to Jim Wardner, who established the town of Wardner on April 4, 1886.

Initially, the Bunker Hill Mine shipped ore to smelting operations in Wickes, Montana; Tacoma, Washington; and Salida, Colorado. In 1898, the Bunker Hill Mine purchased a controlling interest in the Tacoma smelter. In 1905, they sold their interest, although continued to process their concentrates there, as well as at the Salida smelter. A decision was made to eliminate shipping costs altogether and put into motion an agenda to build their own smelter. In July of 1917, the Bunker Hill Smelter opened for operation in Smelterville, which was the largest smelting operation on earth! While other mining systems closed during World War II, Bunker Hill thundered on. During those war years, an antimony electrolytic plant was added. Due to the manpower shortage, two hundred women took over the duties of running the operation.

Kellogg and Wallace seem to vie for being the hub of the Coeur d'Alene Mining District. You can be the judge. My vote goes with Wallace! Both have amazing histories, but Wallace has a beauty and charm unequaled by anyplace else in the Silver Valley. As far as lodging opportunities go, Kellogg wins hands down!

While in Kellogg, don't miss the opportunity to visit the Shoshone County Mining and Smelting Museum (www.StaffHouseMuseum. com). It is located at 820 McKinley Avenue, Kellogg (208-786-4141). This is a great opportunity to learn about the Bunker Hill Mining Operation and smelting, a subject I still don't completely understand. Be sure to call and check on times open, as they fluctuate. The museum typically closes for the season on September 20. Further down McKinley Avenue on the opposite side of the street is the Bunker Hill Mine (1886-1981). One of the oldest and largest mining companies in North Idaho, it is a must-see. The Bunker Hill Mine produced more than 37 million tons of ore!

Kellogg was incorporated in 1907; in 1960 it had a population of about six thousand. The Bunker Hill Mine and smelter closed in 1981, which signaled the closing of many other mines. Years of processing at the Smelterville plant had led to the contamination of the land, air and waterways. In 1983, the Environmental Protection Agency (EPA) assigned this area to an extensive cleanup. In 1996, the smelter complex and refinery were demolished. Since 2007, the EPA has spent $200 million on remediation and cleanup of the site.

The Sunshine Mine, which is located between Kellogg and Wallace,

Bunker Hill Mine

Shoshone County Mining and Smelting Museum

was the location of the worst mining disaster in the history of the United States, on May 2, 1972. Ninety-one miners, trapped eleven floors beneath where a fire started, died from smoke inhalation. Two miners miraculously survived for eight days by moving further back into one of the drifts to distance themselves from the deadly smoke and carbon monoxide. They ate the lunches of the men who had perished in order to survive. The Federal Mine Safety and Health Act (MSHA) of 1977 now requires that underground mines are inspected four times a year. Today there is a thirteen-foot memorial dedicated to the ninety-one miners who perished on that fateful day in 1972.

The Sunshine Mine Memorial is very easy to get to. Heading north on Interstate 90, take exit 54 (Big Creek). The memorial will be to your immediate right as you exit the interstate. There is a beautiful poem at the base of the memorial written by Senator Phil Batt specifically for the men who perished. The name of the poem is, "We Were Miners Then." The monument was dedicated May 2, 1974, and sculpted by Ken Lonn. Please take the time to read the inscriptions. The names of the ninety-one miners who perished are listed on the base of the monument. Take a moment as well to "remove your hats," and honor these men who died in the worst mining disaster in United States history.

To get to the Sunshine Mine from the monument, head due west under the interstate for two miles on Big Creek Road. You will pass through the small community in one mile. The Sunshine Mine will be on your left at two miles (1220 Big Creek Road, Kellogg). The Crescent Mine is directly across the road from the Sunshine. The Sunshine Mine is gearing up to become active. Currently the only activity taking place in the Sunshine Mine is care and maintenance, but that is all about to change. As of this writing, only three mines in the Silver Valley are active: The Lucky Friday in Mullan, the Golden Chest in Murray and the Galena in Wallace. Soon Sunshine Mine will be added to that list!

Of the mines that make up the Coeur d'Alene Mining District in the Silver Valley, the best-known is the Sunshine Mine. In the years of its operation, it has produced millions of tons of lead, zinc and copper, as well as a staggering 360 million ounces of silver! The mine itself is a huge operation, with a six-thousand-foot main shaft and working levels every two hundred feet, which run two miles east and west and one mile north and south. It opened in 1883 and officially closed in 2001.

Silver isn't only used to produce coins, silverware and jewelry; its purposes are unlimited. It is used in electronics, cell phones, computers, batteries, solar panels, appliances, automobiles, electrical conductivity and even in bacterial resistance in medicine.

Sunshine Mine Memorial

Sunshine Mine

Silver Mountain Resort gondola tramway

Since the 1930s, the Sunshine Mine alone has produced more silver than the much-publicized and fabled Comstock Lode of Virginia City, Nevada.

Today, Kellogg is a resort community most famous for the Silver Mountain Resort. Kellogg Peak at 6,297 feet and Wardner Peak at 6,200 feet are accessed by an elaborate 3.1-miles-long gondola tramway which delivers skiers, summertime hikers and nature enthusiasts to the lodge at 5,700 feet. This spectacular tramway takes the blue ribbon for being the longest tramway in the North America. Open all year, the gondolas offer the traveler breathtaking views, no matter what time of the year, as it ascends 2,400 feet up the mountainside. The gondola rides cost from $14 to $18 and last about twenty minutes.

A 3.1-mile-long gondola ride is about as far from a ghost town as you can get, but while you're in the Coeur d'Alene Mining District, why not treat yourself to a spectacular view of the Silver Valley and take in a little of what the twenty-first century has to offer?

After experiencing the gondola ride and viewing the Silver Valley from one of the valley's highest vantages, you might want to consider touring the underground mine in Kellogg; I am referring to the Crystal Gold Mine Tour. The Crystal Gold Mine was originally discovered and mined in 1881. As already stated, the Silver Valley is known today for silver, but in 1881, all the miners were after was gold! Gold ore can be mined, crushed and processed with little more than a gold pan. Although the miners knew there was silver in this mine, it was of no significant value. Silver needs to go through a smelting process to separate the metal from the ore and in 1881, the only smelting operation available in Idaho was in Ketchum, six hundred miles away. The Anaconda Smelter in Montana would open for operation the following year, in 1882, but that was 234 miles away! Other smelting operations would eventually open in Montana, Washington and Colorado, but at the time, they weren't in existence. Even if they were available, the costs to transport the silver ore by horse-drawn wagon would be exorbitant.

During your walking tour, you will be led through the original adit. It is highly educational for young and old alike, and I strongly advise it no matter what your level of experience is. The tour is open seven days a week, March 1 through October 31. Adults are $16, seniors $14, and children $9. Tours are every twenty minutes. The inside of the mine is a constant 50° F, so bring a jacket or sweater. A museum is also available which must be seen to be appreciated. More is written on the Crystal Gold Mine in a separate section.

If you are going to consider getting a motel/hotel while in Kellogg, I suggest Silver Mountain Resort. It is by far the largest lodging facility in the Silver Valley, with 215 rooms, four restaurants, cocktail lounge, bike park and the largest indoor water park in Idaho. The terminal for the aerial gondola (ski lift) is in the hotel itself, so no driving is needed to get to it. Go online or call for more information; www.silvermt.com (208-783 -0202).

Note: Read the paragraph on the Kellogg Tunnel and March Ore Body in the previous section on Wardner.

OSBURN

Located 5.7 miles west of Wallace at exit 57 on Interstate 90 is the town of Osburn. It is second to Kellogg in population, with 1,572 as of 2021. At an elevation of 2,520 feet, Osburn is also in Shoshone County. It is named for Bill Osburn, who had a trading post here.

At a glance there doesn't appear to be a lot to see, but there was a great deal of mining activity that took place here from 1887 to 1969. Osburn is one of the twelve primary towns that make up the Coeur d'Alene Mining District. My first impression is that Osburn's population is made up more of residences than a business sector such as that of Wallace. The Coeur Mine is east of town above the Silver Hills Elementary School on E. Mullan Avenue. The Coeur Mine operated between 1969 and 1991. Consolidated Silver Mine (Consil Mine) is on the west side of Osburn. Consolidated Mill is now used for mine safety instruction.

Interesting piece of trivia: The main shaft of the Consolidated Silver Mine has currently been set up as an escape route from the Sunshine Mine in the event of an emergency.

Some of the information I obtained would not have been possible without the help of Jamee Sperry. Jamee is the director of the Osburn Public Library on Mullan Avenue. My thanks and appreciation to her!

The Blue Anchor RV Park is conveniently located alongside Interstate 90 in Osburn. The 867,000-acre St. Joe National Forest borders the southern portion of Osburn and the Coeur d'Alene Mining District.

KINGSTON

Located along Interstate 90 about two miles northwest of Pinehurst, Kingston is the westernmost city in the Silver Valley Mining District. Unfortunately, I can't find any significant mining contributions

Snake Pit restaurant (oldest restaurant in Idaho).

Kingston has made to the Coeur d'Alene Mining District.

There is very little to see here other than the Snake Pit, the oldest restaurant in Idaho! The Snake Pit is worth the visit. To get there, head north on Coeur d'Alene River Road from Interstate 90 for six miles. The Snake Pit will be on the right side. You can't miss it; 1480 Coeur d'Alene River Road. The Snake Pit holds the title as the oldest restaurant in Idaho and has a sterling reputation for great food and excellent service.

If you choose to, you can continue on Coeur d'Alene River Road from the Snake Pit to Murray; it is thirty miles.

PINEHURST

In Shoshone County, with a population of 1,619, Pinehurst is at the western end of the Silver Valley, six and a half miles west of Kellogg.

From Interstate 90 follow Division Street; it will turn into Pine Creek Road, which continues for 7.2 miles. At the fork, take East Fork Pine Creek to the left. At 4.7 miles, you come to Trapper Creek Road on your right. Directly across from this junction is the Nabob Mine. Further down Pine Creek Road, a well-defined dirt road branches off on the left at Highland Creek (Highland Creek Road), and continues for quite a distance. You may be more adventurous than I am; if so, enjoy. At this junction (Pine Creek Road and Highland Creek Road), you will see a concrete pad. This is the remnants of the Highland Surprise and Nevada Stewart (1904 to 1972). In one more mile, you will see the footings of the Douglas Mill (1917 to 1981) on your left. The pavement will end shortly after.

Dredge tailings can be seen on right along Pine Creek at 4.3 miles.

There is very little to see here.

PULASKI TUNNEL

I'm going off track here from ghost towns and mining camps to explain about this side trip. While in Wallace, it is important to know about this landmark, and to understand the heroism, desperation and self-sacrifice that took place here.

In August of 1910, a great forest fire of unequaled scale waged in Idaho's panhandle (dubbed the Big Burn). Forty-five men from the newly-formed United States Forest Service (USFS), led by Ranger Edward Crockett Pulaski, set out from Wallace in an effort to slow down the raging fire that was threating their community. Unbeknown to Pulaski's crew, the fire was a culmination of numerous fires started by sparks from locomotives, by lightning and worsened by drought, that had already burned large areas in western Montana and northern Idaho. The fire would ultimately burn five million acres, making it the largest forest fire in the history of the United States. On the twenty-first day of August, eighty-mile-an-hour, gale-force winds whipped the fire into an inferno of unprecedented magnitude and fury. Smoke darkened the sky as far as Massachusetts, while ash and embers fell as far as Chicago. Ash alone fell in Greenland.

When Ed Pulaski realized that he and his crew were hopelessly being overtaken by the flames, he ushered his men down a narrow canyon in a desperate attempt to reach a mine opening he was familiar with. The thick smoke turned the daylight hours dark as men stumbled along the canyon bottom, all the time being pushed onward by Pulaski. When they reached the mine opening, Pulaski had the men lay down on their stomachs inside the tunnel. From the seepage on the floor of the mine, Pulaski wet blankets from their backpacks and hung them at the mine's entrance. When one man hysterically tried to run out of the mine, Pulaski held him at gunpoint and ordered him to lie down. Several hours later, forty men emerged from the mine; five men died. If they had tried to outrun the devastating inferno, they would have all certainly perished. The soles of the men's boots

238

Nine Mile Cemetery/monument to the five who perished at Pulaski Tunnel.

were burned through. Pulaski's face and hands were burned, and he was blind in one eye. Due to injuries Pulaski received from the fire, he could no longer work in the field, but instead was assigned to an administrative position until his retirement. In the end, a third of Wallace lay in waste, and eighty-seven people were dead, while millions of acres of prime forest were gone.

Hurricane-force winds were generated by the firestorm, which symbiotically in turn created more heat. At that time, the Western white pine (Idaho's state tree) made up the larger percentage of the forest; this tree is known for its high sap content. Hydrocarbons in the sap of the white pine boiled out of the trees, releasing flammable gas that spread over hundreds of square miles, detonating as it heated. Massive pine trees didn't just burn; they exploded from within due to the excessive heat, hurling gigantic timbers hundreds of feet in all directions. Trees and roots were ripped from the ground and catapulted across canyons a half-mile wide. Just for a moment, try to imagine the following: The energy released from this fire was equivalent to a Hiroshima-sized atomic bomb exploding at a rate of one every two minutes. Nothing in the recorded history of North America has ever equaled this apocalyptic firestorm.

Today, a four-mile round-trip trail meanders under a canopy of Douglas fir trees. Western sword fern, thimbleberry and Scoular's willow grow along the shaded trail. The West Fork of Placer Creek gently flows alongside the length of the trail throughout the year. Well-written informative signage regarding the 1910 fire is posted at numerous spots throughout your hike. There is an 800-foot elevation gain to the destination overlooking the tunnel. Keep a lookout for a tall, charred cedar snag standing upright. There will be a sign pointing it out. It is an actual remnant of the 1910 fire. Another interesting feature along the trail is a Buffalo Blower (a ventilator) from the War Eagle Mine. There will be a sign pointing it out as well.

At Nine Mile Cemetery outside Wallace is a monument and grave site for the five men who perished that fateful day under Edward Pulaski's watch. Ed Pulaski personally tended the grave site of those brave men until his death on February 2, 1931.

Pulaski Tunnel is listed on the National Register of Historic Places. No motor vehicles of any kind are allowed on this trail. Before starting out on this trail, consider putting a couple of dollars in your pocket. Soon after you cross the highway, you will see a "Welcome to the Pulaski Tunnel Trail" sign. Near the sign is an "iron ranger" donation box. It would be a nice gesture to drop a dollar or two into the iron ranger to let the men and women who keep this trail so beautifully maintained know that their actions don't go without notice. I humbly ask you to do this.

An inspirational and enlightening book concerning the 1910 fire and Ed Pulaski is *The Big Burn* by Timothy Egan.

Afternote: The Pulaski is a wooden-handled tool which is a combination mattock and axe. Edward Pulaski is credited with its invention in 1911. This essential tool used widely today by the USFS in fighting forest fires carries his name! You will see examples of the Pulaski along the trail.

CRYSTAL GOLD MINE

I am setting aside a page for this side trip as it is important to your visit to Kellogg and the Coeur d'Alene Mining District. Like the Sierra Silver Mine Tour in Wallace, this is an underground tour as well. This particular mine has a unique history. It was originally worked in the 1880s. Not wanting anyone else to discover it, the original owner presumably dynamited it shut when he left for one reason or another, but never returned.

In 1914, the Monitor Silver Mine began tunneling directly above the Crystal Gold Mine with no idea that the closed-off Crystal Gold

Crystal Gold Mine tour (Lucas seated).

Mine was below them. Seventy-seven years went by until, in 1991, a man named Brandt, who owned the property at the time, was attempting to get to the source of a spring that was bubbling out of the mountainside. He soon discovered that what he thought was a spring was water that had been accumulating for decades inside the closed-off mine. Five years later, after much planning and work, the Crystal Gold Mine was opened to the public for underground tours.

There is no record of the amount of gold that was taken out of the mine, although assays have been conducted recently which reveal seventy ounces of gold per ton in certain areas. If you care to do some quick arithmetic, you will see that this is beyond extraordinary! Due to today's current codes and restrictions, the mine cannot be opened for operation. Today, the Crystal Gold Mine is owned by Ray and Sherry Cropp. It is open seven days a week, May 1 through October 31, for guided tours.

There was an old saying among miners of the 1880s with regard to locating and following veins of gold-bearing quartz: "Gold likes to ride a red dress, or rides an iron horse." During the tour, it will be explained to you what this means! Keep in mind, the methods used in 1880 were significantly different than those used in later years. It will be demonstrated to you how much light a single candle produces in the pitch blackness of a mine. There was no electricity in 1880 and this was all the light the miners had to work by while swinging a ten-pound sledgehammer. It is a fascinating and educational experience for young and old alike, and I strongly urge you to set time aside while in the Silver Valley to experience this unique tour. If you are lucky, your tour guide will be Lucas. At the end of the tour, you will be shown the proper technique to pan for gold (there is a right way). You are then welcome to pan yourself at no charge for one hour to see how much "color" you can find. Children are encouraged.

Although the Silver Valley and the Coeur d'Alene Mining District are known for silver, it was gold that first lured the prospectors to this region. Silver would eventually become the most predominant metal mined. However, unlike gold, silver needs to be smelted. It wasn't until smelting became available in nearby states that excavation of silver was even considered. The early miners knew that silver existed here, but it was of no value to them until it could be processed.

From Kellogg, drive SE on Cameron/Silver Valley Road 1.3 miles to the Crystal Gold Mine and RV Park. It is located directly alongside Interstate 90.

Hard hats are provided at the mine prior to the tour; there is a gift shop on the premises.

Overnight RV parking is available, with full hookups to water, power, and sewage; pets welcomed. Address is 51931 Silver Valley Road, Kellogg; 208-783-GOLD (208-783-4653). www.goldmine-idaho.com; also crystalgoldmine1881@gmail.com.

CATALDO MISSION

Cataldo Mission is so close to Kingston it would be a shame to drive past it, especially if you are continuing to Coeur d'Alene. It is home to the oldest building in Idaho and is a National Historic Landmark. It was constructed between 1850 and 1853 by the Coeur d'Alene Indian tribe and Catholic missionaries, and today is inside Coeur d'Alene's Old Mission State Park. It was named for Father Joseph Cataldo.

From Kingston, continue on Interstate 90 for nine miles to exit 39. Follow the signs to Old Mission State Park.

Cataldo Mission was the first stop while transporting needed supplies and provisions destined for Prichard, Eagle City, and Murphy, after first crossing Coeur d'Alene Lake by steamship in 1880; old@idpr.idado.gov; www.parksandrecreation.idaho.gov.

Cataldo Mission

Loading House at Adelmann Mine.

244

BOISE (NEAR)

ADELMANN MINE

An interesting day trip south of Boise is this short hike to the Adelmann Mine. It is an in-and-out, five-mile hike. The hike is classified as easy with a moderate elevation gain to the mine. Operated by Richard C. Adelmann in the early 1900s, the operation primarily mined gold. Richard Adelmann was a saloon owner, miner and businessman out of Boise.

The trailhead is located on Highway 21 at the Boise River Wildlife Management Area, north of Lucky Peak State Park. From I-84, head north on Highway 21. At ten miles you will reach Highland Valley Summit. Your parking destination is a short distance past the summit, opposite mile marker 15. Vehicles should be parked on the outside of the gate, being sure not to block the entrance. Walk between the buildings and continue straight up the double-track dirt road after crossing through the gate.

About a mile into the hike, you will pass a roadkill pit where the Idaho Fish and Game (IDFG) disposes of animal remains they have picked up along the highway.

There isn't a lot of information on this mine other than it was worked by Richard C. Adelmann in the early 1900s and is a gold mine. The mine itself is of no consequence; you will pass by the caved-in entrance along the trail as you proceed to the loading house. The structure that loaded the ore for transport is both interesting and makes for ideal photography. Iron ore cart tracks can still be seen adjacent from the collapsed entrance to the mine. You will walk past the mine which is located on the double-track road across the ravine from the loading house and ore chute.

This is a popular destination for day hikers. Dogs are required to be on a leash. Signage may be posted that animal trapping exists along the creek that parallels a portion of the double-track road you will be walking on. Arrowleaf balsamroot, morning glory, lupine and skeleton weed accompany you on your way during spring and summer months. Beware rattlesnakes during spring and summer months—another reason to keep you dog leashed. Please give snakes a wide berth and do not harm them.

Due to wintering wildlife, the road is closed from October to May. This property is on BLM land. Be respectful of the mine, as well as of the route getting there, or the privilege of accessing this property may be taken away from us!

MAYFIELD

Located in Elmore County at 3,599 feet, Mayfield is twenty-two miles southeast of Boise. Mayfield was one of the few towns to spring up along the Oregon Trail. It was an agricultural and ranching community, that also served the needs of travelers along the Oregon Trail.

From Boise, head south on Interstate 84 and exit at Blacks Creek Road in nine miles. Turn left and head east. Stay right at Prairie Junction, remaining on Mayfield Road. Mayfield will be on your left in approximately seven miles from the junction, a total of thirteen miles from I-84.

I had the privilege of speaking with Betty Miller, a longtime resident who lives on a ranch off Blacks Creek Road. At ninety-one years of age, Betty remembers Mayfield very well. Betty grew up in Kuna. Once married, she and her husband Clay moved to Blacks Creek in 1951. She says Mayfield was a Scottish settlement consisting of several

Schoolhouse and schoolteacher's residence.

246

farms and ranches surrounding the community hall and school. Sheep and cattle were raised and the land was farmed. Primary crops were hay, wheat and oats. She recalls wheat selling for three cents a pound. Betty said the community was dryland country, meaning there were no watering systems that are available today to water the fields. Instead, they planted at specific times of the season, hoped it didn't freeze and prayed for rain. One of the neighboring farms had daughters who married into a ranching life in Prairie. Over time, others sold and moved. Today, one ranch remains. Cattle can be seen wandering alongside abandoned buildings that once served as the center of the community. Mayfield had no general mercantile or café. Mayfield's residents shopped in Mountain Home, or at a small store in Regina that was located east of present-day Stage Stop and I-84.

You will pass a large structure on the right-hand side of the road. This was a dance hall that also served as the community center, for potluck gatherings and Sunday school. Dances and community functions were commonly held here until sometime between 1957-1962. Reports say the center was built in 1915. Back then, people frequently traveled between isolated communities for dances, rodeos and Sunday church services. There are three buildings on the opposite side the road. The two side-by-side buildings were the schoolhouse and home of the Mayfield schoolteacher. Another stone structure is further south. These structures are on private property and behind a barbed-wire fence. The property is grazing land for cattle presumably owned by the small ranch you passed just before reaching Mayfield.

If you continue on Mayfield Road, a short distance beyond Mayfield is Cemetery Road. Although gated, the dirt road leads to the Mayfield Cemetery. Only a few grave sites exist in the fenced and volunteer-maintained cemetery. One dates to 1891, another, 1873. One marker was illegible due to age.

Mayfield is located along the Oregon Trail Back Country Byway. This dirt byway continues onto Mountain Home and Glenns Ferry. Several interpretive signs are positioned at significant places identifying historical spots. One is Bowns Creek and Inscription Rock a few miles south of Mayfield. Faint but visible, printed in axle grease on a large rock, are names of individuals who traveled this route 150 years ago.

Another way to reach the site of Mayfield is to exit I-84 on exit 71 (Boise Stage Stop Restaurant). Turn east and proceed to Mayfield Road.

NEAL

Located south of Boise in Ada County is the site of Neal. This group of mines was discovered by Arthur Neal in 1889.

For years, cattlemen had spent time on Upper Blacks Creek and not noticed the telltale signs of valuable outcrops that existed. A man named Jake Slater even cut a road though some of it, not realizing the wealth of the rock he carelessly tossed aside. Then, in late 1888, Arthur Neal discovered some rich float while running a string of pack animals from Pine Grove. As it was too late in the season to prospect, he returned in July of 1889 and discovered the outcrop he had hoped for. He partnered with George House and together started developing the lode.

Soon others, attracted by the news, staked claims. Other miners weren't the only ones interested in Neal. Eastern capitalists soon showed interest. Investors from Chicago and New York financed the construction of mills and supplied capital. One private owner who refused outside investors to assist him sold his claim for $225,000 in 1902. Before mining shut down, an estimated $2 million in gold came out of the district.

A gold vein stretching many miles east and west extends through the Neal District and crosses Blacks Creek Road. Every mine in the Neal

Twenty thousand tons of ore dumped by the Atlanta Gold Corporation in 2016.

Old concrete marker designating BLM and Oregon Trail.

Nathan Cook

All that remains of Neal's largest and finest stamp
mill.

District is located along this same vein. In 1987, Don Blow started a mine south of Neal Summit. He worked it for a year and then leased it to Meyer Resources, who drilled for three years. Meyer ultimately walked away, saying, "Too much dirt to move to get to the gold." Then in 2016, Atlanta Gold Corporation excavated an area to the east along the same vein for four years. The open pit can still be seen today.

I was fortunate to get a firsthand tour of Neal from Nathan Cook. Nathan Cook's parents moved from Arizona and settled in Prairie in 1954, when Nathan was five years old. Nathan and his wife, Mary, have remained on that same ranch in Prairie. Nathan was instrumental in acquiring much of this information.

To get to Neal, take Blacks Creek Road off I-84 and head east towards the Prairie/Mayfield junction. At 5.8 miles, you will pass the Golden Eagle Mine, which is an active gold mine. The Golden Eagle Mine is owned by Dan Yanke. From the road, you can see the tower that lowers the six-man crew down the 400-foot shaft to the main tunnel. The hoist house stands next to the tower. The ball mill that crushes the ore is seen to the left. In 2021, the Golden Eagle mined 1,000 tons of ore. Continue for .2 miles to the junction. Take the left fork towards Prairie and Neal Summit.

At 3.8 miles, stop and look to your right. On the opposite side of Blacks Creek was the site of a stamp mill. Ore was dumped from the small hill down to the mill which was powered from water by Blacks Creek. A small concrete slab just beyond the willow bushes is all that remains. The concrete slab is not visible from the road. Continue on Blacks Creek Road to Neal Summit; mileage will be 4.5 miles from the junction. Park here and take a short hike up the dirt road past the locked gate. At a quarter mile, you will see 20,000 tons of ore dumped by the Atlanta Gold Corporation in 2016. It is estimated that this ore contains .2 to .3 ounces of gold per ton. It was abandoned here in 2016, with no plans to process it. If you look at the terrain opposite the ore dump, you will see patches of grass amongst the sage. This was a road used by Meyer Resources in 1991. When they left, they were obligated to re-seed the road they had constructed. This is known as "putting the land to sleep." Prior to excavation, a reclamation act was agreed to with the Forest Service to restore the land Meyer Resources had disturbed.

If you continue on Blacks Creek Road for one mile from Neal Summit, you will come to a double-track road on your right. Take this for a quarter mile to see the only remaining evidence of Neal's twenty-stamp mill. The broken piece of concrete is clearly seen on the left side of the road. This is all that is left of Neal's biggest and finest stamp mill. It was built about 1915 and powered with water. If you continue for another quarter of a mile, you will see the open-pit operation of the Atlanta Gold Corporation. The 20,000 tons of ore that is piled on the ridge above was mined from this location.

The mines at Neal were most active between 1920 and 1930. Homes lined Blacks Creek Road on both sides of Neal Summit. There was also a school, but no evidence of any structures remains today. Mines on Neal Summit were developed between 1890-1892. Production ended between 1934-1935. There were six mill locations in the Neal District. Other than the concrete slab beneath the willow bushes, and the piece of concrete from the twenty-stamp mill mentioned above, no other evidence remains from those mills.

BOISE

The city of Boise with its temporal climate must be mentioned as its origin is paramount in Idaho's mining history.

Henry C. Riggs, who helped plat the city of Boise, was instrumental in having the territorial capital moved from Lewiston to Boise in 1864. The county that Boise is situated in was named for his daughter (Ada).

During the early 1860s, Lewiston was the territorial capital of Idaho.

O'Farrell Cabin in Boise.

Then, in 1864, the territorial capital was moved to Boise. Boise's location was significant in that it was at the crossroads of the Oregon Trail and of routes that led to the Boise Basin and the Owyhees. Most of the prospectors who had settled in Clearwater Valley and Pierce had now moved to Boise Basin, where gold had been discovered in 1862, establishing Idaho City (forty miles northeast). Boise Basin's population swelled, as twenty thousand miners migrated to the new diggings. After the initial placer claims were exhausted, hydraulic mining dominated the Boise Basin for twenty years. Dredge mining followed the hydraulic years, leading to hard-rock mining, which continued into the 1930s. Ultimately, 2.9 million ounces of gold was produced from the Boise Basin.

Although Silver City, which was founded in 1864, is not considered part of the Boise Basin, it nevertheless contributed to the population and to the vast amount of wealth attributed to the state of Idaho. Located in the Owyhee Mountains (eighty-five miles south of Boise), it produced $60 million in silver prior to World War II.

As with the California gold rush, the population increase in the early years of Idaho created agricultural development and ranching, and propelled industrial and economic growth that transitioned into statehood. Idaho became a state on July 3, 1890. Named the City of Trees by the first settlers to see the Treasure Valley from Bonneville Point, Boise is the most populous city in Idaho.

Ironically, the railroad passed Boise by during the mining boom years. The steep grade created by the Boise Bowl in which Boise sits was considered too difficult for a railroad to get in and out. As an alternative, the railroad ran only to Nampa in those early years. A wagon road ran from Kelton, Utah to Boise. Both freight wagons and the Kelton Stage operated along this primary road.

There are many historical places in Boise to enjoy. At 450 W. Fort Street (adjacent to the Veteran's Administration) stands the O'Farrell Cabin, constructed in 1863 and considered to be the first home ever built in Boise. The single-room cabin was moved from its original location one block west of this spot. Hand-cut cottonwood logs were used in the reconstruction, duplicating the original wood used. The yellow paint on the front door was carefully duplicated after determining it was the original color of the interior. The cabin is on the National Register of Historic Places and was restored to its 1912 condition in 2002. It is also considered the first place of Catholic worship in Boise. Three interpretive signs are positioned alongside the cabin explaining its unique history, as well as the early years of Boise. Today, the O'Farrell Cabin is one of Boise's most significant landmarks.

Thanks to the National Register of Historic Places, several sites exist throughout Boise. I advise visiting these following Boise locations:

- Idaho State Historical Museum at 610 Julia Davis Drive
- Interpretive signs at Fairview Park, 2300 W. Idaho Street
- Pioneer Cemetery, 460 E. Warm Springs Ave.
- Old Idaho Penitentiary, 2445 E. Old Penitentiary Road
- Morris Hill Cemetery, 317 N. Latah
- Fort Boise Military Reserve Cemetery, end of N. Mountain Cove Road off E. Reserve Street

KUNA CAVES

This is not a mine, nor does it have anything to do with a ghost town. However, if you are an enthusiast of mines (as I am) this very well may be something you would enjoy seeing. In reality, it is a lava tube. Located in a remote area of Kuna, the tube is fifty feet deep. There is an opening at ground level with a caged ladder leading down to the bottom of the tube.

To be honest, I don't understand why the BLM hasn't destroyed this

Entrance to Kuna Cave (lava tube).

for reasons of liability. It is a fun side trip, though, so if you would like a little adventure, do this before it is officially closed to the public. The inside of the lava tube is not maintained and is littered and scrawled with graffiti. If you are up for it, google Kuna Caves. It is off Black Cat Road.

This lava tube was created during the Holocene Era about 12,500 years ago. Reports from older residents in the area say that there was once a system of multiple tubes running as far as the Snake River, but the Army Corps of Engineers dynamited the maze many years ago to keep people out.

PEARL

Located in Gem County, at 4,153 feet, is the site of Pearl. From 1894 to 1910, Pearl was an industrial gold-mining community. On December 7, 1867, a local rancher showed up with some exceptional specimens of gold quartz ore from two separate veins near Willow Creek. After some preliminary assessment was done, it was decided that no immediate action would be taken, and the district remained dormant until the Panic of 1893. Pearl saw considerable growth the following year. Being the closest gold-mining community to Boise, Pearl had three mercantile stores, four saloons, a butcher shop, two hotels, a church, livery, school, fire station, blacksmith and an Odd Fellows Lodge.

The Panic of 1893 was an economic depression from 1893-1897. It was caused by several things, including a wheat failure and a run on gold in the U. S. Treasury. In addition to this, the opening of numerous silver mines in the western United States had led to an oversupply of silver. Due to this, an interest in gold mining immediately resumed. Between 1894-1896, excellent gold recovery was seen. About 20,000 ounces of gold came from Pearl's early operations.

Colonel William H. Dewey took over the Lincoln Mine in Pearl in November 1896. Dewey's son, Edward H. Dewey, took over operations by deepening the shaft to the 500-foot level, but encountered sulfides. Other mining attempts between the late 1800s and early 1900s proved unsuccessful. Pearl became a ghost after 1910, although a few outlying ranchers remained. The many buildings that once lined the street are gone and no evidence of the town remains. Pearl saw renewed activity in 1980 with the testing of old lodes, but no evidence of mining exists today.

There is an Idaho Historical Roadway Sign (#447) at the top of Freezeout Hill on Idaho State Highway 16 south of Emmett. The sign reads, "Gold mines high on the ridge above here maintained an industrial community at Pearl from 1894 to 1910 when ore ran out."

The best way to reach Pearl is by exiting Highway 55 at the top of Horseshoe Bend Hill onto Pearl Road (milepost 57). The dirt road leads to both Highway 16 and to the community of Eagle. Rock Creek Shooting Range located two and a half miles in is a sport clay-shooting range set on three hundred acres. Further beyond is the site of Pearl. Today, everything is fenced, and private property/posted signs abound. A few mining dumps can be seen on the hills above the road. As you pass through the site of Pearl, you will see Willow Creek running alongside Pearl Road, supplying water for wandering cattle. The drive on Pearl Road from Highway 55 is enjoyable and scenic, but avoid the spring months due to excessive mud!

BUFFALO HUMP DISTRICT

PIERCE (IDAHO'S FIRST GOLD RUSH)

Located in Clearwater County, Pierce sits at 3,094 feet. It is thirty miles east of Orofino and stands as the birthplace of gold mining in the state of Idaho! In August of 1860, Elias D. Pierce and Wilbur F. Basset led a party of eleven miners deep into the Clearwater River region, a land dominated by the Nez Perce Indians. On a tributary of the Clearwater River called Orofino Creek (also called Canal Gulch), they discovered substantial quantities of placer gold. After news spread, sixty men came into the region and wintered that same year despite the presence of Nez Perce. This would be the first discovery of gold in Idaho (then Washington Territory). The settlement of Pierce was established that winter.

News of the strike spread quickly as hopeful prospectors poured into the area, despite the threat of Indian interaction. By 1881, ten thousand miners and settlers had rushed to Pierce. The placer claims along the Orofino were the first in Idaho to be worked on a large scale and placer mining continued into 1875. It is estimated that between $5 and $10 million in gold came out of the Pierce District.

Although mining continued into 1875, the news of gold in the Boise Basin in 1862 had a significant impact on Pierce. By 1864, Idaho City (in the Boise Basin) had become the largest city in the Pacific Northwest, and many of the Pierce miners had moved on to southern Idaho. As in all mining camps, the Chinese had a significant presence. It is estimated that eight hundred Chinese took possession of claims here after the white miners abandoned them.

Between 1892 and 1910, lode mining took place, although it was never hugely successful. The Wild Rose Mine was the most notable, with an estimated yield of $250,000. Since lode mining was never a profitable venture, Pierce will always be known as a placer mining district.

Between 1906 and 1930, large-scale bucket line dredging took place along Orofino Creek and Canal Gulch.

Due to a complicated boundary issue, Pierce was the first county seat for Shoshone County. It was later changed to Murray and then again to Wallace. Today, Pierce is in Clearwater County. The Pierce Courthouse constructed in 1862 is Idaho's oldest public building. As of 2021, Pierce had a population of 551. Clearwater County formed in 1911.

The 190's saw the logging industry come to Idaho. The Clearwater National Forest is the largest Western white pine stand in the world. By early 1910, the logging industry was flourishing, not only in Idaho but in Washington, Wisconsin and Minnesota. Several lumber mills were established in Headquarters, Idaho, ten miles north of Pierce. Plentiful stands of timber sustained Pierce long into the twentieth century, preventing it from becoming a ghost and vanishing like so many other boomtowns of the era. By 1990, the lumber mills of Headquarters closed, but Pierce had already been established as a solid community. While in Pierce, visit the J. Howard Bradbury Memorial Logging Museum at 103 S. Main Street. The museum is open mid-June through mid-October, Fridays and Saturdays.

On Highway 6, the community of Potlatch is known for its lumbering history. Between 1906 and 1981, the Washington, Idaho and Montana Railway operated its celebrated mile-long train, delivering a steady stream of Western white pine logs to the Potlatch Lumber Mill, and hauling the finished lumber to market. Declining lumber prices caused its closure.

The ten-mile section of Highway 11 leading into Pierce from Weippe is named the Gold Rush Historic Byway.

Elias D. Pierce did not become wealthy during the course of his prospecting years, but the city of Pierce that he is named for has the distinction of being the second-oldest city in Idaho, Franklin being the first.

MOUNT IDAHO

Mount Idaho started out as a thoroughfare to the boom town of Florence, when a forty-five-mile-long toll road was carved out of the hills by Mose Milner, aka California Joe, in 1860. The area of Mount Idaho was inside what would become known as Camas Prairie, named for the blue flower of an indigenous plant native to moist meadows of the western United States. The bulb of the flowering plant was an important food source for Native Americans in the Pacific Northwest, including the Nez Perce tribe. It was so important to the Nez Perce that it played a part in the Nez Perce Indian War, when the military confined them to a reservation in the 1870s.

A refreshing tale of Mose Milner is told by Lambert Florin in his book, *Ghost Towns of the West*. One day, a traveler stole a horse from

Mose. When Mose discovered the theft, he followed the stranger and shot him in the head with his rifle. A note was then pinned to the dead man's shirt warning others about dishonesty. The note was even signed, "Mose Milner, Mount Idaho." No lawyers, court costs or lengthy trial. Mose had his horse back and the thief was dead.

After an encounter with a mountain lion disabled Mose, he decided it was best to sell his toll road and cabin to Loyal Parsons Brown, who later partnered with his brother-in-law, James Odel. Brown would become Mount Idaho's most celebrated citizen and benefactor. He opened and operated a freight team in Elk City to haul freight and mail to Lewiston. Brown was responsible for bringing the first apple trees from Walla Walla, Washington, to plant in the fertile Camas Prairie. The first supply store was opened in 1872 by Loyal Brown, as was the Brown Hotel. In 1862, a post office was established and later, a mercantile. A stage line soon ran between Lewiston and Mount Idaho.

Mount Idaho was the scene of the Nez Perce Indian War of 1877. A treaty had been agreed to in 1855, allotting land for a reservation to the Nez Perce. When gold was discovered by Elias Pierce in 1860, gold-starved miners invaded the reservation, giving no thought to the Nez Perce. While Nez Perce tempers flared, another treaty was proposed in 1863. Chief Joseph of the Nez Perce tribe was one of the chiefs who never signed the treaty.

As settlers moved into the Camas Prairie region, in 1877 the military gave Chief Joseph thirty days to confine his people to the Clearwater Reservation. Chief Joseph and the White Bird tribe met to discuss terms of returning to the Clearwater Reservation when, unbeknownst to them, three young braves set out alone, murdering several settlers. This became known as the Salmon River Murders. A war soon escalated, with numerous casualties on both sides. The Brown Hotel was used as a hospital for the white settlers and soldiers. It was a terrible conflict of brutality, eventually ending with the Nez Perce retreating into Montana in late June. The terrible conflict lasted for less than two weeks, but the event has been burned into the annals of Idaho's history for all time!

Being the first settlement in Idaho County, Mount Idaho was soon appointed the county seat of Idaho County and had its peak between 1878 and 1880. Loyal P. Brown constructed a lumber mill. From this mill, lumber was used to construct the county courthouse, jail and Masonic Hall.

Mount Idaho's economy relied hugely on miners traveling to and from Florence, along with other local mining communities. As the Florence gold claims dwindled, so, too, did trade with Mount Idaho. Another blow came when Loyal Brown denied the owner of a large printing company who wanted to purchase land, forcing the company to build in Grangeville instead. As Grangeville steadily grew, Mount Idaho failed economically. As a result, most businesses were forced to leave Mount Idaho and move to Grangeville. Today, Grangeville is the largest city in Idaho County. The county seat was moved to Grangeville in 1902.

Today, Mount Idaho has transitioned into parcels of real estate throughout the Camas Prairie. It is located 3.5 miles southeast of Grangeville off Mount Idaho Grade Road; elevation is 3,640 feet.

A cemetery remains today of Mount Idaho's early residents, with many casualties from the Nez Perce War (the Battle of the Clearwater).

ELK CITY

Gold was discovered in Newsome Creek along the Nez Perce Trail by an overflow of prospectors from Pierce in 1861. In that same year, the townsite of Elk City was established along the South Fork of the Clearwater River. Between 1861 and 1895, supplies and provisions came from Lewiston along the same Nez Perce Trail. For centuries, the Nez Perce Indians used the trail to travel to Montana and Wyoming to hunt buffalo. Today, Elk City falls inside of the Nez Perce National Forest and is at the eastern end of Highway 14.

Many of the miners left Elk City when news spread of the new strike in Florence in that same year of 1861. However, by 1862, several discouraged miners returned to Elk City. It was at this point in time they realized that by bringing water to their Elk City claims, a greater amount of gold could be obtained. A series of aqueducts or ditches were dug, one being the American River Ditch, which brought water from the American River north of Elk City. This imported source of water was needed to operate their rockers, sluice boxes and, eventually, hydraulics. The town flourished in the next few years. The Union Mining District was formed and named by Union sympathizers. The name was later changed to the Elk City Mining District. Rich placer gravels were worked in numerous gulches and drainages throughout Elk City. In the early years prior to women coming to the camps, miners were content with a simple existence of living in a tent or under a lean-to. As winter approached, they constructed sturdier cabins to withstand the heavy snows, but this was done strictly out of necessity. When wives joined their husbands in the newly developed camps, a completely different tone was set. Wives brought culture, social gatherings, schools and a different perspective on their community. This bond of women and men working together is what established the towns that we know today.

Elk City

Elk City was booming now with six saloons, numerous stores, two blacksmiths and three butcher shops, a lumber mill, newspaper (*Elk City Mining News*) and a population of one thousand. Between 1872 and 1884, the Chinese had established an unusually large population, until the Chinese Exclusion Act of 1882 impacted existing Chinese, as well as those attempting to enter the country. As a result, the Chinese population declined. The Chinese Exclusion Act was the first significant law restricting immigration into the United States. It expired in 1892, but Congress extended it for another ten years under the Geary Act.

By the 1870s white miners introduced improved mining methods. By 1891, machinery for a dredge was packed in on mules, employing dozens of men. A conservative estimate of gold recovery by 1902 was set at between $5 million and $10 million.

The first post office opened in 1888. By 1895, the Elk City Wagon Road, following the same route as the Nez Perce Trail, was completed from Clearwater, which made possible the freighting of heavy mining equipment. A stage line made daily runs, with stage stops at Switchback and Newsome Stations. In 1934, a single-lane forest road was completed following the same route. Today, a volunteer group called "Friends of the Elk City Wagon Road" maintains the historical route for all to enjoy. A guided historic road trip is done every July out of Clearwater.

By 1898, placer gold was depleted. Hard-rock mining continued from 1902 to 1932. The American Eagle was one of the largest producers, located eight miles southeast of Elk City. Other mines east of Elk City are Blue Ribbon, Sultan, Hercules, Steckner, Alberta and Pasadena Mines. Between 1913 and 1914, the population was reported to be four hundred. Both dragline dredges and bucket dredges operated from 1935 to 1940. Lode mining continued up until World War II, when all gold mining was halted throughout the United States.

Although the population fluctuated at the turn of the twentieth century, telephone service connected Elk City in 1901. State Highway 14 was completed in 1932 from Grangeville to Elk City. Until that time, the only means available to get to Elk City was over the Elk City Wagon Road. Today, Highway 14 borders the beautiful South Fork of the Clearwater River.

Gold dredging was first introduced to Idaho in the early 1880s and continued into the early 1960s. Idaho was the nation's fourth leading producer of dredged gold after 1910. The two principal methods were bucket-line dredging and dragline dredging. Dredging operations took place along the Clearwater River, Red River, Crooked River and American River.

Hydraulic Mining was used extensively in Cal-Idaho Pit and Buffalo Pit. A historical road sign just outside of Elk City on Highway 14 explains Buffalo Pit. The destructive erosion created eighty years ago by the hydraulic monitors and water from the American River still show the environmental scars that are a result of this method of mining.

Although the lumber industry came to Elk City in the late 1800s, the impact the Shearer Lumber Mill made on Elk City has never been equaled. In 1955, Gwen and Capitola Shearer opened the Shearer Lumber Mill, which employed eighty people. Today, a memorial plaque stands in front of Shearer Park commemorating the contributions the Shearer family has made to the community of Elk City.

Today Elk City is a small community with a population of 202. It is in Idaho County, at an elevation of 4,006 feet. The Elk City Hotel provides nice accommodations and boasts the town's only gift shop and museum. You can make a reservation online or call the hotel at (208) 842-2452. Directly across the street from the hotel is the Elk City General Store. I strongly suggest the Elk Horn Saloon for a cold beer and meal. The Elk Horn's knotty pine interior and warm atmosphere extend a genuine sense of hospitality, as does a black shaggy dog named Oliver, who may be on hand to greet you. If you are lucky, Larry the bartender will be there to answer any questions. The state of fare on their menu is limited but excellent. Elk City also has a VFW Post 8311 and American Legion Post 153.

The annual Elk City Days is the second weekend in August. There is a traditional baseball game between the Forest Service and townsfolks, logging events, and a parade.

The Elk City Cemetery is on a small hill at the intersection of Elk Creek Road and Sweeney Road. It is all but forgotten and no longer used. A typhoid epidemic hit Elk City in the late 1800s. Some of the graves are of children who succumbed to the fatal disease.

Elk City is fifty-three miles east of Grangeville on State Highway 14. Gold panning in numerous creeks and rivers surrounding Elk City can still produce color for patient individuals, as it did for the prospectors of the 1800s.

The junction at Highway 14 and Crooked River Road start what is known as the Gold Pan Loop Tour. Orogrande/Dixie Road make up the second portion of the loop to Dixie. This final leg to Dixie can be extremely rough and unpredictable. A high clearance vehicle is essential; use caution. See Gnome Mill Site (this chapter) for more information.

Approximately six miles south of Elk City on the paved road leading to Dixie (Highway 222) is Gold Point Mill. The location is marked by a large historic sign on the right side of the road. It was a Depression-era, steam-operated stamp mill that remains in extremely good condition. It is worth the time to investigate.

GNOME MILL SITE (GOLD RUSH LOOP TOUR)

From Grangeville, head east towards Elk City on State Highway 14 for forty-seven miles. Turn right onto Crooked River Road. Eight miles after leaving State Highway 14, several structures can be seen along Crooked River Road. A historical marker points out the site. Structures can be seen directly across from the sign.

A driving tour laid out by the USFS starts as soon as you turn onto Crooked River Road. The tour is called the Gold Rush Loop Tour. The first sign seen after turning onto Crooked River Road is the Crooked River Mill Site, although there are no structures. Another mile will bring you to the Gnome Mill Site. Elevation at the Gnome Mill is 4,303 feet.

The Gnome Mine produced fifty thousand tons of ore from 1932 to 1937. The stamp mill processed twenty-five tons of ore per day, using cyanide to leach the pulverized ore to separate the gold. A community grew here and received its name from the mine. Several buildings from the community of Gnome, gradually giving way to the elements,

Gnome

Collapsed structure at Gnome.

stand near the roadside; these make for excellent photography. Dredge tailings appear next to and around some of the structures, giving the impression that they were built on top of the tailings after dredging ceased in that area. These were the years of the Great Depression, when gold prices had escalated. As you continue along Crooked River Road, dredge activity can also be seen along Crooked River. A bucket dredge operated here between 1937 and 1940.

After visiting the small community of Gnome, continue on Crooked River Road. The Orogrande Airstrip in a short distance past Gnome Mill Site on the left side of the road.

At ten miles you will see the Jerry Walker Cabin on your right. The small cabin can be rented through the Red River Ranger District (208-842-2245). It has two bedrooms with two single beds each, but no running water. A vault toilet is located at the rear of the property. Occupancy is four people.

From the Jerry Walker Cabin it is one mile to Ogogrande. A few private residences exist in Orogrande, but nothing from the gold mining years. One mile past Orogrande is Old Orogrande.

Jerry Walker Cabin

OLD OROGRANDE

Old Orogrande is located one mile south of Orogrande on Crooked River Road. The phrase "oro grande" is Spanish for "coarse gold." The site is in Idaho County at an elevation of 4,659 feet. The most notable feature in Old Orogrande is the Colgrove Hotel, built in 1899 by James Colgrove. James Colgrove also opened a post office and store here in the same year. Old Orogrande was a supply point for the mining communities of Concord, Frogtown, Humptown and Calendar, twelve miles southeast. Today, the only summer residents of Old Orogrande are Ben and Maryann York. Their home is next to the Colgrove Hotel. They are very hospitable and friendly but politely introduce yourself first if you have any questions.

The higher-altitude camps of Concord, Frogtown, Humptown and Calendar were known as the Buffalo Hump Mining District, and in 1899, boasted a population of five hundred. An interpretive sign posted at Old Orogrande gives a brief description of the formidable district. In 1899, a supply wagon from Grangeville took eleven days to make the grueling round trip.

Old Orogrande is located twelve miles south of State Highway 14 on Crooked River Road and is part of the Gold Rush Loop Tour. The first twelve miles of Crooked River Road from Highway 14 is on a maintained gravel road. The loop continues from Old Orogrande to Dixie, twenty-one miles. To reach Dixie from Old Orogrande, you will need high clearance and 4WD!

After leaving Old Orogrande and continuing on Gold Rush Loop Tour, you will start to pass mile markers. At about 3.2 miles is a hairpin turn to the right. In a short distance up this cutoff, you will encounter the remnants of cabins. This is the Penman Mine. Proceed on foot or drive to see the ore chute, debris and equipment. A small spring runs at both levels all year long. Several cabins remain. The remnants of the Penman Mine offer some great photographic opportunities and give a glimpse into what life was like at this remote mining camp. Elevation at Penman Mine is 6,187 feet.

As you continue your drive to Dixie, you will pass through some incredible isolated country. Savor every moment and keep a lookout for wildlife! I appreciate all forms of wildlife and will do anything I can to help preserve it. When I am in the outdoors, I consider myself as being in their home and show proper etiquette and courtesy. You will be traveling through a burn area. It is always wise to carry a length of chain or tow strap along with a saw in the event you encounter a tree that has fallen across the road.

Colgrove Hotel

Penman Mine

Do not confuse Ororgande (Idaho County) with readings you may encounter of Oro Grande (Custer County). Due to the similarity in names, there is some confusion. Oro Grande was located west of Challis and north of Custer on Loon Creek. Gold was discovered here by Nathan Smith in 1869, setting off a rush. By 1870, tents and log homes along with a whopping population of 1,500 had formed the community of Oro Grande. The camp was short-lived and, as with most camps, after the whites left, some Chinese remained. On February 12, 1879, Sheepeater Indians were blamed for the killing of the remaining five Chinese in Oro Grande. The accusations grew into a fury, eventually leading to the Sheepeater Indian War, when the Sheepeater Indians were pursued for many months, leading to their ultimate surrender in October of 1879. Although no Sheepeater Indians were officially charged with the killings, it was later discovered that white miners had murdered the Chinese for the small amount of gold they possessed. Nothing remains today of Oro Grande, although several geologic features in the area bear the name Sheep/Sheepeater. One other feature that resulted directly from this unjust act was the naming of China Creek, which is a tributary of the West Fork of Mayfield Creek, near China Creek Recreation Site.

HUMPTOWN, FROGTOWN, CALENDAR AND CONCORD

Old Orogrande is the gateway to Humptown, Frogtown, Concord and Calendar. These turn-of-the-century mining camps lay twelve miles up Humptown Road/Crooked River Road, and make up the Humptown Mining District.

I was told by a competent source who lives in Old Orogrande that it is impossible to get a 4WD vehicle up this road without tearing it to pieces. For that reason, I have not been to the Humptown Mining District. I will get you as much information as I can. It is possible to get rock-climbing Jeeps up the boulder-strewn road but even then, damage may occur. Regardless, ATVs during summer months and snowmobiles during the winter months can make the trek.

It is ten miles from Old Orogrande to Orogrande Summit (7,266 feet) before the terrain levels off. That is an elevation gain of 2,600 feet. Beyond Orogrande Summit are the sites of Humptown, Frogtown, Concord and Calendar.

The discovery of lode quartz led to five hundred miners rushing to the area in spring of 1899. The community of Humptown was established that year and named for the nearby mountain, Buffalo Hump. Humptown elevation is 7,736 feet. By July, 1900, there were two hotels, a livery, five saloons and numerous tents. Reports also

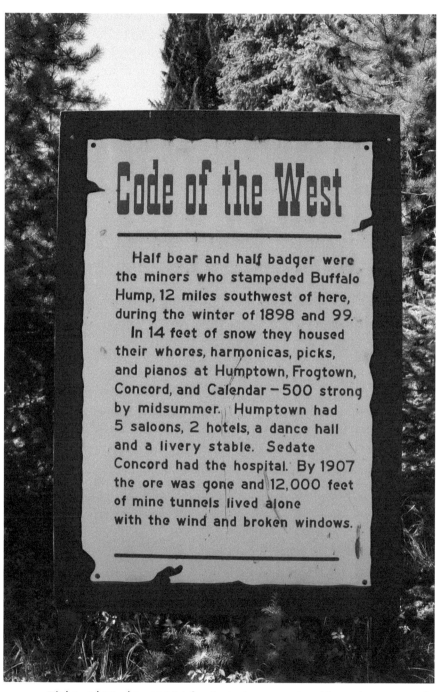

Code of the West

Half bear and half badger were
the miners who stampeded Buffalo
Hump, 12 miles southwest of here,
during the winter of 1898 and 99.
In 14 feet of snow they housed
their whores, harmonicas, picks,
and pianos at Humptown, Frogtown,
Concord, and Calendar — 500 strong
by midsummer. Humptown had
5 saloons, 2 hotels, a dance hall
and a livery stable. Sedate
Concord had the hospital. By 1907
the ore was gone and 12,000 feet
of mine tunnels lived alone
with the wind and broken windows.

*This sign is posted at entrance to the steep grade
leading to the Buffalo Hump Mining District.*

state that a stamp mill was introduced and operated until 1915. The St. Louis Mine, south of Concord (NF 202), was operating between 1940 and 1942.

The Buffalo Hump Mining Company was incorporated in the state of New York in 1899 by D. J. Rockefeller. Charles Sweeney was the first president. Interesting note: authentic stock certificates for Buffalo Hump Mining Company can be purchased online.

The area is extremely remote but beautiful. Crystal Lake and Hump Lake, which are both cold runoff lakes, are inside the Humptown Mining District. Buffalo Hump Mountain, the tallest in the district, is 8,938 feet. The sites of Humptown, Frogtown, Calendar and Concord lay along FR 233/NF 202. Concord is the southernmost location at 7,580 feet. Numerous mines are peppered throughout the district. There is a campground listed on the DeLorme Map and Idaho Road and Recreation Atlas, at Wildhorse Lake FR2331. The entire Humpback Mining District was lode mining.

In recent years, some of the old mining claims have been purchased and residences have been built. With those homes, private property notices are in place. In cases like this, respect private property.

DIXIE

Named by Confederate sympathizers during the Civil War, Dixie is thirty-six miles south of Elk City inside Idaho County at 5,620 feet. Orogrande/Dixie Road (Forest Road 222) continues past Dixie for twenty-seven miles to the Salmon River.

There are conflicting reports on when Dixie started, although a historical road sign in Dixie states that Dixie was founded on August 24, 1882, when two miners hiked over the divide from Elk City and found gold in Dixie Gulch.

Dixie was almost deserted by World War I. Increases in gold prices between 1932 and 1937 saw a resurgence in old claims. One source says that a population of five thousand was reached and that $1.5 million in gold had been recovered by 1924.

The most notable structure in town is Silver Spur Lodge Outfitters. It does operate as a B & B throughout the year, although they are usually booked with hunting trips between September and Thanksgiving, which is their busiest time. Rick and Debbie Koesel are your hosts and provide all meals for their guests. At one point there was a hotel in town, but it was purchased by the Silver Spur Lodge and is now used by the them. Nine rooms are available in the lodge with six additional rooms at the hotel. For summer guests, outdoor activities include horseback riding, fishing, hiking, or a historical gold-mining tour. If you wish, a guide will lead you on horseback into the beautiful backcountry. Also available are overnight camping trips. A guide will lead you to a scenic spot in the Frank Church River of No Return Wilderness, the Gospel Hump Wilderness or the Nez Perce National Forest, where an overnight camp with tents will be set up. Meals and cleanup are provided by your guide. All you do is enjoy the heavenly blanket of stars while keeping warm by the campfire. For hunters, typically between September and Thanksgiving, drop camps and guided hunts may be scheduled.

Rick and Debbie have operated the Silver Spur Lodge for twenty-two years. The lodge provides WiFi and extends every courtesy possible to their guests. For information, go to www.silverspurlodge.com, or call (208) 842-2417. Silver Spur Lodge is thirty-six miles south of Elk City and eighty-two miles east of Grangeville. Air charter service is also available.

From Elk City, Forest Road 222 is paved, apart from the last four and a half miles before reaching Dixie. Red River Hot Springs is an hour's drive.

Dixie had a post office up until 2010. Mail is now delivered by the postal service three times a week. There is no gasoline, groceries,

Dixie (Silver Spur Lodge Outfitters on left).

or lodging other than the Silver Spur Lodge. A livery stable in town was built in 1896 and is still used today. An RV park at the north end of town supplies ice and ice cream sandwiches. I was surprised at the beautiful private log homes that were being built. Currently, the population stands at thirty-five year-round residents.

NORTH SALMON REGION

GIBBONSVILLE

Located in Lemhi County, twenty-six miles north of Salmon, Gibbonsville is situated in the Bitterroot Mountains and Salmon-Challis National Forest on Highway 93, at an elevation of 4,570 feet, and is thirteen miles from the Montana border. Before Gibbonsville was a mining community, Lewis and Clark traveled through here in September of 1805 as they followed the North Fork of the Salmon River. Much of Highway 93 through Gibbonsville and beyond is part of the Lewis and Clark National Historic Trail. Frequent interpretive signs are seen along the highway, explaining Meriwether Lewis and William Clark's epic journey, which began in 1803. Their futile intent was to find a water route through the Rocky Mountains to the Pacific. The 8,000-mile unprecedented journey, which took three years, was the first overland American expedition to reach the Pacific Ocean.

Gibbonsville was named for Major General John Gibbon, who was a graduate of the United States Military Academy and who taught artillery at West Point. Gibbon played an enormous role throughout the Civil War but was most remembered for his 1877 conflict with the Nez Perce, and the Battle of the Big Hole at Big Hole River in western Montana.

Placer gold was discovered here in 1877 along Anderson Creek. However, it was lode mining that catapulted Gibbonsville into the single highest gold-producing community in Lemhi County. At its peak, Gibbonsville had over six hundred miners working in the mines, the largest being the A. D. & M. There were also numerous businesses, including eight saloons, two sawmills, five stamp mills, a blacksmith and a newspaper. Two railroads boosted Gibbonsville's productivity. One was the Northern Pacific branch line from Missoula, which came within thirty-five miles. The other was the Gilmore and Pittsburg, which reached Salmon in 1910.

Production ceased in 1899 but started up again in 1906. Total production of $2 million made Gibbonsville one of Idaho's top gold-producing mining camps, which continued into the 1920s.

Today, Gibbonsville's colorful and boisterous past has transitioned into more of a bedroom community. A great place to get information is the Gibbonsville Relic Museum on Gibbonsville Road. The Relic Museum was once the community school for Gibbonsville.

If you're in Gibbsonville and would like a bite to eat, try the Broken Arrow Café and Resort, 3148 US 93, Gibbonsville. This is a family-run Mexican restaurant that offers great service. Open Thursday through Sunday.

SHOUP

Twenty-one miles north of Salmon on Highway 93 is the small town of North Fork. Follow the posted sign to Shoup by turning left just past North Fork General Store onto Salmon River Road (FS Road 030). Follow the paved road for seventeen miles to Shoup. The paved portion of the road will end in 16.7 miles. This scenic drive will lead you beside the Salmon River, eventually ending at Corn Creek Campground in forty-six miles. As you ascend the road you will pass clumps of rabbit brush and woolly mullein. Keep a lookout for a historical plaque on the left, marking the spot where Meriwether Lewis and William Clark stopped along the Salmon River in 1805. At approximately ten miles, you will pass the Indianola Ranger Station at the junction of Indian Creek Road (FR 036). This road will lead you to Ulysses.

In the later part of the twentieth century, Shoup became known as a fishing resort. Until quite recently, the "Shoup Store" offered lodging, a general store, a café and river rafting. Unfortunately, it is now abandoned. It also boasted having the only operating gravity-fed gasoline pumps in the country! The abandoned general store is still there, as are two glass-domed (gravity fed) gasoline pumps. As of this writing, there are no longer any amenities here. Shoup is located in Lemhi County and sits on the bank of the Salmon River at an elevation of 3,389 feet, in the Salmon-Challis National Forest. A historical marker sits directly across from the Shoup store next to the Salmon River.

The history of Shoup is interesting. After arriving too late to profit in Leesburg, Sam James and Pat O'Hara pushed northward to the Salmon River. Not finding the amount of color they had hoped for in the Salmon, they worked their way up the cliffs overlooking the Salmon and discovered a vein of gold-bearing quartz that sent their hearts aglow! This would become the Grunter Mine. O'Hara and James sold their interests. James stayed on in Shoup and discovered other lodes, including the Kentuck on June 17, 1882. Both the Kentuck and the Grunter would become Shoup's leading mining

274

properties. The Grunter Mine was a mile east of the Kentuck on the same vein. The Grunter is an open-pit mine on the north side of the cliffs above the Salmon River. By 1890, more than three hundred claims had been filed, not all yielding a profit. Some of the mine's names were Hummingbird, Spring Load, Gregor, True Fissure and Lost Miner. Most of Shoup's supplies came in by river boat and barge from Salmon City.

Named for Governor George Laird Shoup, Idaho's first governor, by 1888, Shoup had the usual array of business, including a ten-stamp mill, two hotels, a post office, two boarding houses, a mercantile, a blacksmith, sawmill, saloons and, surprisingly, an opera house! By 1902, fifty-five stamps had come into production. Shoup is inside the Blue Nose-Mineral Hill Mining District.

If you continue a short distance up the road from the abandoned Shoup store, you will see remnants of the bunkhouse and other dwellings for the miners, as well as the Gold Hill Mine entrance. This is private property owned by Jim Hulihan, whose residence is here as well. The twenty-five-acre parcel runs from the road up the side of the hill and beyond the ridge. Jim's father lived here for many years until age forced him to step aside. Apple, elderberry and elm trees grow around Jim's residence. A short distance further, you will see a sign pointing out the Clipper Bouillon Mine, which is located on the opposite side of the Salmon River. The Clipper Bouillon Mine was

Shoup General Store

discovered by Mark Ainslie in 1887. If you look carefully, you will see a stamp mill located on the river's edge (opposite side). Mill workers used to get to and from the stamp mill by way of a rope bridge. There is no easy access to the opposite side of the Salmon River. If you want to get to the other side to investigate, you are on your own!

If you walk behind the Shoup store and work your way up a trail to the left, you will come out on top of the ridge overlooking the Salmon River. There is a small cemetery here on the bluff. The Grunter Mine is further along the trail. The Grunter Mine is on Jim's property.

There are numerous campgrounds available along the Salmon River if you continue up Salmon River Road, as well as The Ram's Head Lodge and Café, which is located fifteen miles beyond Shoup. The Ram's Head Lodge and Café has been open since 2018 (208-329-5081). The Salmon River Lodge and Resort is also located further up Salmon River Road at Corn Creek.

It is possible to continue onto Cobalt via Panther Creek Road. The junction is about nine miles past Shoup off Salmon River Road.

ULYSSES

Located on Indian Creek Road north of the Salmon River was the town of Ulysses. Gold had been discovered here in 1895 along Indian Creek. Miners from Michigan with copper mining backgrounds who had incorporated created a syndicate. Together they purchased some of the better claims along Indian Creek, turning it into one mining operation, and established the Kittie Burton Gold Mining Company, which revolutionized mining in the area. In 1901, they purchased the Kittie Burton Mine, which was on the ridge to the west. A few months later, they took control of the Ulysses Mine, which was on the east side of the valley. The entire area became known as the Indian Creek Mining District. A fifteen-stamp mill which started production in 1902 was enlarged to a thirty-stamp the following year. It was located in the bottom of the canyon and powered with water from Indian Creek. A cable tram system carried ore buckets from both mines to the Kittie Burton Mill. Being near Shoup, the two camps competed with one another.

Accessing Shoup had been easy due to its location by the Salmon River, but Ulysses was challenging. First, machinery had to be transported by flat-bottom boats from Salmon City. Aside from hauling the heavy equipment four and a half miles up the steep grade to Ulysses, the river created a navigation problem because it was littered with equipment from recent wrecks. A fire in September of

1904 set production back in Ulysses. At that point in 1904, Ulysses claimed to be Idaho's largest active gold mine. The Kittie Burton's main adit extended 975 feet through hard rock The ore body was the largest and richest in Ulysses and reflected high hopes for the stockholders.

Mining operations were financed by stockholders of the Kittie Burton and Ulysses Mines. It eventually turned out to be a disappointment due to low-grade ore, with Shoup proving to be more successful. Combined, Shoup and Ulysses produced $2 million in gold!

Today, Ulysses is in Lemhi County, at 5,299 feet. It sits alongside Indian Creek, which is the main tributary flowing into the Salmon River inside this section of Salman-Challis National Forest. The best time to visit is spring, summer and fall. Twenty-one miles north of Salmon on Highway 93 is the small town of North Fork. Turn left just past North Fork General Store onto Salmon River Road (030); follow the paved road for eleven miles to Indian Creek Road (FS 036), at the junction of the Indianola Ranger Station. Turn right onto Indian Creek Road and proceed four and a half miles to the site of Ulysses. The Kittie Burton Mill was scrapped, and the building itself collapsed many decades ago.

Newspapers have a long history of exaggerating facts, misrepresenting truth and misleading the public. At the turn of the twentieth century, newspaper articles wrote sensational headlines telling of a fabulous gold strike in the camp of Ulysses near the Salmon River. Subscribers in the East, believing what they read, left their families and came to Idaho. One such person who had just graduated from divinity school left his wife and nine children to come to Ulysses on the strength of what he had read in the newspaper. He became known throughout the camp as the "Distiller of Spirits." He eventually returned to his family but not with the wealth he had hoped for.

As in most camps of the western United States, it was the men who sold claims, supplies and provisions who benefited the most with financial gain.

Ulysses was a unique camp. It had a boardinghouse, grocery, school, post office and, surprisingly, no crime! Ulysses didn't have a saloon. If the miners desired whiskey or beer, they traveled the four and a half miles to Indianola where there was a saloon. There was also a stage stop in Indianola. Another thing that made Ulysses unique was its strong family setting. During celebrations such as Fourth of July, there was storytelling and there were singing events. The town of Ulysses was professionally operated, and a safe place for families to live and raise their children. At its height, Ulysses had a population of one thousand, this is at the same time Salmon City's population was six hundred. There were multiple residences up and down Indian Creek south of Ulysses that no doubt contributed to that number. Peak production occurred in 1904.

In 2008, Frank Albrecht and his wife purchased twenty-two mining claims representing 350 acres in the Indian Creek Mining District, with the intention of building a home. After the Mustang Fire of 2012, Frank completed building their house on the same spot the Kittie Burton Mill had been located. Prior to Frank and his wife arriving, looters had scavenged tremendous amounts of the materials left behind from Ulysses' early years. Stories of trucks with trailers carrying off machinery, relics and even the corrugated roofing from many of the structures were common. Without the roofing to stabilize the wooden structures, they collapsed in time. Any wooden structures that were overlooked by the looters were lost in the Mustang Fire. There are still scattered metal remnants if you know where to look. Cable from the tram still exists, but the towers burned. Since hauling heavy machinery up the four-and-a-half-mile grade to Ulysses was an arduous task, it was equally difficult to get it out when the mines closed and the residents moved away. For this reason, a great deal was abandoned and left behind. The war years saw scrap drives that could have accounted for some of the looting, but many of the reports surrounding the plundering took place long after World War II. What a terrible shame that this incredible part of Idaho's history was carted off and lost for all time.

Frank knew that very little was written concerning Ulysses, so he decided to do something himself. He wanted the story told as to what occurred, so through the historical society, newspaper articles, state museum and descendants of people who lived and worked in the area, he compiled a history of the Indian Creek Mining District. As of this writing, his book has not been published; however, it will be titled, *Truth, Deception and Gold: Indian Creek, Lemhi County, Idaho*. For information concerning his book, contact the Lemhi County Historical Society, or the Salmon Public Library, both in Salmon, Idaho.

Side note: As you ascend Salmon River Road, keep a lookout for a historical plaque on the left marking the spot where Meriwether Lewis and William Clark stopped along the Salmon River in 1805.

SOUTHERN IDAHO

IDAHOME

Located in Cassia County, at an elevation of 4,426 feet, Idahome is southeast of Burley on Highway 81, seven and a half miles north of Malta.

The town formed when Twin Falls placed a flour factory here. Because of the flourishing wheat crops, the railroad made this a stop. The Twin Falls Mill and Company held a contest to name a new brand of flour. The entry chosen was "Idahome," clearly a combination of the words "Idaho" and "home." By 1916 the community was established, and the town grew around the railroad terminal. Idahome was the name of the flour mill which produced Idahome Flour. As the town grew, it took on the same name. Idahome's economy was based on agriculture, specifically flour. There are also reports that Idahome pursued silver lead mining. By 1918, the population had grown to three hundred. A schoolhouse, lumberyard, grocery, airport, oil company, bank, café, sugar beet factory, newspaper and telephone service, and of course a grain elevator and mill, were soon part of the fledgling community.

Then, suddenly in 1919, the flour company moved to Burley. With the abandonment of the flour company, in addition to highway traffic replacing rail service, the last remaining wheat farms moved on and the town of Idahome became a ghost. Vandalism, scavengers and the elements stripped away the wooden structures, leaving only the lofty silo and another concrete ruin, the only evidence showing that Idahome ever existed.

Today, an Idaho Historical Roadway Sign (#449) marks its location alongside Highway 81. Behind the sign is the colossal concrete grain silo towering over the desert floor. Now home to wayward pigeons, the grain silo stands silently as a sentinel. It is all that is left of the once-prosperous community.

The best way to reach Idahome from Burley and Heyburn is to take the Idahome exit (237 exit) off Interstate 84 heading south. Turn right and head west to Highway 81. The site of Idahome is located at the junction.

Idahome wheat silo

STREVELL (NAF/CITY OF ROCKS LOOP)

Strevell is indeed a ghost, but only a few foundations exist. The fact is, I had seen it on a map as a "ghost town," and it intrigued me. You can make a loop from Burley on Interstate 84 or Highway 81 and continue south. Located on the Idaho/Utah border, Strevell was an active community based mostly on agriculture, which supported a grocery and drug store, post office, school, restaurants, service garages, the two-story Strevell Hotel, and a home baseball team.

The community of Strevell had a noteworthy past! At one point, the FAA (Federal Aviation Agency) decided that Strevell would be the ideal place for an emergency airstrip, for aircraft low on fuel or simply lost to make landings. An elaborate beacon light was installed that signaled aircraft within eighty miles in any direction to make emergency landings. However, with the advent of new, more sophisticated technology, the emergency light was abandoned in the 1960s.

An abrupt end to farming came from drought in 1911. Afterwards, the town turned more to a "port of entry" into Idaho by relying on fuel and lodging for weary truckers and motorists entering Idaho. Especially important, Strevell was the only stopping place between Burley and Snowville, Utah, twenty-seven miles to the southeast. In the 1960s, the newly-opened Interstate 84 bypassed Strevell to the east, which resulted in an immediate decline for the tiny community. Three gas stations—Chevron, Texaco and Phillips 66—along with Mary's Café, soon closed, and Strevell was left to the elements.

Hotel Strevell closed in 1940. Thirty years later it was purchased and moved north up Highway 81 to the former townsite of Bridge. It is very recognizable, as it is the only structure on the east side of Highway 81 below Malta. Today it is a private residence.

To reach Strevell, take Interstate 84 south of Burly and exit at Yale Road onto Highway 81. Driving distance to Strevell is 38.7 miles.

The site of Strevell is marked by a large dirt road (3600) on the right. This well-maintained dirt road leads to Naf, Yost, Almo and City of Rocks National Reserve. Directly adjacent to this (dirt) road on Highway 81 are the foundations of Strevell.

After exploring the few ruins of Strevell, why not make your drive worthwhile? Five miles west on (3600) is the quaint site (town) of Naf. Get your camera out, as it's a good spot for photos. Naf was originally settled in 1870s by Mormon settlers. It is in Cassia County at an elevation of 5,289 feet. The Naf Mercantile still operates intermittently. Today, the arid community supports small ranches nearby.

Walkway leading to Mary's Café.

Continuing past Naf on (3600) for twenty-four miles, you can visit City of Rocks National Reserve. The City of Rocks National Reserve is a 14,407-acre preserve nestled in the Albion Mountain Range, and offers camping, twenty-two miles of hiking trails, world-class rock climbing, fascinating granite formations, and a home to 750 species of plants and animals. A half mile beyond the entrance to the City of Rocks is the City of Rocks Visitor Center in Almo.

Take the time to stop here first and watch the eight-minute video the park service provides that explains the ancient geologic formations that make up the City of Rocks, as well as information concerning the California Trail that passed through this area between 1843 and 1882. There is no charge to enter the City of Rocks National Reserve, and it provides a glimpse into when nineteenth-century Americans followed their dream of manifest destiny, and pushed west in the largest mass-migration in the history of the United States. Particularly interesting to me are the names of numerous settlers written with axle grease on the rocks near their campsites as they traveled to California, at two primary locations. It is a humbling experience to stand in front of these names, knowing they were written by individuals just like us who stood on this very ground 140 years ago.

After leaving the City of Rocks National Reserve, you can continue your loop north on the 77 Spur (aka Elba Almo Road). In nineteen

Town of Naf (population: 1).

283

miles, you will hit the 77 Cutoff. You can continue from here to Burley, approximately thirty miles from the visitor center in Almo.

For information go to: http://gatheringgardiners.blogspot.com/2014/04/strevell-idaho.html.

Travelers of the California Trail wrote their names in axle grease at this spot in City of Rocks 140 years ago.

EASTERN IDAHO

CARIBOU CITY

Located in Bonneville County in eastern Idaho, at 6,000 feet, is Caribou City. It was named after Jessie Fairchild. Fairchild and three partners, F. S. Babcock, John Keenan and Frank McCoy, discovered placer gold in nearby Pisgah Mountain in 1871. Fairchild told such incredible stories of his years amongst the Canadian caribou herds in British Columbia that his partners nicknamed him Caribou Jack. His name was eventually linked to Caribou City, Caribou County and the Caribou National Forest. He was mauled to death by a grizzly bear and is buried in Soda Springs Cemetery.

John Keenan discovered gold in McCoy Creek the same year, giving rise to Keenan City. Together, the two cities attracted hundreds of eager miners and prospectors. Caribou City reported a population of fifteen hundred, while Keenan City boasted five hundred white miners, with about the same number of Chinese miners.

Like other names of the era, Caribou City conjures up images of a raucous town with muddy streets and batwing doors leading into a saloon smelling of whiskey and overly-perfumed women. The surrounding towns of Soda Springs, Henry and Herman flourished with the sudden onslaught of miners. General stores, livery stables, hotels, schools, saloons and brothels developed quickly. Initially a tent city, Caribou City developed quickly, giving way to a large boardinghouse and several businesses. In 1907, the USFS established Caribou National Forest, changing the original spelling of Cariboo.

Hard-rock mining continued into the 1880s, eventually giving way to hydraulic mining. Melting snow during the spring months supplied the high-pressured water needed to eat into the mountainsides and capture the gold-bearing gravel in large sluice boxes positioned below.

Interpretive signs are positioned at the Caribou City site, explaining to the visitor where the numerous mines existed and giving a layout of the townsite. Although the boardinghouse has perished, ruins of cabins can still be seen. Caribou City is located three hours north of Soda Springs and east of Grays Lake.

The best time to visit is late spring, summer and fall.

285

CHESTERFIELD

Located in Caribou County at 5,446 feet, Chesterville was a Mormon settlement. The scattered buildings and cabins of Chesterfield have been lovingly restored to their original splendor by the Chesterfield Foundation, a nonprofit organization that was established in 1979. Although not a mining town, Chesterfield is indeed a ghost and was established inside the Portneuf River Valley along the Oregon Trail by Latter-day Saints. The community relied on agriculture and livestock for their livelihood. The most impressive of the restored structures is the Holbrook Mercantile, a Latter-day Saints brick meeting house, and a tithing office. Chesterfield was added to the National Register of Historic Places in 1980.

The word tithing means "a tenth part." Tithing is a donation or offering, typically one-tenth of one's income for the service of God.

Prior to 1900, four hundred people lived here. By 1940, the town was abandoned. The primary community failed primarily due to the severe winters and to individuals and businesses moving to larger cities that had more to offer. The tiny town has a peaceful charm and visitors are welcome to walk inside many of the buildings. The Chesterfield Cemetery is located a short distance south of town.

A bronze historical plaque dedicated in 1966 by the Daughters of the Pioneers stands near what is called Oregon Trail Campsite. Interpretive signs are scattered throughout the abandoned town identifying different structures.

From Soda Springs, head northwest on Old Highway 30 to Bancroft. Turn right onto Main Street, which will merge into Chesterfield Road; continue for ten miles. The town is open to visitors from Memorial Day to Labor Day, 10:00 a.m. to 6:00 p.m. You can visit during the winter months, but the buildings will be boarded up.

Chesterfield is a delightful ghost and is both educational and easy to locate.

BIBLIOGRAPHY

Adkison, Norman B. "Bustling, Booming Mount Idaho Now Nothing but a Ghost Town." *Lewiston Morning Tribune* (Lewiston, ID), July 1, 1962.

Florin, Lambert. *Western Ghost Towns*. Superior, 1970.

Hart, Arthur. "Nampa's Dewey Palace Hotel was Legacy to a Remarkable Man." *Idaho Statesman* (Boise, ID), April 17, Statesman 2016.

Idaho Road and Recreation Atlas. Benchmark Press, 2021.

Miller, Donald C. *Ghost Towns of Idaho*. Pruett, 1976.

Mines, Idaho Bureau of. *The Gold Camps and Silver Cities of Idaho*. 1963.

Olsen, Wayne C. *"Early Mining on Mackay Peak," Wayne's Reflections*, March 16, 2019, https://mountainsage.blogspot.com/2019/03/early-mining-on-mackay-peak.html.

Paulson, Don. *Mines, Miners, and Much More*. Twain Publishers, 2015.

"Pierce, Idaho–Our State's First Major Gold Rush," Rare Gold Nuggets, October, 2016, https://raregoldnuggets.com/?p=3384.

Raisch, Bruce A. *Ghost Towns of Idaho*. Self-published, 2008.

Reichert, Bruce, dir. *Outdoor Idaho*. Season 19, episode 7, "Gold Rush Days and Ghost Towns." Aired on March 7, 2001, on PBS. https://www.pbs.org/video/outdoor-idaho-gold-rush-days-ghost-towns/.

Robison, John, Public Lands Director, Idaho Conservation League, public lecture.

Sparling, Wayne. *Southern Idaho Ghost Towns*. Caxton, 1978.

Thalman, Ray R. "The Rise and Fall of Chilly, Idaho." *The Arco Advertiser* (Arco, ID), January 8, 1999.

Wolff, Fritz E. "Driving the Kellogg Tunnel: Two Miles to Glory—or Ruination?" *Western Mining History*, https://westernmininghistory.com.

Yarber, Esther. *Stanley-Sawtooth Country*. Publishers Press, 1976.

Elsensohn M. Alfreda. *Pioneer Day in Idaho Country,* Caxton Printers

Museums:

Lost Rivers Museum, Mackay, Idaho.

Owyhee County Historical Museum, Murphy, Idaho.

Nampa Train Museum, Nampa, Idaho.

I am indebted to Ed Reagan for the gift of his Legacy Book; to the City of Rocks Visitor Center in Almo, Idaho; and to information kiosks for the following: Idaho City, Sunbeam, Mine Hill, Stibnite, Florence, and the Pulaski Tunnel Trail.

ABOUT THE AUTHOR

Born in southern California, Bob recognized his interest in ghost towns at an early age. Whenever he had time, he could be found poking around abandoned gold camps and towns in the Mojave Desert, Death Valley and throughout the Eastern Sierra Nevada.

When Bob retired and after he and his wife made Idaho their home, he focused his passion on ghost towns that make up the Gem State.

This book is a culmination of his exploration of the magnificent camps, mines and towns that were a result of one of the richest gold and silver strikes ever seen in the United States of America. In Northern Idaho, you will learn, more silver was extracted from one tiny district than anywhere else on our planet. One town in central Idaho even played a significant role in our victory during World War II.

Read now his story of when Idaho was young, and gold and silver were king!

Author in front of Cossack compressor building (Mine Hill, Mackay).